D1832312

# Sociology of Education

# Sociology of Education

## Theories and Issues

Dr Kaushik Chattopadhyay

KALPAZ

**© Author**
All rights reserved. No part of this work may be reproduced, stored, adapted, or transmitted in any form or by any means, electronic, mechanical, photocopying, micro-filming recording or otherwise, or translated in any language, without the prior written permission of the copyright owner and the publisher. The book is sold subject to the condition that it shall not, by way of trade or otherwise, be lent, resold, hired out, or otherwise circulated without the prior publisher's written consent in any form of binding or cover other than that in which it is published.

The views and opinions expressed in this book are author(s) own and the facts reported by them have been verified to the extent possible, and the publishers are not in any way liable for the same.

ISBN: 978-93-5324-936-6

First Published, 2022

*Published by*

Kalpaz Publications
C-30, Satyawati Nagar,
Delhi – 110052
Ph.: 011-47034999, 9811692060
www.kalpazpublications.com
E-mail: kalpaz@hotmail.com

*Printed at:* Gyan Press, Delhi.

# Contents

**To**

**My father like health activist**

**Dr. Kusadhwaj Ghosh**

**Who taught me**
**the 'what', 'when' and 'how' in social life.**

# Preface and Acknowledgements

*Sociology of Education: Theories and Issues* is a collection of essays that explore the field of education through the lens of sociology. This effort is not just "what 'most people' think it is," rather it is "what sociological researchers do" in a very literal sense. It is profoundly pragmatic in nature and similar to the "down-to-earth activity," where the initial point is modernity. Specifically, the Enlightenment's attempt to discover and describe the natural order-of-things is important here. Self-incurred tutelage was released by constructing a typology of living and non-living nature of the universe by man. Scientific observations and experiments divided and sub-divided things and after completion of complex causal calculation and verification, facts were socially established in a given order.

By classifying, ordering and calibrating, for example, modern science proposed three distinct domains of nature: the animal, the vegetable and the mineral. This kind of classified process of bracketing knowledge clearly provided the disciples of modernity with a useful scientific starting point in their attempts to make sense of the life world. In the middle ages, the religious institutions adopted strategies ranging from assimilation through tolerance to persecution in its relationships with other belief systems. Theological teaching was a major part of global schooling that ensures the rise of new category of pedagogy. What is new after industrial revolution? Two important things emerge. Firstly, European schooling ensures scientific teaching rigorously. Secondly, rise of a new middle class with a new value system in society creating a new horizon of social learning.

It is especially important to understand that teaching and learning was not separate from other areas of knowledge, and that many of the same conditions held consistent in all fields. The larger context of education in modernity cannot be achieved unless masses or common people are able to benefit from scientific and technological advancement. For this, the prerequisite condition is that common people should be enlightened enough to take advantage of new discoveries and inventions.

For modernisation the two extremes of the social hierarchy become deformed: on one side, the working class tends to divide into marginalised social groups and groups assimilated into the middle class; on the other side, the upper class distinguishes itself less and less from the constellation of the middle ranks, and the economic power of the traditional bourgeoisie is eroded by the political power of the "professional class." The cultural criteria of differentiation (lifestyles, consumption patterns) intersect with economic and social criteria (income, wealth, occupational role) and are freed from their structural conditionings. From this point of outlook, the presence of behaviours in contrast to middle-class values can be viewed by educational sociologists as diminishing social control, what commonly refers to as cultural attenuation, or the loosening of social control due to diminished enforcement of conventional values.

However, the crisis in modern education does not result from the low salary of the teachers, the poor buildings, obsolete equipment, and too few schools. The crisis results from the school's inability to decide what it is going to do with the students and what to teach them. In other words, it is uncertainty and ambivalence of purpose that create the crisis. Modern education lives in the past and has not kept pace with the changes that have overtaken our civilisation. Our schools have failed to give due consideration to the content of education needed to fit the masses to operate in a democracy.

All these points of sociological aspects are discussed here, including other several co-related issues. Not just only from a theoretical point of view, here I have tried to look at all other empirical issues of sociology of education. The central goal here is to establish its subject matter. The sociology of education, which is not merely a branch of the pure science of sociology, like educational sociology, is called here for researches: (a) on the functions of the social "facts" of education and their relationship to social change; (b) on the role of teachers in relation to their students and their communities; and (c) on the development of studies of the functions of education in the larger society with the assumption being that social life itself exists on different levels. Thus, the book captures the essence of both the empirical and conceptual reflection, which leads one to conclude that the educative process helps the individuals not only to occupy different "levels" of existence, but also to conceptualise change as a dynamic process involving both structures and human agents.

I still cherish the fond memory of my departed parents. Had they been here now, they should have felt elated on this occasion. I always carry the blessings of my parents. Without my parents I would not have become what I am now. I am grateful to my mother-in-law, who was my constant and strong well-wisher.

My two elder sisters, Dr. Banani Chatterjee and Smt Tandrani Banerjee, and my nephews, Surojit and Satyajit, and my niece, Krittika with her little *Angel* motivated me in my work.

I am specially thankful to my wife, Sucharita (Juna) who is my companion and always remains a source of inspiration. To all others who have assisted me in writing this book including my students, I convey my sincere thanks.

Sri Bimalbhushan Chakrabarti, who was my *Kakai*, had been a source of impetus in writing my books and articles. With my *Kakai,* I express my gratitude to my teacher and research guide, Prof. Samir Dasgupta, Department of Sociology, University of Kalyani. He taught me how to express one's own ideas in sociological terminology. Dr. Dasgupta was a sociologist, versatile writer, dramatist, director and what not. I feel myself honoured to have published some joint papers/books with him.

I am indebted to my teachers, seniors and friends, namely, Prof. Swapan Kumar Bhattacharyya, Prof. Pabitra Sarkar, Prof. Debi Chatterjee, Prof. Pradip Kumar Bose, Prof. Pujan Sen, Prof. Samita Manna, Prof. Debjani Sengupta, Dr. Sujata Sen, Dr. Partha Sarathi De, Dr. Basabi Chakraborty, Dr. Amiya Kumar Mudi, Dr. Sibasish Banerjee and my colleagues of Prof. Syed Nurul Hasan College, Farakka, Murshidabad.

I am specially thankful to Prof. Jayanta Mete, who renders me courage and support by providing carefree comfort zone. Thank you Dr. Debabrata Debnath, Dr. Ajoy Adhikari, Dr. Dolon Das, Dr. Ajit Mondal, Dr. Rajib Saha, Dr. Subhajit Biswas, Sri Basu Acharya, Amal Banerjee for your motivation to work in newer dimensions.

"Sahajpath"... you are always in my heart as a continuous source of brainwave to enrich myself. I am also obliged to Smt Rama Biswas, MLA of Ranaghat Dakshin (Bidhan Sabha Constituency) of Nadia District, WB, for her immense moral support and encouragement in my empirical venture.

I express my gratefulness to all those who have in some way or other assisted me in writing this book.

In fine, special thanks go to Amit Garg, Proprietor of Kalpaz Publications whose insistence and eagerness forced me to complete this book in a short time.

**Kaushik Chattopadhyay,**
Assistant Professor,
Department of Sociology,
Prof. S. N. H. College,
Farakka, Murshidabad.

Dated, Kalyani,
The 17th June, 2021

# Chapter - 1

# Introduction

The sociology of education is an interdisciplinary field of scientific enquiry. This interdisciplinarity has also become a buzzword in the present methodical field of global research and analysis. It deals with the education related issues sociologically. As new interdisciplinarians of this field, sometimes point at the problem that academic work generally within narrow and possibly arbitrary or artificial disciplinary boundaries, which takes place sometimes prevents academic bearings in mind to the close connections of different phenomena and also of the different disciplines and their subfields.

Lester Frank Ward, one of the six founding fathers of American sociology and the first president of the *American Sociological Association*, argued in 1883 that, education is a principal source of human progress and an agent of change that can foster moral commitment and cognitive development to better society (Bidwell, 1979). This field was referred to as educational sociology, and it focused on practical issues and the formulation of policy and recommendations. The name sociology of education was introduced in the late 1920s by Robert Cooley Angell (1928). Angell believed that the sociology of education is the study of how public institutions and individual experiences affect education and its outcomes. To him, the educational institutions are sources for scientific data and sociology cannot promise to produce answers or suggest changes to solve school problems. The sociology of education is mostly concerned with the public schooling systems of modern industrial societies, including the expansion of higher, further, adult, and continuing education.

Today, however, there is a need for sociologists with both emphases: "one group to carry out objective research and the other one to work with schools in interpreting and implementing scientific findings. The latter group needs to have special training in scientific methodology, as well as practical knowledge of how schools work" (Ballantine, 2001: 16). If we go through the works of Jean Anyon, Michael W. Apple, Henry Giroux, Joel Taxel and P. Wexler, we can understand the characteristics, which distinguish the American sociology of education in the late 1970s and early 1980s from British sociology of education. But there exists no such explanation in contemporary academic discourse that focuses on how does the new sociology of education become distant to traditional school of disciplines.

Research fields always offer new interdisciplinary study programmes. They can lead to the formation of new interdisciplinary enquiries and eventually new disciplines, or they may result in a completely different post-disciplinary organisation in academic fields. In fact, there has been undoubtedly a continuous and strong growth of interdisciplinary teaching and research programmes in the contemporary social sciences. It has been identified by many social scientists as the desirable direction towards which the social sciences should develop themselves, both in terms of teaching and research.

In the present phase of network social connectivity, education identifies itself as a field of battle between virtual and real time that entails a rewriting of geo-politics, geo-strategy, geo-finance, and geo-democracy. Cyberspace is a new form of perspective in the field of sociology of education and it is that perspective of real-virtual time with a digital element allowing one to remotely touch, see, hear, and perhaps feel (Assie-Lumumba, 2011). The fluidity of knowledge and real-virtual dichotomy focus "globalisation" as a flashing mirror hiding the phenomenon of virtualisation.

This treatise initiates some basic points which help to understand the fundamental relationship among society, education and sociology, and assist to establish the sociology of education as an interdisciplinary science. The following analysis clarifies the meaning and definitional dimensions of sociology of education from a position of third eye view. Here the focus is on the meaning of sociology of education. A comparative analysis has been done between the definitional characteristics of their time and space to understand the way in which the new sociology of education incorporates new metaphors within its boundary.

## Sociology

Etymologically the word "sociology" is derived from the Latin word *socius* (companion) and the Greek word *logos* (study of) meaning "the study of companionship." Sociology is "a science concerning itself with the interpretative understanding of social action and thereby with a causal explanation of its course and consequences" (Weber, [1968]1978: 4). The philosophy of science depicts a strict adherence to the systematic observations and logical explanations and goes beyond just these to include interpretation–learning meaning what people find in what they do. The complexity of everyday experience, for sociologists, is not naturally self-evident and simple. Howard S. Becker suggests that sociology can best be understood as the study of people "doing things together" (Becker, 1973). This definition reminds us that neither society nor the individual exists in isolation but that each is dependent on and intertwined with the other.

In the broadest terms, sociology can be defined as an orientation that reveals "the strange in the familiar" and "places individuality in social context" (Macionis and Plummer, 2008:2–5). Sociology is, therefore, a scientific study of human behaviour in groups, having for its aim the discovery of regularities and order in such behaviour and expressing these discoveries as theoretical propositions or generalisations that describe a wide variety of patterns of behaviour. As a sub-discipline of social science, sociology primarily concerns itself with social relationships, whose network is called a society. This society is the sole concern of sociology.

Emile Durkheim, one of the sociology's French pioneers, showed that social forces are at work. "If society is to be considered as the normal goal of moral conduct, then it must be possible to see in it something other than a sum of individuals; it must constitute a being *sui generis,* which has its own special character, distinct from that of its members and its own individuality, different from that of its constituent individuals. Briefly, there must exist, in the full meaning of the word, a social being. On this condition only society is abled to perform the moral function that the individual cannot" (Durkheim, 1961: 60).

Though, there are other perspectives in social sciences that focus on some unique aspects of the society, but the central concern of sociology is the social relationships of mankind. Sociology also uses scientific method in its study. Methodically, Durkheim points out, the educator must foresee and prepare for the development of the new sentiments. Here, science is an accumulated body of systemised knowledge and widely accepted processes dedicated to the discovery of generalisations and theories for refining and building on the existing knowledge. The scientific method which is universal (though now objected to by some scientists) consists of formulating a problem to be investigated, formulating some hypotheses and conducting a research which must be public, systematic and replicable.

Sociology also involves the study of human groups and how they operate through established institutions and institutionalised patterns of behaviours which are more or less adapted to the specific functions of society assigned to each institution. Members of an institution or a group interact with one another at the individual level. The patterns of behaviour are the sum of the activities of one member on another in the group. Thus, sociology is also seen as the study of the formation and transformation of structure and the relationship of groups and group members with one another, noting that where there are collectivities there are tendencies for participation, cohesion and conflict.

We can understand sociology from various points of view. Some of them are seemingly paradoxical, as proposed by Roland Meighan and Iram Siraj-Blatchford (1986: 10) in their book: *A Sociology of Educating*. These are:

(1) It is a relatively new discipline, yet its quests and questions are among the most ancient forms of reflective thought.

(2) If sociologists were not available, some form of substitute reflection on social behaviour would probably emerge: yet sociological thought and inquiry are also resisted and resented.

(3) Everyone tends to feel familiar with the world of the sociologist: as members of the social world we should be the experts on it. Yet common-sense views are frequently disturbed by the inquiries of sociologists.

(4) Sociology, in attempting to free us from the determining effect of social frameworks, may only make the strength of the structures more apparent and the sought-after freedom more elusive.

(5) Sociology attempts dispassionate inquiry, yet cannot eradicate values from its investigations, the investigator or the subject of the investigation. The sociologists, like good detectives, must suspect everything and everyone, including themselves.

(6) Sociologists themselves are far from united on many issues related to their discipline, yet have some unity in their undertaking to meet argument with argument and to acknowledge the value of the constructive doubt, and in their willingness to live with the creative uncertainty of a constantly changing subject matter.

(7) If this buffet, this smorgasbord, is to your taste, welcome to sociology!

Sociology has been defined and redefined by a set of theoretical and methodological tools which are contending idiolects, and has also been subject to various breakaways and splits that have created new sub-fields, even distinct, new disciplines. These contending "discourse communities" "produce knowledge and establish the conditions for who speaks and who gets heard" the innovative paths. From the point of view of an educational sociologist, a primary task of educational institutions is to transmit society's knowledge, and part of that knowledge consists of the means by which new knowledge is to be sought. Learning how to think independently and creatively is probably one of the most valuable tools the educational institution can transmit. This is especially true for the scientific fields in institutions of higher education. Sociology considers education as a social institution through which a society's children are taught basic academic knowledge, learning skills, and cultural norms.

## Education

The term education is derived from the Latin word "educare" which means to "educate", to "bring up" or to "draw out" the latent powers of child. Confirming to this meaning, French sociologist Emile Durkheim defined education as "the action exercised by the older generations upon those who are not yet ready for social life. Its object is to awaken and develop in the child those physical, intellectual and moral states which are required of him both by his society as a whole and by the milieu for which he is specially designed" (cited in Ottaway, 1955: 216). To educate means "to develop man's faculties, especially his mind so that he may be able to enjoy the contemplation of supreme truth, beauty and goodness".

William Graham Sumner (1906: 638) defined education as the attempt to transmit to the child the mores of the groups, so that he can learn, "what conduct is approved and what disapproved, how he ought to behave in all kinds of cases, what he ought to believe and reject". Education is a social institution through which a society's children are taught basic academic knowledge, learning skills, and cultural norms. Education, is thus, the social process by which an individual learns the things necessary to fit him to the life of his society. Formal education describes the learning of academic facts and concepts through a formal curriculum. Arising from the tutelage of ancient Greek thinkers, over centuries, scholars have examined topics through formalised methods of learning. In contrast, informal education describes learning about cultural values, norms, and expected behaviours by participating in a society. This type of learning eventuates both through the formal education system and at home.

Education, like health, is often seen as an unproblematic social good to which everyone is entitled as a right (Giddens, 2009: 833). Most people who have gone through an education system would probably agree that education has been beneficial for them. To the sociologist, education takes place in the society as a social institution, and is a social thing that enables and promotes human beings in acquisition of skills, knowledge, etc. to widen personal horizons. Emile Durkheim (1956) proposed that the society, as a whole, in a particular social milieu, determines the ideals, which education realises. Education perpetuates and reinforces those elements, which maintain homogeneity and diversity at a time with a balancing condition. For example, education plays an important role in socialisation and social control by embedding social norms, values, customs, rules, etc. On the other hand, education helps human beings to acquire new knowledge and to quake past knowledge to reproduce new ways. This practice exposes the status of education as to ignite revolution and change.

All of the major institutions, including education, are studied by Durkheim through the first way and convinced that the complexity of division of labour helps to develop education system that could pass on the skills required in filling the various specialised roles. In the traditional society, where repressive laws prevail, occupational skills could be learnt within the group and social life. Durkheim did admit social change, where education, by no exception, performs its special task as "the methodical socialisation of the young generation." By this he destined the development in the child certain values and certain intellectual and physical skills "which are demanded of him by both the political society as a whole and the special milieu for which he is specifically destined" (Durkheim, 1956: 71). Only in this way, as he anticipated, the cohesion and survival of the society be assured.

Durkheim saw education as a means of organising the individual self and the social self. The internalisation of values and discipline represents the child's initiation into the society. This is why it is very important to study and analyze education using sociological approaches. For the sociology of education, he depicted a theoretical view to analyse how education is embodied in subjects, to explore the consequences of this embodiment for the moral health of society, and to recognise that embodied beings are not simply a location for society, but possess creative capacities which can also revitalise and begin to change the social space in which they exist.

Education is a process of transmission of social heritage. In its broadest sense, education may be defined as the process whereby the social heritage of a group is passed on from one generation to another and whereby the child learns the rules of social behaviour. It is a conscious training of the young to their later adoption of adult roles. It is synonymous with socialisation. In a limited sense, education is training by a body of instructors within the institutional pattern of the schools, colleges, and universities. While it is clear that education plays an integral role in individuals' lives as well as society as a whole, sociologists view that role from many diverse points of view. Functionalists believe that education equips people to perform different functional roles in society. Critical sociologists view education as a means of widening the gap in social inequality. Feminist theorists point to the evidence that sexism in education continues to prevent women from achieving a full measure of social equality. Symbolic interactionists study the dynamics of the classroom, the interactions between students and teachers, and how those affect everyday life. In this section, you will learn about each of these perspectives.

The role of sociology in education is to establish the sociological standpoint and show its appreciation to education. Mannheim (1956: 99) stated that the "group consciousness is the modern practice of educating the person in a socially neutral atmosphere, while its absence in the traditional type of education inhibited the rise of a new and independent group orientation." Education does not operate in a vacuum. To have a better society, we should analyze the society to show its strengths and weakness and plan the educational programmes on these effects. One of Mannheim's observations was that academic teaching had contributed to "the suppression...of... awareness." Over-specialisation had the effect of "neutralising the genuine interest in real problems and in the possible answers to them." The student, he claimed, is "rendered entirely uncritical by this method of teaching where everybody takes responsibility for a disconnected piece of [knowledge] only and is, therefore, never encouraged to think of situations as a whole" (Mannheim, 1943:65-6).

In *Man and Society in an Age of Reconstruction,* Mannheim (1940) proposed that, sociologists do not regard education solely as a means of realising abstract ideals of culture, such as humanism or technical specialisation, but as part of the process of influencing men and women. Education can only be understood when we know for what society and for what social position the pupils are being educated. "Education has always had the formation of man as its subject matter. It has always wanted to mould the rising generation according to some conscious or unconscious ideal, and always sought to control every factor of personality formation" (Mannheim, 1952:230).

Firstly, educators always know, in personal contact between human beings lay a very profound factor influencing psychic development. The personality of teacher, parents, friends, in certain circumstances exercises a more profound effect on a child than his institutionalised, cultural surroundings. Personal contact, the inspiration exercised by the vital personality of a leader, has a directly awakening, rousing effect and cannot be replaced by mere objective cultural products.

Secondly, educators have also recognised the importance of the last-named group of educational factors—the objective products and achievements of a culture. These are of two kinds: (a) specialised areas of knowledge and skills by which human action is made more efficient; (b) the moral and aesthetic values generally treasured within a culture which, though not directly functional or utilitarian, assist in forming attitudes and ideas.

Finally, educators are aware of the importance of the breeding of automatic, quasi-instinctive habits, the undeviating character of which can often be lent more stability to both individuals and groups than "ideas" which have already ceased to be convincing, or stringent social demands which, by their very rigidity, often fail to achieve the intended effect.

All these ways and means of influencing human beings have in common, a tendency to confine themselves to possibilities afforded by the mutual relations of individuals, and thereby remove the task of education from the social and historical sphere, making it, so to speak, intimate and personal. It was indeed known that education did not take place only in the more or less artificially isolated spheres of school or home, in the intimate relations between man and man, between "me" and "you."

In 1970, Paulo Freire remarked that education is suffering from narration sickness. The unfinished character of human beings and the transformational character of reality necessitate that education be an ongoing activity. In *Pedagogy of the Oppressed* Freire suggested that the education is constantly remade in the praxis. "In order to *be,* it must *become.* Its 'duration' is found in the interplay of the opposites: *permanence* and *change*" (Freire, 1970: 84).

Following Basil Bernstein (1996: xix) however, we are reminded that education "is central to the knowledge base of society, groups and individuals" and that education, like health, is a "public institution, central to the production and reproduction of distributive justice." Sociology of education deals with such matters. Biases in its form, content, access and opportunities, therefore, have consequences not only for the economy: they reach down "to drain the very springs of affirmation, motivation and imagination." Schools play on, help shape and form the aspirations, the core feelings, emotions and intellect of every individual who passes through them. Education has "a crucial role in creating tomorrow's optimism in the context of today's pessimism. But if it is to do this then we must have an analysis of the social biases of education" (Bernstein, 1996: xix), including how structures and practices within them relate to social practices outside.

The end of all education is, first, the completion of the individual; second, implied in the first, adaptation of the individual to such cooperation with the society in which his lot is cast that he works at his best with the society in perfecting his own type, and consequently in creating conditions favourable to the development of a more perfect type of individual. The task of education, therefore, is not merely to develop people adjusted to the present situation, but also people who will be in a position to act as agents of social development to a further stage. On the other side, as Alvin Toffler (1970: 361) remarks, "[T]he most criticised features of education today—the regimentation, lack of individualisation, the rigid systems of seating, grouping, grading and marking, the authoritarian role of the teacher—are precisely those that made mass public education so effective an instrument of adaptation for its place and time."

## The Objectives of Education

Education has a great social significance. Since the earliest times, philosophers had devoted to it a good deal of attention, defining its nature and objectives. In modern times too, eminent educational philosophers and outstanding teachers have accorded education a high place in their works. Moreover, the aims are concerned with purpose whereas objectives are concerned with achievement. Usually an educational objective relates to gaining ability, a skill, some knowledge, a new attitude etc. rather than having merely completed a given task. Thus, the objective of education is learning, not teaching.

Education, according to Matthew Arnold, is the acquisition of culture, and culture is the study and pursuit of perfection. Perfection consists in the complete development of the whole man; and when man is developed socially, politically, intellectually and morally, to the limit of his possibilities, he may be said to as educated (Delaura, 1973). Following Arnold, the objectives of education may be briefly described as follows:

(i) **To complete the socialisation process:** The first and the foremost objective of education is "to complete the socialisation process." Modern family has failed to perform the role of a socialising agent. Evidently, now, it is felt that the schools should play the role to instill in the child the qualities of honesty, fair play, consideration of others, and a sense of right and wrong. Here, through his critical method, Arnold views education by emphasising on moral conduct as a measure of personal and social value (Mazzeno, 1999).

(ii) **Transmission of cultural heritage:** Education is the road to culture (Arnold, M., et al., 1994: 139). It should aim at the transmission of cultural heritage, that is, the knowledge of the past, its art, literature, philosophy, religion, and music. Through history text books and indirectly through celebration of patriotic holidays the child is acquainted with his cultural heritage.

(iii) **Reformation of attitudes:** Culture should reform politics. Education should aim at the reformation of attitudes wrongly formed by the unscrupulous party leaders. Secondary education carries on the objectives of primary education, with an added emphasis on the values and norms of a democratic way of life. The fundamental goal of higher education is to educate concerned and active citizens. Reforms in educational policy give emphasis on it. On the other side, within a family group, the child often comes to absorb a host of attitudes, beliefs, loyalties, and prejudices. To reform these beliefs and prejudices is the function of education.

(iv) **Occupational placement:** Education should enable one to undertake a productive task and earn enough for himself and his family. Education achieves this objective by developing skills among the pupils. The learners achieve eligibility by acquiring knowledge and skills needed to occupy their respective places in a labour force stratified by class, race, and gender. By this point of objective, in contrast to the liberal view of education as the great equalizer, radical educators saw the objectives of education quite differently: Education is not about equality, but inequality.

(v) **To instill the sense of competition:** Education runs by a system of schooling. The main emphasis of schools is upon personal competition. Each child is compared with his classmates by the percentage of marks or division. The school not only ranks all those within its walls, but also shifts its raw material, passing some and rejecting others on the basis of intelligence and diligence. Thus, it acts as a social selector. For this reason, the radical perspectives have argued that the main functions of schools are the reproduction of the dominant ideology, its forms of knowledge, and the distribution of skills needed to reproduce the social division of labour.

The Radhakrishnan Commission Report on University Education in India adds, "[T]he purpose of all education, as admitted by thinkers of East and West, is to provide a coherent picture of the universe and integrated way of life". This is a liberal view of schooling. According to this view, if education can achieve this objective, any product of our educational institutions could well play his role in life and help in building a better world. The liberal notion of education predicts that the naturally evolving structure of human progress must stand above class and sectional interests. In contrast, there is counter-logic in democratic liberal ideology that provides the basis for resistance and conflict. This liberal democratic ideology contains concerns for human rights that are often at odds with capitalist rationality, its ethos of commodity fetish, and its drive for profits (Giroux, 1983: 281). On the other way, the radical perspectives have tended to treat schools as "black boxes." It is remarkable that education is sometimes used as a medium of indoctrination. In the communist countries, the students are taught lessons in communism, while in Islamic countries they are taught Islamic fundamentalism. In India, although the old forms of social stratification based on caste are coming to an end, yet social stratification is making its appearance in a new form.

In India, the objectives of education have always been influenced by the philosophy of political life of the dominant ruling party of that time. After colonial phase, the public school system has brought forth a new student group of the upper class children. An "elite" class of children, reared up in western lifestyle has come up. Education has accelerated the rate of social mobility in independent India. An educated youth, on the basis of his constitutional rights, finds no avenues open in the village and consequently migrates to the city where he procures a lucrative job that enhances his social status. This modernness is more "open" than the traditional one, and it is one of the reasons of education explosion.

## Social Character of Education in Relation to Society

The education as a system, first of all, may be viewed as a part of the total social system. It both reflects and influences the social and cultural order of which it is a part. However, in modern society, education is viewed as formal training. Arnold W. Green, (1960) writes, historically, education is meant for the conscious training of the young for the later adoption of his roles as an adult. The term education has different meanings. Each person interprets the word in terms of his past experience, his needs and purposes. The parents, the teachers, administrators, religious leaders, politicians and artists interpret the term education in their own ways. For example, to a student, education means acquisition of knowledge, receiving a degree or diploma. A statesman may claim that it means to train individuals as ideal citizens. A teacher may interpret education as means of creating a new man and new society.

Education is indispensable to individual and society, as without it there would be loss of all the accumulated knowledge of the ages and all the standard of conduct. An individual must learn the culture of the society or the accepted ways of doing things. He must be socialised into the prevailing culture and must learn the rules of conduct and expectations about future behaviour (Majoribank, 1985). Education provides a conscious teaching programme that helps to inculcate values, norms and social skills which will enable the individual to develop his personality and sustain the social system.

Education is both the living of life (in the network of social relationships, in the classroom and outside) and a preparation for life. Preparation for life involves: (a) capacity to earn a livelihood, (b) capacity to enrich one's life through the enjoyment of the cultural heritage and of one's inner resources, (c) capacity to function efficiently and constructively as a member of society, as a citizen of the State. Education involves: (a) mastery of the tools of learning, such as reading, writing, arithmetic and (b) mastery of our relations to our inner self, to our neighbour, to the universe.

Education is an induction into the learner's culture. It is a deliberate instruction through which we acquire a large part of our social and technical skills. By modern convention, however, education has come to mean "formal training by specialists within the formal organisation of the school." Education, according to the Western scholars, is deliberate and organised activity through which the physical, intellectual, moral and spiritual potentialities of the child are developed, both in individual, as an individual and also as a member of society. Education as social institution plays a vital role in our society (Apple, 1982). The function of education is multidimensional within the school system and outside it. It performs the function of socialising the individual for a variety of social roles and development of personality. It is also an important part of the control mechanisms of society. Education is a necessity right from the simple society to modern complex industrial society. Thus, education is both acquisition of knowledge or art of teaching and learning of values, norms and skills.

The most important function of education is socialisation. Society, here, provides a conscious teaching programme to inculcate values, norms and social skills that will fit the new individuals for their normative role in society (Selakovich, 1984). Society creates educational institutions such as school and colleges to perform certain functions in accomplishing this general end. Education plays an important role in the development of personality. The object of education, as said by Durkheim, "is to awaken and develop in the child those physical, intellectual and moral states which are required of him both by his society as a whole and by the milieu for which he is specially designed". Education helps the development of the qualities of an individual, like physical, mental and emotional make-up as well as his temperament and character. By doing this, education minimises inequality on the one hand; and on the other by developing a skill parameter, it reconstructs a new kind of social hierarchy (Coleman, 1968). American sociologist Talcott Parsons, from a structural-functional perspective, sees the schools as neutral places organised to provide students with necessary skills and knowledge they will be needed to function in the wider society.

The sociological analyses of education give us a deeper understanding of the form and purpose of education in a society and the interactions of people within educational organisations. Sociologists study structures and organisations of social systems, including education, family, religion, economics, politics, and health. Social institutions, such as education, constitute the major structural components of any society. Sociologists of education focus on the institution of education and the structure, processes, and interaction patterns within it (Ballantine and Spade, 2012). These aspects of education vary greatly across societies.

## Educational Sociology

Professor Lester Frank Ward (1883) in his *Dynamic Sociology* undoubtedly demonstrated once for all that education was the initial or proximate means of progress in human society. He had considered education as social function. As sociologists have succeeded in delimiting their own field of labour, they have reached a fair consensus of opinion concerning the basis of all sociological study. The point of departure in such study is the social group, whether the group is large or small, temporary or permanent, simple or complex. It is therefore, the social group as an educational unit upon which we must build an educational sociology. Walter Robinson Smith (1917: 15) proposed that the educational sociology could be considered as "one of the most important differentiations of the science of sociology."

The principles of sociology provide a basis for development of a scientific educational sociology. It is that sub-field of sociology, where the science of society describes and explains the institutions and the social relationships within which the individual gains and organizes his experiences. Educational sociology, thus, may be defined "as the application of the scientific spirit, methods, and principles of sociology to the study of education" (Smith, 1917a: 15). By such study, the social laws which are governing education may be obtained and applied in the ways which may improve our educational practice.

Whatever contribution educational sociology may make to educational theory will be reflected in the improvement of the arts of teaching and of the school administration. It stressed on the importance of social objectives. It is the scientific study of how people live in social groups, especially including the study of education that is obtained by living in the social groups and education that is needed by the members to live efficiently in social groups. It suggests measures for solving the various social problems through the medium of education.

This idea of educational sociology is not new. As early on 1893, Dr William Torrey Harris, whose training and interests were psychological rather than sociological, wrote: "But no philosophy of education is fundamental until it is based upon sociology — not on physiology, not even on psychology, but on sociology. The evolution of civilisation is the key to education in all its varieties and phases—as found in family, civil society, State, and Church, as well as in the school" (cited in Smith, 1917b: 763). In 1900s, the psychological aspects of educational science were sufficiently emphasised but it is only recently that its sociological aspects have begun to receive attention.

The central aim of the educational sociologist can thus be defined as being to study the process of education, and the institutions by which it is carried on, in relation to the economic, political, cultural and other institutions of the society in which it functions. The educational sociology makes an effort to achieve the aims of sociology through the educational process which appears between the individual and society. From this idea, the first use of the term educational sociology in connection with a school course was by Professor John Morris Gillette while in the Valley City Normal School. Professor Gillette identified educational sociology as an applied science of sociology (Ellwood, 1914). The teacher also naturally prefers to see his pupils improve and acquire sound knowledge. Charles Abram Ellwood (1914: 379) suggested that the education of the individual is the initial means of social progress and the final reliance in all attempts at social reconstruction. But education may dissolve the social order and block all social progress. Education without the proper controlling ideas and ideals cannot be the key to social progress. Thus, educational sociology is the study of the interaction of the individual and his cultural environment.

The first course in educational sociology had been given by Henry Suzzallo as early on 1910 at Teachers College, Columbia University, and in 1916 a Department of Educational Sociology was established in the same institution under the chairmanship of David Snedden. Another important step was taken in 1920s, i.e., the establishment of the Department of Educational Sociology, under the chairmanship of Enoch George Payne, in New York University's School of Education and the publication of the *Journal of Educational Sociology*. An important factor in clarifying the field of educational sociology and transferring it from a social philosophy of education to the science of social interaction has been the development of research in the whole field of the social sciences (Brown, 1954: 48).

Volumes have been written on the comparative research techniques of the physical and the social sciences. The approach of educational sociology is not alone individual or societal: it is both. Thus, educational sociology is the study of the interaction of the individual and his cultural environment, which includes other individuals, social groups, and patterns of behaviour. The importance of culture in determining personality was emphasised in the definition of educational sociology. Since social control is the central problem of education, the processes by which it determines human behaviour constitute the central problem of educational sociology.

Thus, the nature of educational sociology is both theoretical and practical. It is the scientific study of how people live in social groups, especially study of the education that is obtained by living in social groups and the education that is needed by the member to live efficiently in social groups. In this perspective, in 1928, Enoch George Payne had published his *Principles of Educational Sociology: An Outline,* and conceived education as reaching out to embrace the total experience of the person, and its chief function, as social control. For this reason, in a real sense, he is considered as the "father" of educational sociology.

## Sociology of Education

A journey from pedagogical science to the sociology of education through the stepping stone of educational sociology as an applied discipline is an extension of sociology of knowledge. By studying an educational system sociologically, it means to consider the relation of societal thought and group interest in moulding that education and also to evaluate objectively the possible ramification or consequences of an education system to be society at large. "In our age it is not enough," writes Mannheim (1962: 33), "to say that this or that educational system or theory or policy is good. We have to determine for what it is good, for which historical aims it stands and whether we want this educational result." Thus, "the study of education must concern itself with a clarification of both of what education is and what it aims at being. The definition of what education is involved, an analysis of techniques and the definition of aims is concerned with an assessment of values which help to decide, among other things, what methods should be used" (Mannheim, 1962: 44).

The primary aim of sociology of education, in Mannheim's term, is now: (a) to understand the prevailing education system, (b) recognising its strength and limitation, in order to set and (c) a reform planning, as part of the reconstruction of man and society. "Our investigation into the sociological foundation of education cannot be a purely academic one, piling up facts for their own sake. There is something definite we want to know. We are in search of something which should never be lost sight of in our research. We want to understand our time, *which* the predicament of this age and what healthy education could contribute to a regeneration of society and man" (Mannheim, 1962: 160).

D. F. Swift (1966: 93) noted three important things that occur in human life. Firstly, everything which comprises the way of life of a society or group of people is learnt. Nothing of it is biologically inherited. Secondly, the human infant is incredibly receptive to experience. That is, he is capable of developing a wide range of beliefs about the world around him, skills in exploiting it and values as to how he should manipulate it. Thirdly, the infant is totally dependent from birth and for a very long period thereafter upon other people i.e. he is incapable of developing human personality without a very great deal of accidental or intended help from other people.

In 1969, Swift defined the sociology of education as a "discipline" that "dealt with social improvement" (1969: 2). Swift, therefore, established the relationship between society and education as the process by which individual member acquires many physical, moral and social capabilities demanded of him by the group into which he is born and within which he must function. This process has been described by sociologists as socialisation. Education has a broader meaning in society than socialisation. It is all that goes on in the society which involves teaching and learning whether intended or unintended to make the child a functional member of that society.

The individual in the contemporary society can only be who he is, at any stage of his development, by interacting with the social and physical environment. Here education becomes a practice of freedom. Education can, therefore, take place in a society. It is society that constructs personality, which is regarded as an organised whole and all inclusive, comprising the physical, mental, emotional and spiritual characteristics of a person. The character and temperament of individuals are subsumed in this definition. The children are born with some inherent qualities bestowed on them by heredity. Personality development depends partly on these natural factors and partly on the environment. The education of individuals, therefore, depends on both the factors – heredity and environment. Education is seen as the whole life of a community viewed from the particular standpoint of learning to live the life. This total way of life of a community is regarded as the culture of that community. Culture is, therefore, the content of education.

Thus, the social environment influences the education of the child, his or her genetic constitution notwithstanding and vice-versa. Education is determined by the culture of the community. Sociology of education deals with such systematic study of social behaviour and human groups. It focuses primarily on the influence of social relationships on people's attitudes, abilities and ethical behaviour and on how societies are established and changed. In reality, the educational system of many countries must reflect the philosophy of that society. Education should be based on the needs, demands and aspirations of the society for it to function properly. It should be related to the level of culture, industrial development, political organisation, religious climate, family structures, differentiation, stratification and degree of urbanisation. It should not only fulfill the individual's and society's needs but their future aspirations also.

In addition to its internecine struggles, the developments and discontinuities within sociology and the sociology of education, both reflect and respond to changes in societies – national and global. However, there are neither inevitable nor simple relationships between social and political contexts and the preoccupations and dispositions of the academy. To Ottaway (1962: 4), the sociology of education is concerned with the influence of the social environment on the growing child, but this should not allow us to forget that it is always an individual with his own unique gifts and qualities who is being educated. Briefly, sociology of education is defined as a study of the relations between education and society (Banks, 1971). It is an analysis of the sociological processes involved in an educational institution.

Schools are the primary institution for instructing, training and socialising the next generation. To study school as an organisation is another central interest in the sociology of education today. Besides the responsibilities of transmitting what is already known, the schools are also supposed to develop students' intellectual skills and creativity and foster the production of new knowledge and technology.

Innovation involves creating new knowledge and finding new ways to use existing knowledge (Foucault, 1974a). Even in the most traditional tribal societies, innovative ideas and inventions that provide a better way of performing a task or enhance the quality of life usually gain acceptance. In technologically advanced societies, schools—especially large research universities—play an important role in creating new knowledge and technology. Sociology of education negates the traditional schooling and lay stress on changing pattern of school edification accordingly to the changing society and its need.

Although the sociology of education has shown remarkable progress since the 1950s in the area of empirical research, it has lagged behind in the development of theories about schooling. In the study of schooling, sociologists involving in educational research must seek the relations between the complexities of teachers' and pupils' cultures, their actions and intentions and their relationships with forms of curricula organisation and content, the organisational contexts of schools and the communities and wider societies in which they are located.

As an activity, education sails on society, and its aims and methods depend on the nature and character of that society in which it takes place (Dore, 1976). Educational institutions respond slowly to change, and schools should often perform the delicate balancing act of trying to preserve the status quo and teach tradition while promoting social innovation and cultural change. The sociology of education reduces its focus to an unproblematic "what most people think it is," and its approach to a preference of research method, apparently uninformed by any theoretical or methodological "fads or fashions," and able to ignore the wider political and situational factors that generate the "practical" troubles of time and money. This kind of voluntarism turns the study of this discipline into a search for the weight of personal preference, periodically disturbed by mercurial changes in fashion.

The primary goal of researchers in the sociology of education is to conduct basic and applied studies that increase understanding of the role of schooling in society and the effects of schooling on individual lives. Contrary to rationalists, Marx saw "practice and experimentation as the prerequisites of knowledge" (Matthews, 1980: 4). That is to say, it is sociology of education that excludes itself from the possibility of being the object of sociological study. And that, really, is the key point; isolating a selection principle and reflecting on its effects enables us to do for our discipline what we claim to do for others. Mahatma Gandhi's proposal for "basic education" presents a significant example of the influence of the sociology of knowledge on the school curriculum (Kumar, 1989).

An important aspect of Gandhi's proposal was the introduction of productive crafts and skills. In functional terms, the idea was to relate the school to the processes of production in the local milieu, with the aim of making the school itself a productive institution. In symbolic term, by proposing the introduction of productive skills and the knowledge associated with them in the curriculum, Gandhi was advocating the allocation of a substantive place in education to systems of knowledge developed by, and associated with, the oppressed groups of Indian society, including what are now called the Scheduled Castes and Scheduled Tribes.

The sociology of education has come a long way in understanding different sources of inequality of educational opportunity. Most importantly, the dominant conceptions of structure and agency as developed by Anthony Giddens (1984), employed in the sociology of education are characterised by a dualism which makes it difficult to conceptualise adequately the processes involved in social change.

## Definitional Analysis of Sociology of Education

During the second half of the 19th century, in the most developed countries, the situation began to change as a variety of kindergarten programmes emerged to prepare preschool-aged children for socialisation and the beginning of elementary school learning and as federal legislation addressed the needs of children with disabilities. In the beginning of the second half of twentieth century, the sociology of education becomes a new name for studying the social aspects of education that has always been the concern of the educator in some form or another.

As a discipline of social science, the sociology of education makes its definition as an interdisciplinary field of study. Social scientists tried to define it in their own ways. For example, we can consider A.K.C. Ottaway and Oliver Banks for their definitional analysis. Ottaway (1962: 1-2) writes, "[T]he sociology of education may be defined briefly as a study of the relation between education and society." Sociology of education is thus a social study whose method is scientific. It is a branch of social science. It is the study of origins, organisations, institutions and development of human society.

Ottaway's definition refers to that study which concern with the educational aims, methods, institutions, administration, and curricula in relation to the economic, political, religious, social and cultural forces of the society within which they function. A historical approach may be used in sociology of education, when it studies initial and specific conditions for any institution, organisation or society to develop properly. There is need to trace the situational social needs as origin or background. This definitional emergence explains how society and the institutions develop. It looks at interactions within the society and also among society and other institutions. There are also possible outcomes or achievements of these interactions.

Banks (1971: 4) writes, "[T]he sociology of education, however, is more usually confined to studies of industrial societies, which offer certain distinctive and challenging problems." She further writes "most fundamental perhaps is the increasing importance in advanced industrial societies of specialised educational agencies which share with, and in certain circumstances replace, the pre-industrial socialising agencies, of which normally the family is the most important."

Banks incorporates industrial societies and their problems as the centre of the study of sociology of education. The sociology of education has been developed as a largely macrocosmic study of educational institutions. This study with its different dimensions tries to understand the institutional or organisational roles which help in the promotion and maintenance of social cohesion and social unity, or social differences and deviance. Actually, Banks identified different ways of viewing education and its forms. Sometimes education becomes a matter of luxury. On the other way of looking where it helps human beings to become self-made. It is not only that the family shares in the socialisation process. Alongside the school and, indeed, other agencies performs the same action as well. A number of studies in social psychology, as well as in sociology have shown the complexity in socialisation process.

As a scientific study of human behaviour in group life, having for its aim, the convening of regularities and order in each action and expression in these landscapes as theoretical propositions that describe a wide variety of patterns of social-selves in learning environment. This definition shows that there is a very close relationship between the individual and the society. It looks at how children become full-fledged socialised. Furthermore, the definition discusses social relations in a learning environment and network of such relations which are known as society.

In 1971, Michael F. D. Young published his *Knowledge and Control: New Directions in the Sociology of Education* as an edited volume. In introduction, Young focused on the problematic nature of knowledge and the manner of its transmission, acquisition, and evaluation in schools. The definitional task of sociology of education, as Young states, is "to relate the principles of selection and organisation that underline curricula to their institutional and interactional settings in schools and class-rooms and to the wider social structure" (1971: 24).

The field of socio-linguistics may be a source of originating of sociology of education. It is specifically true for Basil Bernstein's view. He identifies the rules of the play of education. After demystifying education, Bernstein wants to reveal its true nature. The power relation has been exposed and it is shown how these relations underlie and shape discourse and practice and distribute forms of consciousness. And if the play is to be summed up—what is education?

According to Bernstein (1990), "education is a relay for power relations external to it." The degree of success of the relay is not the point here. The educational system's pedagogic communication is simply a relay for something other than itself. Pedagogic communication in school, in nursery, at home, is the relay for class relations; the relay for gender relations; the relay for religious relations, for regional relations. Pedagogic communication is a relay for patterns of dominance external to itself.

In sociology of education, Bernstein's theory of codes increased attention to mother–child interaction, language as a vehicle of power and control in society, and language as a socialising factor and regulator of knowledge inside and outside schools. Sociology of education should reveal these paradigmatic dimensions of contemporary schooling. Bernstein was optimistic about that. He defined the sociology of education as "the analysis of the intrinsic features constituting and distinguishing the specialised form of communication realised by the pedagogic discourse of education" (Bernstein, 1990: 143). Bernstein's theoretical framework was initially based upon integration of elements of the work of Durkheim, Mead and Luria, but he expanded this at a later date to incorporate the insights of Althusser, Bourdieu, and Foucault (Wright, 2014: 16).

Many of the analyses of the sociology of education, especially those carried out by the diverse group of theories of reproduction, assume, taken for granted, the very discourse which is subject to their analysis. These theories, in particular, observe pedagogic discourse as a medium of other voices: class, gender, and race. The discourses of education are analyzed for their power to reproduce dominant/dominated relations external to the discourse but which penetrate the social relations, media of transmission, and evaluation of pedagogic discourse. One of the oldest and most reliable findings in the sociology of education is the relationship between educational sources of the family, race, ethnicity, and academic achievement. Clearly, there is some mechanism by which differences in family background translate into individual success and failure in the classroom, starting in the early grades.

It is often considered that the voice of the working class is the absent voice of pedagogic discourse, but we shall argue here that what is absent from pedagogic discourse is its own voice. If theories of cultural reproduction or transformation of culture formulate ordering or disordering principles, then those principles relate to the message of pedagogic discourse, not to ordering/disordering principles intrinsic to its logic as a specialised discourse. Thomas S. Popkewitz (1991: 2) views sociology of education in an exclusive way, when his central thesis is to understand reform as a part of the process of social regulation. Quoting an unknown historian he defines the sociology of education as that branch of "knowledge," "where social control is a residue."

Kathleen Lynch (2006: 100) defines sociology of education as "a normatively-oriented discipline with a much greater focus on educational reform than radical change." New sociology of education can be defined as the scientific analysis of the social processes and social patterns involving the educational system to develop the curriculum of future. It is the study of how social institutions, organisations and forces affect educational processes and outcomes, and vice versa. It extends to a critical theory of learning. Indeed, it is the study of how public organisational services and individual experiences affect education and its outcomes. It is mostly concerned with the schooling systems of contemporary global societies. It explores the ways in which the organisation of school curriculum and knowledge itself as the "official" curriculum, work to sort students.

## Educational Sociology vs. Sociology of Education

"Educational Sociology" and "Sociology of Education" are two branches of study that are sometimes understood as one and the same branch, but actually not so. They indeed show some differences between them when it comes to the subject of their study and the nature of the branches of study.

Educational sociology has as its chief province the scientific determination of educational objectives. It constitutes an applied or linking science between the fields of sociology (as a pure science) and social economy (as the science of all phases of human well-being) on the one hand, and the practice of education on the other hand (Snedden, 1922: 33). If a general definition of educational sociology is required, it might be given as the application of the scientific spirit, methods and principles of sociology to the study of education. The scope of the subject would require an analysis of our educational systems as they exist, together with an evolutionary study of the way they came to be what they are, and the outlining of a programme necessary to bring them into harmony with the progressive demands of a rapidly moving society. This is no mean task and calls for the efforts of many minds in a never-ending process of construction, adaptation, and reconstruction. It will not even then make education simpler, but it ought to make it more effective to apply.

Sociology of Education depicts an analysis of the sociological processes involved in the educational circumstances. It does not emphasise on the study within the tradition of education and it is not the application of specific principles and findings of sociology to the administration and processes of education. It is the study of how individual experiences affect education and its outcomes. In order to better explain the social phenomena of education, Emile Durkheim (1956) made explicit the following research areas which he considered appropriate for sociologists in conceptualising the meaning of sociology of education:

1. Identification of the current social facts of education and their sociological function.
2. Identification of the relationships between education and social and cultural change.
3. Cross-cultural and comparative research in various types of educational systems.
4. Investigation of the classroom and school as an ongoing social system.

Despite the clarity of Durkheim's position, many sociologists accepted his research direction (Brookover and Erickson, 1975: 5). Since long, as a founding father of "sociology of education", he has scientifically defined sociology of education as "a system of education that is preoccupied more specifically with preparing man for social life" (Durkheim, 1956: 36). This definition of sociology of education is suitable because it speaks much of what goes on in education system. This French idea negates the American idea of "Educational Sociology", which applies, in a confused way, to the sociological study of education and, at the same time, to the introduction of sociology into classrooms, as a subject-matter. The subject-matter of sociology of education is forming the citizen, what may be called: "Citizenship Education."

The United States' term "Educational Sociology," was called in Germany as "Social Pedagogy" and in the UK, as the "political arithmetic" tradition (Ball, 2004: 3). The central concerns of "educational sociology" were descriptive and structural. It focused upon patterns of educational opportunity and social mobility within industrial democracy – "the problematics of social stratification and status attainment" (Apple, 1996: 127). Educational sociology must include two fundamentals aspects: (1) a general application of the principles of sociology to the school as an institution; and (2) a specific application of these principles to educational practice (Smith, 1917b: 766). It did not consider education in autonomy as a matter of moral instruction in its effects in the elementary school. This sociological study of education holds that the teacher should be a strict disciplinarian and should exert complete control over the conduct of his pupils. It must deal with society in its efforts to incorporate the learners within itself. Educational sociology will also teach us, while the work of culture is necessarily carried on by specialised training; socialisation is a more fundamental process than vocational training (Ellwood, 1927: 29). Linguistic, intellectual, and vocational training should all be recognised as means, but not as ends.

On the other hand, the sociology of education was utterly opposed to any sort of education which attempts to develop the individual propensities of the child or which allows him any degree of free initiative in the schoolroom. The sociology of education touches the power of reason to apprehend, order, and relate the phenomena of social life. "If there is one fact that history has irrefutably demonstrated it is that the morality of each people is directly related to the social structure of the people practicing it" (Durkheim, 1961: 87). This fact identification from a positivist perspective goes through the way of sociology of education where education could and should include moral education based not upon religion, but upon a sociological study of the nature of the existing social morality. Thus, sociology of education rejects the psychological metaphors of educational sociology, and gives spaces for the development of philosophy of science. It also deals with the branch of study that made of the relationship between education and society as a whole.

The educational sociology is the branch of study that deals with the various methods providing better education to society through an in-depth research of our culture and society. Educational sociology as a subject has to take both the sociologists and the educationists into consideration. This makes the subject an invaluable asset to all the students and researchers of social sciences, particularly sociology and education. It is a general belief that such of those who are involved in a deep study of education will benefit more from the branch of educational sociology, which is conceptually much older than the concept–sociology of education.

This sociology of education is the study of how public institutions and individual understandings affect the teaching-learning processes and its outcomes. The study of the development of public schooling systems and its impact on modern industrial societies forms the subject matter of the branch of study of sociology of education. Topics such as higher education, further education, adult education and continuing education can be included in the branch of study of sociology of education.

In the sociology of education, education has been viewed as a basically optimistic human effort characterised by aspirations for improvement and betterment. It is concerned with such general concepts such as society itself, culture, community, caste, class, environment, socialisation, accommodation, assimilation, cultural lag, sub-culture, globalisation, status, role and so forth. It helps us to understand the effectiveness of different educational methods in teaching students with different kinds of intelligences.

Education is thus, a fundamental endeavour of every individual. It is interesting to note that the experts of the sociology of education opine that education is looked upon as an endeavour by which children can develop according to their needs. The potential in the children plays a great part in the role of education. As a human endeavour, it is also characterised by aspirations for progress and betterment. It is also perceived as one of the best means of achieving greater social equality.

## Concluding Remarks

Education has something to do with knowledge. Explicitly or implicitly, "education" is going to have something to do with a theory of knowledge, along with 'epistemology'. "This nexus is very clear in Plato" (Matthews, 1980: 24). In the *Republic,* Plato had rejected the conception of education professed by those who say that they can put into the mind knowledge that was not there before. This is the antithesis of Locke's *tabula rasa,* which must receive all its knowledge from external sources. The work of Francis Bacon, John Locke and David Hume should be interpreted in relation to the massive upheavals in the science of their time.

We must trace matters further back to the old Hegelian idea that "the state is, by its nature, an educator" (Althusser, 2006: 146). One of the central Marxist claims is that the understanding of an object, circumstance or institution involves examining its history, the process of its coming into being, the circumstances of its production. This suggests a wish to restrict the curriculum to the basic skills and to "value-free" knowledge. It is a reminder that Marx believed in the possibility of objective knowledge. This contrasts with the neo-Marxists of the 1970s and 1980s who argued that "*all* knowledge is class knowledge" (Barcan, 1993).

Pierre Bourdieu, like Louis Althusser, gave the school central importance in the transmission of power and inequality. Bourdieu took the idea of "hegemony" much further. He is labeled as Marxist by some, a Weberian by others, and even a follower of Durkheim. This neo-Marxism contributes four closely related concepts to the sociology of education, that is, hegemony, legitimacy, ideology and reproduction. New sociology of education ran into this transitional phase of intellectual crisis. As an academic discipline sociology of education was born in the context of an emerging pluralist, multicultural, cosmopolitan society. The major commitment of the new sociology of education was to a new sociology of knowledge.

This paradigm shift has occured in the field of sociology of education in the early 1970s. In UK, it was the beginning of formation of the "New Sociology of Education" (NSOE), which was different and altogether more controversial approach to the discipline of knowledge praxis. The NSOE was new in its application of the "interpretive approach" for schooling and perhaps best exemplified by the early work of Michael F.D. Young (1971). While borrowing much from the interpretive schools, such as symbolic interactionism, phenomenology, ethnomethodology, and Marxism, the new paradigm has emerged in Britain partly as a reaction to the lack of success of earlier reform policies based on traditional research (Bates, 1980). It promises to advance understanding of educational processes related to classroom interaction, classroom language, and the curriculum.

Young's edited collection on a critical history and prospects for the future of sociology of education has included contributions from Basil Bernstein and Pierre Bourdieu that marked a change in direction for the sociology of education exploring for the first time the teachers' role in reproducing social inequalities. The political arithmetic approach in UK had positioned the teacher and the school as neutral agents in this process, but the work of Young and his collaborators has demonstrated another side to education. It was no longer seen as primarily a progressive force for greater equality and increased personal autonomy as intended by those behind the raft of educational policies introduced as part of the expanding post-war welfare state. Instead it, as Lauder et al. (2009: 573) suggested, was "deeply implicated in the reproduction of (social) inequality."

This newness in sociology of education helps us in understanding of how power, resistance and human agency can become central elements in the struggle for critical thinking and learning. Schools will not change society, but we can create them as pockets of resistance that provide pedagogical models for new forms of learning and social relations—forms which can be used in other spheres more directly involved in the struggle for a new morality and view of social justice.

# Chapter - 2

# The Essence of Sociology of Education

After WW-II, there has been a growing tendency to give more and more attention to the sociological aspects of educational theory and practice in courses for the training programmes. These investigations have been carried out in a greater extent by the sociologists than the educationists. There are many advantages, since educational sociology is best regarded as a part of general sociology, and a more intimate part instead of recognising it as a separate branch or offshoot of sociology (Ottaway, 1960: 190). The emphasis in modern sociology has come to be the study of social institutions and the relations between them.

The social nature of education was no new discovery, but Emile Durkheim was the first to recommend the comparative study of educational systems, and teaching methods, from a modern sociological point of view, and as a part of the science of education. The emphasis on educational campus and community relationships provided a shift from merely applying sociology to the alleviation of educational problems to the inclusion of the use of sociological theories and methods to enhance our knowledge about education in particular, and social behaviour in general. This orientation toward the acquisition of knowledge is referred to as the "sociology of education" theme in contrast to the earlier "educational sociology" theme.

The essence arises from the boundaries of sociology, which are notoriously difficult to define. The studies, which are most likely to overlap or interrelate with it, are social history, social anthropology and social psychology. The historical fact that education must have a social purpose, and it embodies a set of social values and ideals, which are always been expressed in the works of educational thinkers. Thus, the studies of curriculum are considered to be always culturally and temporally specific.

The curriculum may also be seen as development, or as a "hypothesis testable in practice."

The historicity of the work culture consists in knowledge, skills, and standards which are utilised in making of tools, institutions, and group organisation. Its vehicle is language in some form (Ellwood, 1927: 26). This sociological perspective feels convergent on a need for a systematic sociology of the school, with comparative studies of different campuses representing social units of different kinds. The role and function of the campus as an agency for the socialisation of the young requires much more explicit definition. Durkheim views that the famous educational theorists are "revolutionary spirits," who aim at social change (Ottaway, 1955: 214). Durkheim insists that each society has its own conception, or ideal of man, which nevertheless changes at different points of time in history and at any given time, is related to the needs of the society.

Unlike social anthropological perspectives, the sociology of education tries to analyze the social structure and culture of the campus. The researchers know that the culture is necessarily carried on by specialised training, but socialisation is a more fundamental process than vocational training. The techniques of our various vocations are necessary for carrying on the work of civilisation, but even more necessary are the fundamental social attitudes which we practice in the community life. The participant observation method becomes helpful for the researchers to carry on their research work. Hence, sociology of education makes it clear that the ideal outer environment of the school campus is the same as in the school, which is a campus of systematised, rationalised, and morally controlled social process.

Human nature is very flexible, and society selects the qualities it wishes to develop from the range of man's possibilities, and gives precedence to those of most value to its purposes. A qualitative perspective considers that any education will develop individual aptitudes and qualities, which are inherent in human nature, but the direction in which the individual is led to specialise is not determined so much by his nature as by the environment in which he finds himself. This social psychological perspective concentrates on the studies of small group analysis, sociometry, group dynamics and the like. Many of the campuses can be classified as face-to-face groups, peer groups, or a pace of meeting together at particular times, or a "frog pond" (Davis, 1966). The observation of a small group, or the classroom, is such a study of social interaction, which is not properly falls in the field of social psychology rather than that of sociology. It depends on the nature of the facts studied. If the facts are concerned to the reactions of particular individuals to the social group then they are psychological facts; but if they are concerned to the nature or structure of the social group itself, or the group in relation to other groups then they are sociological facts.

The essence of sociology of education varies on the changing dimension of the theoretical perspectives in sociology. The "new sociology of education" includes both phenomenological and structuralist accounts in its explorations. From this nature of sociology of education, we therefore, expect not only great help in solving the practical problems of educating campuses, but also a revitalisation and humanisation of the science of sociology itself.

## The Campus

Modern society provides campus for education. All education proceeds by the participation of the individual in the social consciousness of the race. This process begins unconsciously almost at birth, and continually shapes the individual's powers, saturates his consciousness, forms his habits, trains his ideas, and arouses his feelings and emotions. Through this unconscious education the individual gradually comes to share in the intellectual and moral resources which humanity has succeeded in getting together. He becomes an inheritor of the funded capital of civilisation.

This informal family education is a part of the larger function of the transmission of culture. As the social order has become more complex, formal education has assumed an important place in its continuity, as well as in the growth of culture itself. The purposes of education may have been altered as the cultural outlook itself has changed, but everywhere education assumes an important place in the life of the individual in fitting him for a place in his community.

The formal education in primitive culture is based on verbal traditions—the folklore, the mythology, and history of the society—in which the training of manual skills is essentially based on the material cultural elements of a clan. In that tribal group-life, the learning processes are controlled by the myth and magic of supernatural power and the safety measures are very much concentrated on the moral customs, ceremonies, norms and values of the kin-group.

The complexity in this formal educational procedure was incorporated in a modern manner particularly after increasing need of specialisation, and especially when the writing had given man a means of preserving his culture in more objective form (Young, 1934). The rise of democratic nationalism put a more distinctive mark on modern education in which family education became a part of informal education.

The most marked complexity was started after the introduction of secondary and higher education. The sex ratios among our school population also depicted several interesting changes. This growth in formal education with several social changes was gradually encroached different other areas of society by constructing a triadic relationship between teachers, pupils and their guardians.

The entire configuration of social relationships in school campus was reassessed by the new codes of moral conduct. Colleges, universities, night schools, folk schools, etc., the institutional frames of a society, must be examined in the light of two matters: contemporary theories of education under the impress of modern science, and the rise of new competitors of formal mass education—newspapers, magazines, books, motion pictures, and the radio.

The devotion of democracy to education has become a familiar fact. Under the influence of John Dewey (1959), there has grown up a "school" of educational theory which places great faith in intellectual and emotional training of the child and the adult with a view of improving the worth of the common man, making him more intelligent about his world, and more able to cope with its innumerable problems. For Dewey (2004[1915]), the mind of man is but an instrument to aid him in adaptation to his environment, an idea born of biology and the machine age. Since a democratic society repudiates the principle of external authority, it must find a substitute in voluntary disposition and interest; these can be created only by education.

A society marked off into classes need to be especially attentive only to the education of its ruling elements. A society, which is mobile, which is full of channels for the distribution of a change occurring anywhere, must see to it that its members are educated to personal initiative and adaptability. Here, the child became the center of educational activity and his growth as an intelligent unit in democratic society was the main concern. The personality of the child grows out of his interests in integration with the democratic culture.

In America, there is great faith in "conscious control," in enthroning the "intelligence," and in setting up a "responsible criticism" of our society at any point where it seems advisable. From this point of reason, in contrast to Dewey's view, Fred J. Kelly (1914) went further. For him the schools should assume responsibility in setting up our social, economic, and political goals. The school, therefore, becomes in a sense the testing or "proving" ground for the basic sociological problem of the relation of the societal order to the personality and in regard to their reversible interaction.

## The School as a Special Environment

The process of education can be studied a science or an art, but both of these are distinct from the study of *pedagogie* which consists of theories of a particular kind. To define the process of education, that is, to define its nature and role in the most generalised form, we must consider what the practices of different societies have in common. "There are always adults and children, and education is the action exercised by the first on the second. Children always have to be prepared for membership of their social group. In all societies this action has two aspects. In the first place it is diverse whenever there is a division of labour in the society, since this requires a different preparation for different types of future work. Different social classes, where these exist, have different cultural standards and objectives: the education of the *bourgeoisis* not the same as that of the *ouvrier*" (Ottaway, 1955: 215). Yet this diversity is based on a set of educational practices more or less common to all. Thus, in the second place each society has a basis of common culture which must be learnt by all, and is expressed through its manners, morals, religion and way of life.

If we think education as a process of living, and not as a preparation for future living, then it becomes a fundamental method of social progress and reform. It signifies the sum total of processes by which a community or social group, whether small or large, transmits its acquired power and aims with a view of securing its own continued existence and growth. The educative process that runs in a school environment, continuously reconstructs the social experience with the purpose of widening and deepening its social content.

The function of educative institutions is to help in growing of a helpless young animal into a happy, moral, and efficient human being. A school educates students for the *status quo* and when the students go forth they do not find anything so settled that it can be called anything of a static kind. The fundamental need of the school system, in its formation stage, was dependent upon its limited recognition of the principle of freedom of intelligence. "There is no reasonable expectation for an important improvement in the quality of education unless something dramatic is done to ameliorate the socio-economic conditions of existence" (Burkhead, 1967: 89).

Until the public-school system is organised, the school has no power to modify the social order. In public-school system, people send their children to learn in a systematic way about the social basis of living (Boocock, 1973). But, sometimes this schooling system, to a very large extent, overlooked the methods and subject-matter of their teaching. This fact determines the fundamental criticism to be leveled against current schooling system, specifically when educational sociology was founded and educational institutions had received little sociological investigation and adequate sociological treatment.

In the second half of the nineteenth century, it was assumed that the school product would be a loyal patriot, a well equipped good citizen. At this modern era, education became a tool of creation of a discriminating mind, a mind that cultivates the habit of suspended judgment, of skepticism, of desire for evidence, of appeal to observation rather than a sentiment with nostalgic emotion, a discussion with known bias, or an inquiry with conventional idealisations. Social science considers that the evolution of civilisation is the key to education in all its varieties and phases, as found in family, civil society, state, and church, as well as in school. The schools are given special emphasis because of their direct influencing role in formation and growth of attitudes and dispositions, on the one hand, and the emotional, intellectual and moral behaviour on the other.

In a school or formal classroom context, democracy is not a behavioural value or a means of better learning; rather it contextualises a deeper perception that must focus on the freedom to act as the only means of self-realisation available to the individual learner. The environment of school creates for all a new and broader space of acts, and takes a special form by intermingling different races, differing religions, and several customs. The school environment consists of the sum total of conditions which are concerned in the execution of the activity characteristic of a living being. The inclination to learn from life itself and to make the conditions of life such that all will learn in the process of living is the finest product of schooling.

In Durkheimian perspective, the major function of formal schooling is to produce social beings, when schooling to construct a social being is defined as the "system of ideas, sentiments, and practices which express in us not our personality, but the group or different groups of which we are part... ." The social being is distinguished from the individual being, who is characterised by "all the mental states which apply only to ourselves and to the events of our personal lives" (Durkheim, 1956:124). Thus, the school, as a social environment, and as a product of its larger social surroundings, describes the relationship between the student and teacher, roles and the patterns of activities and interaction typical of school life. Sociology of education focuses on the dynamic structural and functional components of the school: the role structure, the social context and value climate, and the types of exchanges of information, technological influence, and technical rewarding characteristic of classroom interaction. It also views school as the place where society recreates itself in the young.

## The School as an Institution of Society

As a social organism, the school displays a differentiation of parts and a specialisation of function with a closed system of social interaction. In this interaction process, knowledge enables a student to adapt the social environment and thus, helps to achieve his socialisation. Indeed, it is through school education that the culture of the group is communicated to the child, thereby acquainting him with the traditions, customs, values, and patterns of conduct prevailing in his group. As an organised system with social relationships, like institution, a school embodies certain common values and procedures, which meet specific needs of the society.

Emile Durkheim, allegedly the founding father of sociology of education, sees education as a social fact "external to individual and constraining his/her behaviour" (King, 1983: 16). While examining their usefulness to society rather than individuals, social facts also have to find an appropriate way to serve "the general needs of social organism". Durkheim was the first sociologist who saw education as social institution. The major functions of education, therefore, are to provide necessary social glue in order to maintain solidarity; to supply necessary technical knowledge and skills in accordance with the needs of work-place and changing technological conditions; to socialise and humanise people "by providing the normative and cognitive frameworks they lack" (Blackedge and Hunt, 1985: 10). Not only that, the school also develops democratic thinking of the child as well as ability to think rationally and independently. Leadership role through group interaction and other association in the school enhances this trend.

In sociology, institution is a pattern of network or system of interrelated rules and provides a set of guidelines for social behaviour and structures. Institutions provide continuity and meaning to life. Members of a society internalise the rules of the various institutions of which they are a part in the normal process of life-long socialisation. As a vital and formalised establishment governed by quantified rules and regulations, like an institution, school formulates standard of behaviour to maintain the demand of the participants. Different functionaries of the school system are assigned specific roles to maintain a proper cultural flow.

The real component units of cultures which have a considerable degree of permanence, universality and independence are the organised systems of human activity called institutions. Professor Bronislaw Malinowski (1931: 625) has described the importance of institutions in these words, "Every institution centres around a fundamental need, permanently unites a group of people in a co-operational task and has its particular body of doctrines and its technique or craft. Institutions are not correlated simply and directly to new functions, one need does not receive one's satisfaction in one institution". Societies must reproduce new members, socialise them, give them a sense of purpose, and provide for the maintenance of order and the production and distribution of goods and services. Each of these functions is performed through some social structure such as family, school, state, church, or business enterprise.

School is a place of formal learning. It is a very vital social institution. This institution provides occasion and process of transmission, communication of group heritage, common to all society. It conserves and transmits culture to the younger generation and it trains and socialises the individuals. This performance serves societal needs and helps to identify school as a social institution. A school, as a social institution, is a structure of society that is organised to meet the needs of people chiefly through well-established procedures. It is an organised system of relationships which embodies certain common rules and procedures and meets certain basic needs of the society.

The school is a unity of interacting personalities (Waller, 1932). Here, the student can demonstrate his/her perception of cause and effect relationships by identifying major changes in society. Like other social institutions, schools are forms of procedure. They are dependent upon certain recognised and established set of rules, traditions, and usages. These usages and rules may be given the name of institutions. They are the forms of procedures that are recognised and accepted by the society and they govern the relations between individuals and groups. To attempt to isolate causal mechanisms involved in those interacting relations of human beings, have their locus in the institution of the school. On this way, the giving and receiving of instruction constitutes the nucleus of the school as an institution.

The following characteristics may be identified in the concept of school as an institution of society:

(i) Institutional frames of school are the means of controlling individuals by meeting some persistent needs or desires of collective behaviour established in the social heritage.

(ii) Like other institutions, schools are dependent on the established forms or conditions of procedure characteristic of collective activities of men that can demonstrate sensitivity of human needs by identifying social problems and cultural differences.

(iii) Like an institution, school has some proceedings that are formed on the basis of customs and dogmas to maintain social structures and machinery through which human society organises, directs and executes the multifarious activities required for human needs.

(iv) As an institution, school is more stable than some other means of formal social control and it is the organisation of rules, traditions, and usages, which are essential to generate more knowledge about the methods of social control.

(v) Every institution has some rules that must be compulsorily obeyed by the individuals. In a school's functional structure, the hierarchy of controlling system maintains its stability by obeying and moulding the ideas and attitudes.

(vi) Schools, as educational institutions, are formed to satisfy the socially recognised primary wishes of men. Schooling for all would help to foster the physical, emotional and spiritual talents of everyone, as well as their intellectual abilities.

(vii) Institutions, like schools, are the forms of procedure that are recognised and accepted by the society to produce a subservient workforce of uncritical, passive and docile workers.

(viii) Institutions exist for the society and govern the relations between members of the society. School as an institution transmits both general values, which provide the "necessary homogeneity for social survival," and specific skills, which provide the "necessary diversity for social co-operation."

## The School as an Organisation of Society

Every organisation is dependent upon certain recognised and established set of rules, traditions, and usages. These usages and rules may be given the name of institutions. There may be several institutions within an organisational structure. An organisational structure is the term applied to the particular arrangement of the interrelated institutions, agencies and organised patterns, as well as the statuses and roles which each member assumes in the group conduct.

Organisational structures are a significant factor in school systems, for lags in the structure aggravate many educational problems. Hence, many of the changes which will occur in education in the near future will involve the changing forms of organisation; these changes not only are likely to affect the way of functioning of schools, and the conditions under which teaching occurs, but they will have enormous implications for the status of teachers within the school bureaucracy and possibly in society as a whole as well.

Apart from the structure of the school, Durkheim (1956) also observed the functions of education in society and their co-relations. In the school, as an organisation, the students, teachers, advisors, officers, employers and the members of parent-teacher association provide the school to fulfill its functions. The relationship between these people can be analyzed sociologically as a whole (Etzioni, 1995; Schneider, 2005). From the perspective of sociology of education, the schools are considered as organised educational centres to conduct educational functions.

Durkheim (1956) identified formal school, for its complexity in modern society, as an organisation and believed that it was the duty of education to make responsible and reliable citizens out of school children. To effectuate parents and teachers need to work hand in hand to achieve a common goal. From this goal achievement index, we can find that some schools succeed while others fail. Goal displacement is a consequence of bad schools, which differentiates them from effective schools and confirms a dialectical position to the good schools.

In bad schools, the performance of pupils and teachers is not as expected. This may be due to poor quality of education. Effective schools are those which produce good results due to effective teaching but do not make learners to be accepted members of the society in terms of their behaviour. Where as in good schools there are higher expectations, good monitoring, safe and orderly environment. Typically the school is organised on some variant of the autocratic principle. Details of organisation show the greatest diversity. The sociology of organisation in 21st century identifies three main components of social organisation of the school. These are the curriculum, the assignment process, and the environment.

The curriculum is the body of knowledge or information that is presented to students in school. The assignment process tends to be fairly stable, when for a learner to perform as expected to achieve a common goal, there should be a conducive environment. In other words there should be mutual relationship. To elaborate more on sociological ideas, where ever there is a group of people, there is participation, cohesion and conflict. These lead us then to an understanding that sociology of education becomes the study of association in terms of participation and cohesion in school organisations. The schools are "service-providing organisation" (Parsons, 1961: 39), which consists of relatively stable patterns of interaction organised around tasks, such as in the case of schools administering tests, operating the library, or maintaining an athletic programme. The interaction defines relationships between the parties involved, each of which is expected to behave in particular ways.

The functions of school systems are, in large part, the functions of organisations in general. School systems are organised to the extent that there is an orderly procedure for replacing members who leave the profession or the system and some available means of socialising them into the school culture before and after admission. The work of the system is divided into orderly but variant patterns, and procedures are available to allocate personnel, with or without their complete consent, into various segments and programmes. Selection standards are designed, or they simply evolve, and a promotion system provides an orderly career for both the higher and lower participants of the organisation.

Schools are considered as organisations, because they contain groups as well as individuals occupying clearly defined statuses and taking on clearly defined roles. Each person in this educational organisation occupies a position that has a specific set of duties and responsibilities, and those positions can be "ranked" according to their relative power and importance. In global school, complex divisions of labour generate problems of coordinating the whole process, which in turn promotes the growth of a cadre of administrators and administrative assistants; but, even so, much of the responsibility for organisation falls on the lower and middle participants (the students and especially the teachers), whose power and authority over the decision process is not always in coordination with their responsibilities. This is an organisational lacuna, which is common and visible feature of everyday social life.

The schools are considered as organisation in sociology, because (1) they may large in size; (2) complex network of positions is created for a specific educational purpose; and (3) they are characterised by a hierarchical division of labour. Thus, the school is an organisation by which educational activities are conducted regularly and continually (Hunt, 1972). As an educational organisation, the school provides the students to gain knowledge, ability and attitude in accordance with the aims and principles of the educational system. The school is a social organisation on its own as well as it can be handled within the context of the relations and its place within the society. Within this context, the roles of teachers and students, authority relations and disciplinary action in the school are important (Brom and Selznick, 1963). To the teachers, education is a planned and conscious activity of modern era that aims to train experts who need it. Actually, schools are the indispensible part of the general social system of any and every society. All kinds of innovations and changes in the society or in the world directly have an effect on education and school in terms of process, organisation, structure and functional dimensions.

### Challenges to Schooling for Education

The expansion of educational provision was stimulated by and helped to consolidate the creation of national cultures. The educational system helped to produce, to validate and to disseminate secular knowledge and an individualistic and materialistic culture. Moreover, mass systems of education have played an important part in the structuration of social classes and in the consolidation of distinctive patterns of racial and gender divisions, contributing to the reproduction of complex patterns of asymmetrical life chances. Albeit of these, people behave the way in society because their behaviour does not meet with social disapproval. Culture has provided a number of checks on irrational conduct and suggestibility. Cultural aids such as schooling or scientific training lessen the chances that a man will behave irrationally or irresponsibly. The members of this schooling processes are characterised here as a part of informal education.

As schools in the 20th century became an increasingly core societal institution, sociologists directed continuous and concerted effort toward understanding both their structure and their effects on individuals. Over the past century, sociologists who developed the theoretical framework for the discipline of sociology of education as a whole (e.g., Emile Durkheim, Max Weber, Talcott Parsons, Pierre Bourdieu, James Coleman, and John Meyer) also directly focused and wrote on the role of education in society. It was because, schools were complex institutions, and sociological theorising was multidimensional and multilayered (Arum, et al. 2015: xii).

The current focus of educational research on improving cognitive development, measured often narrowly by standardised test score performance, has distracted attention away from other critical problems associated with contemporary schooling of any country. Problems of moral authority strike at the core of public education, because schooling in primary and secondary levels is as much about the socialisation of youth as it is about teaching rudimentary cognitive skills. Emile Durkheim (1961 [1925]: 148), one of the founders of modern sociology, argued that "the nature and function of school discipline . . . is not a simple device for securing superficial peace in the classroom—a device allowing the work to roll on tranquilly". Schools, instead, are often the first social institution outside the family responsible for contributing to the process of molding youths for productive adult roles in society. Discipline, according to Durkheim (1961[1925]: 149), "is essentially an instrument—difficult to duplicate—of moral education".

From this perspective, "public schools are as much about shaping individuals' attitudes and dispositions as about imparting specific sets of cognitive skills" (Arum, 2003: 3). On the other side, better behaviour in private schools was the result of higher rates of intergenerational connections and closures in private school communities (social capital). From James Coleman and Thomas Hoffer (1987) perspective, the difference in disciplinary climates was more likely the result of the difference in the legal environment that public and private schools face. Private schools were more easily able to expel unruly students and in general enforce stricter disciplinary practices with fewer threats to the legitimacy of their actions. Education, in the field of economic-sociology, feels interest in this perspective of privatisation of knowledge and market economy.

Education, like the notion of progress itself, has had to accept a more tentative and less grandiose role. Schooling is important for the skills and knowledge it conveys and develops, and for the part it plays in the construction of identities (Bilton, Bonnett, et al., 1996). The shifts in educational philosophy since the Second World War - from education for the sake of a fairer society, to education for the economy; and from equal opportunities and child-centred learning to unequal assessments and common standards - have involved both continuities and discontinuities in educational policy and practice.

The expansion of education in the decolonisation years after Second World War has provided some opportunities for upward mobility by working-class pupils, and has helped to confirm pupils from middle-class backgrounds in middle-class jobs. There is a great deal of variation in educational performance across ethnic and racial groups, especially when gender and social class are also taken into account.

The usefulness of educational accounts that focus upon the cultural inheritance of particular groups of pupils depends upon how sophisticated is their notion of culture, how they see the relationship between culture and material circumstances, and whether they can avoid stigmatising certain children as "culturally deficient" (Douglas, 1967). What is taught in schools is always subject to selection and, therefore, choice. These choices will always be disputed - by educational specialists, politicians and citizens alike.

Within this context of our modern civilisation, education faces numerous challenges. It can be summarised from *Fundamentals of Sociology* of Vidya Bhushan and D.R. Sachdeva (2012: 144-145).

First, it faces the problem of the curriculum and the methods of executing it. What shall be taught at the school and college level? What subjects a student will be required to offer and what contents will be included in each subject? We find our universities and boards changing the syllabi of different classes off and on under the pressure of political and other extraneous considerations, leading to confusion and sometimes even to repetition.

Second, the present schooling system sharpens only the memory of the students. It lacks in providing practical based knowledge acquiring habitus. To be meaningful, education should attempt to develop body, mind, and heart.

Third, the educationists have to find an answer to the following issues:

(a) To what extent shall formal education follow the lead of the social education movement, which attempts to inculcate values through indoctrination, and even propaganda?

(b) Does formal education include extracurricular or co-curricular activities in the campus?

(c) Can we bypass the moral education from our formal education?

(d) To what extent should the state control the management and aid the finances of an educational institution and prescribe what is to be taught at the school and higher levels?

(e) Should the so-called "public schools" be abolished to implement the theory of democracy in education?

(f) What should be the place of examinations in testing the achievements of the students and what should be the system of examination?

Fourth, certain subjects are never brought to the attention of the child on the plea that they are beyond his comprehension. These "tabooed" subjects are taught at the secondary or college level. What happens to the child who does not go through college? Does the exclusion of certain subjects from the school curriculum not handicap his growth as a full man?

Fifth, what should be the place of vocational education in our system of education? Should education concern itself with turning out expert craftsmen or should it give emphasis on liberal education?

Last, how can education preserve our culture and also train people to explore and introduce new values in our everyday life?

While the status attainment paradigm has been extraordinarily influential in the sociology of education, this crisis in schooling for education approach is not the only source for the development of concepts applied to the study of education. Contemporary sociological research on schooling has also been strongly influenced by thinking about educational processes in terms of human capital, cultural capital, and social capital.

## Education is Sociological

Education is a process that aims biological, emotional, mental, social and moral development of human beings (Thornburg, 1984). In our contemporary world, this process was formed to a regular and planned structure which is carried out in a planned and scheduled way. The school is the important component of this structure. The school where education is carried out collectively is one of the most important centers of an organised educational venture. It will be beneficial to know and use some sociological concepts to understand behaviour of students, teachers and school directors in these centers (Willower and Carr, 1965).

Education shares a basic rule with sociology. Educational phenomenon cannot be regarded as an individual action; rather it is a social phenomenon or even a social being. The research field of sociology of education belongs to sociology instead of pedagogy. That is to say, the core concepts of sociology reflect the modern social phenomena, like "science," "rationality," "democracy," "advancement," "development," and so on. Sociological researches and writings give emphasis on the trends of social phenomena, like scientific innovation, welfare state, social mobility and educational opportunity in modern society. These efforts also focus on the consequences of these educational processes or the ways in which people perceive their class situation, their life-chances and the experience of social change.

When sociology was founded, one of its chief founders Auguste Comte (1798-1857) had obvious intention to make it like physics to study society by the methodology adopted from natural sciences. He gave the positivist perception of sociology to the top position in his construction of the structural hierarchy of sciences. The substantial content of Comte's research, social statics and social dynamics are two of his perspectives. According to him, humans' moral improvement helps to stabilise and advance society and it should be achieved in modernity through the knowledge of natural laws (Pickering, 2009). Another French founder of sociology, Emile Durkheim made a clear methodical distinction between traditional society and modern society and pointed out that the educational act, as the unilateral action of the adult generation upon the immature, plays a central role in the process of modernisation.

Modernity as a social and mental structure promotes the application of science in production. On the other hand, modernisation is a process in which society, culture and individual acquire tested knowledge respectively, and apply it to everyday life. Thus, when modernity is identified as a set of characteristics of social organisation and corresponding ideology, then modernisation is a kind of movement, something people ask for with will, and a kind of mobilisation through "body pedagogics."

Like Durkheim, Max Weber explored those forms of "body pedagogics", which refer to any conscious activity that is designed by an organised form of knowledge to enhance individuals' understandings of their own and others' corporeality. Both Durkheim and Weber sought explication of the social importance of the cultural body pedagogics, which is a basic characteristic of a society. Both Durkheim and Weber saw the need for rationally organised agencies of education; and both believed that the requirements of modern society dictated State control. Weber opened the way for a "comparative sociology of education"; and it was precisely this comparative perspective that caused him to recognize "the selective function of education in addition to that of value transmission" (Sieber and Wilder, 1973: 9).

Based on this recognition, Weber (1991) identified culture not just as a matter of cognitive or symbolic knowledge, it also entails an education into socially sanctioned bodily techniques, dispositions and sensory orientations to the world. The control, guidance and direction, which are provided by education through the development of rationality, help to form intellectual and emotional dispositions in children. The possibility for counter-rationalities that embrace veridical meaning rests on the work of Karl Marx, who had explored some of the links between education and social inequality. In sociology of education, Marxists have examined the relationship between education, the economy and the contemporary labour market.

Sociologists have responded to the changes that occur in educational systems, where they are involved in debates concerning the relationship between school and work, patterns of schooling especially in the secondary sector, comprehensive education and the content of the school curriculum (Burgess, 1985). Sociology of education as a field developed focus on two separate levels of analysis. At macro level, sociologists worked to identify how various social forces (such as politics, economics, and culture) created variation in schools as organisations. At further micro level, researchers sought to identify how variation in school practices led to differences in individual-level student outcomes.

In addition to these distinct levels of analysis, researchers further developed separate foci on various aspects of the functioning of education in society. While some researchers focused on economic aspects of education (e.g., how economic forces shaped school practices and how schools determined individual productivity and earnings), others focused on related issues of socialisation, allocation, and legitimation. While approaching research in sociology of education, these distinctions are useful to keep in mind (Arum, et al. 2015: xii-xiii).

The study of education applies a sociological approach in understanding education system in which school system is the main focus of sociology of education. To this effect sociologists look at the structure of the school and interactions in the campus level. He/she looked at the way individuals interact, that is teachers with fellow teachers, teachers with pupils, administrators with fellow administrators, administrator with teachers and pupils and pupils with fellow pupil. He/she looked at how discipline can be maintained in schools to understand the problems of education from a sociological perspective.

Education is sociological not because of its character that gives emphasis to the interactions' level within the school, but because of its nature to study the relationship between the school and the community. Sociology of education looked at the outcome of these interactions because individuals have influence on other individuals and society has ample scope to influence the community level educational system.

Within sociology itself, there is a continuing distinction between theoretical approaches which concentrate upon social structures and how they constrain individual action and those which emphasise the way people in interaction construct their world on a day-to-day basis (Henry, 1988). We suggest that the sociology of education should take both approaches into account. By these two approaches, sociology of education should not only deal with the relationship between modernity of education and modern society, but also the connection between modernity of education and rationality. As a result, sociological theorists in sociology of education should be responsible for the exploration of these relationships.

## The Nature of Sociology of Education

Educational sociology is a field of study that deals with the role of education in the development of knowledge, skills, values and attitudes that help to transform society towards a better social, economic and political order. So the problems, like social mobility, social status, gender relations, school dropout, etc. are the issues that generally compacted in educational sociology. For that reason, the educational sociologist is concerned with the analysis of the social factors that affect the development of education and feels interest to study the school-community relations. Thus, when educational sociology is preferred to stress on the practical applications, the sociology of education, on the other side, is often used to denote theoretical exposition of the social problems related to education.

D. A. Hansen (1967: 22) argues that the distinction is useful and can minimise confusion about the nature of the sociology of education. "Such confusion is avoided and more critical gains promised if the term "educational sociology" is used to refer to the pursuit of a normati theory of education and to research that is primarily directed to furtherii that normative theory or to direct application. "Sociology of education would then refer to the pursuit of empirical theory and to research that i. essentially directed toward furthering it." Thus, the early development oi the sociology of education is seen primarily as a normative subject, which is concerned with specifying what education or schools "ought" to be or do in carrying out the educative function.

Before the Second World War, educational sociology as a field of study was increasingly improving in England. The sociology of education emerged as an important sub-discipline of sociological theory after the Second World War, particularly in Britain. It was Karl Mannheim, who helped in establishing the sub-division of sociology of education within the English academia. Here the work of sociologists in identifying the patterned relationships between social class and school achievement was in part responsible for important policy reforms in British education, in particular the gradual eradication of the iniquitous 11+ exam and the moves towards comprehensive schools. This reformation mode was also true for American educational system. Joseph Slabey Roucek (1956; 1958) stated that in the years between 1920 and 1940, a well-defined and well-structured "school" of American educational sociology did not come into existence.

It did not exist because of the fact that "writers put most of their attention not only on social values, norms and sociological adaptation in education considering educational sociology to be a sub-branch of education (rather than of sociology) but also they offered assistance to educators to identify and to make its goals and methods clear and comprehensible. They are known to be "educationists" rather than being known to be sociologists in the field. Due to such reasons, social philosophy was mixed with sociology and it got hard to differentiate them from each other. As the number of educators who are prone to be more like a sociologist increased in "Applied School", they attempted to bring sociological principles into prominence; they believe and suggest, in general, that educational sociology is a sub-division of sociology" (Aslan, 2020: 188).

According to B. Y. Card (1976), sociology of education gained the most promising popularity as a term immediately after it was rejected to be called "educational sociology" by the American Sociological Association, which was believed to try to develop and control and manage

United States in the 1960s. And in Canada, the Francophone ...one traditions felt the need to verify the usefulness of the ... education by testing it empirically as a potential innovation. ...ogy of education was developed in Canada as a cumulative ...ent of sociological knowledge, and as a social science adapting ...oulded by its power context. After the Second World War, "the ...gy of education has grown from a "no-thing" to a "thing-in-itself" ...adian society" (Card, 1976: 3).

...For the sociologist of education whose work was normally confined ...he study of education systems in the industrially developed "Western ...orld," entered into the intellectual landscape of developing societies in ...ost-war phase. As a social invention, sociology of education had penetrated in this developing world specifically when the structure of core institutions such as universities, was still being transformed by their internal and external forces. The major contours of the sociology of education landscape, as far as the developing "Third World" is concerned, "are determined and can only be understood sensibly in terms of the two opposed and entrenched theoretical paradigms of *modernisation* and *dependency*" (Ball, 1981: 301).

In this phase, the sociology of education was taking shape globally for certain elements in it. If we categorise those elements of sociology of education of this phase, the following three categories may be conceived under which most of the elements would be assumed. These three categories are: (1) *personnel* - with their specific origins, attitudes, interests, habits, training, statuses, and roles; (2) *knowledge* - the knowledge persons concerned with the discipline considered as useful and valid, also the aggregate of concepts, beliefs, ideas, and modes of thinking associated with the discipline; (3) *patterns of interaction* - the institutionalised patterns of classroom teaching, research, consulting, participating in policy-making, production of journals and textbooks, developing and participating in professional associations, plus non-institutionalised, collective behaviour that may in diverse ways affect the invention and diffusion processes.

Globally, in 1960s, the result of the early interest in sociology among educators and educational administrators was that they saw sociology could serve as a tool to generate information about and answers to pressing educational problems. These relationships help in fostering widespread interest in sociology of education research. Indeed, during the years between 1950 and 1965, educational sociology was observed as progressively transforming itself into a scientific specialty quite clos connected with sociology rather than education; throughout that proce it was started to be called "sociology of education."

Some policy-relevant educational research is open to analysis from a variety of perspectives. The nature of sociology of education is determined by some predominant issues of society. In a wide range of national contexts, one of them is race and ethnic relations, with the shifting of focus depending on the composition of minority groups within particular settings. Lawrence J. Saha (2008: 305) observes that: "In the United States, sociologists are particularly interested in the educational attainments of African-American and the Hispanic populations. But in general, similar attention has been given to all minority groups, especially since movements of populations across national boundaries have increased, both voluntarily and non-voluntarily. The study of racial and ethnic minorities has included indigenous, migrant, and refugee populations. Sociologists of education in the United States, Britain, Canada, and Australia have been particularly active in this research." In developing countries, like India, much of the early work in the sociology of education either drew from structural functionalism and other conflict models that had been abandoned in the West, or produced unique work not widely known outside of specific national or regional contexts.

In Africa, the establishment and growth of sociology has been patchy—Nigeria is probably the only country with a full-fledged sociological community of its own. In India also, sociology has established itself, but again there is little in the way of exchange of work. Here the programmes of "relevance" education have "made a major impact on their respective national systems of schooling" (Sinclair & Lillis, 1980: 37). These offensives against the domination of western curricula range from Gandhian Basic Education in India to innovations in basic secondary education in Cuba. They are all marked by attempts to weaken the boundary between school and community, by the establishment of work-related programmes, and by attempts to weaken the boundary between educational knowledge and "the everyday community knowledge of teacher and taught", by introducing material on nutrition and health, crafts and agriculture, into the curriculum.

In some other contexts the range of questions that may be explored through sociology of education research remains restricted as a result of various political, financial, or logistical factors. The overall field of research in the sociology of education is diffuse and dynamic.

, regional, and linguistic factors influence the kinds of ‹ientations adopted in particular settings, but the prevalence ‹inant research traditions and interest in several common ‹is (such as relationships among education and social change, ‹ in educational access and outcomes, and the impact of on on education), as well as often top-down policy agendas, re is considerable convergence in the focus of research. Just as ‹e differences in how sociologists understand and explain ‹ional problems, researchers in the sociology of education employ e range of research approaches and methodologies in their work.

The sociology of education thus focuses its attention on understanding w the institution of education functions in relation to other social ‹stitutions in society. It studies how the various institutions such as caste, ‹amily and in general the structure of the society shape the institution of education and in turn how they are shaped by the institution of education. Thus, the nature of sociology of education is to focus on the various social functions that education may have such as socialisation or the reproduction of the inequalities based on race, class, gender and caste.

While much of the sociology of education has focused on identifying how schools affect students, an equally interesting and productive line of research has focused on how social factors structure school organisation. Cultural explanations for variation in school practices are inherently appealing (Tobin, Wu, & Davidson, 1989), but sociologists have attempted to move beyond these simplistic explanations to uncover the deeper underlying structural causes for school variation. Sociological analyses of the external environment of schools have also focused on one major problem area, the impact of social class on education. More studies have probably been devoted to this problem than to any other area in the sociology of education (Gross, 1959: 144).

The theoretical dimension of structural functionalism is highly significant for its formative impact on the development of the sociology of education. It has drawn attention to crucial questions about the relationship between education and other spheres of social life as well as to the role that persistent social inequalities play in advanced societies. Talcott Parsons (1959: 277-8) has presented one of the most influential structural functionalist accounts of education in his discussion of the socialisation and allocative functions of schooling. The researchers, who are dealing with modern social institutions reveal the nature of education in capitalist society—that education is the tool of the dominant classes;

and this perspective has provided by the conflict theory in sociology of education with theoretical basis and foundation in reality. The meritocratic and democratic visions promoted by liberal and functionalist analysis are criticised as ideologies that serve the interests of dominant social groups.

The sociology of education is concerned with those theories and concepts which are the abyss between the chalk-talk and pupil (Bernstein, 1961). Sociologists continue to address these issues from different stances. The nature of the sociology of education varies on the basis of coming of these different aspects. For example, a critical pedagogy, as a form of cultural politics, involves more in learning pedagogical techniques and the knowledge required by the mandated curriculum. More than most other approaches within the sociology of education, critical pedagogy is grounded in the actions of classroom practitioners. The analytical nature of this stance is based on the characteristics of rationality from the psychological point of view, what Georg Simmel treated sociologically as the capability of human beings to pursue goals in a conscious and tactful way.

The critical pedagogy is the study of oppression in education. This perspective focuses on the rectification nature of sociology of education. It is based on two propositions: (1) oppression exists, but the forms of oppression may differ; and (2) the transformation of oppressed is possible, the oppressed can liberate themselve by knowing the causes of oppression. Paulo Freire (2005[1970]) argued that, to be human, we need to be self determined. His work was to humanize man, humanize through conscious action and transformation of the world. To act upon his/her oppressed situation one needs to develop critical consciousness. The struggle for humanisation is possible to break the dehumanisation of the banking concept of education. Education should raise the awareness of the students so that they become subjects, rather than objects, of the world. This is done by teaching students to think democratically and to question continually and make meaning from (critically view) everything they empirically learn.

Different empirical verifications cover recent theoretical developments in sociology of education, as well as applications of theory and research on a broad range of themes highlighting educational issues in several national contexts. "Reproduction Theory," "Resistance Theory," "Theory of Relative Independence and Will," "Cultural Capital Theory" and so on have strong echoes of Marxism. A neo-Marxist perspective on the sociology of education has been developed to explore the relationship pitalist objectives and the educational system, where reparation of students is guided to be future workers on the s in the hierarchy of capitalist production.

t Gintis and Samuel Bowles (1980: 52-3) outline the dence principle that links schooling with the economy: "Given significant success of capital directly and indirectly structuring and in the face of the undemocratic nature of economic life, s could not fulfill their egalitarian and developmental objectives. oncluded that the only means towards the achievement of progressive cational reform is the democratisation of economic life, allowing for emocratic and emancipatory school system which does not conflict ith the formation of adults capable of effective participation in the system of production."

In the sociology of education, for instance, feminist analysts have criticised classroom studies for ignoring the central role that gender plays in the construction of students' school experience and school outcomes (Weiler, 1988: 41-42). More radical versions of feminism, in the process, have also inspired researchers and educators to take seriously the questions about sexuality, body practices, social identity, and related issues that have typically been excluded from education and related discourses. Queer theory, influenced by postmodern critiques of language and practices seen to categorise and regulate people arbitrarily, adopts a more radical stance by contending that no sexual or gender identity is normal.

Judith Butler (1990), in particular, argues that specific categories such as male, female, lesbian, gay, or transsexual act as labels that fix expectations about behaviour and identity and thereby constrain and channel our actions in specific ways. Gender, for Butler, is performs as we express various dimensions conveyed through these categories in our dress, speech, and other actions. Butler's theory of performativity has been influential well beyond research on gender and sexuality in the sociology of education, informing studies in such areas as race, ethnicity, class, disability, youth cultures, and teachers' work (Ball, 2004b; Youdell, 2010).

Basil Bernstein (1996) made a significant contribution to the study of communication with his sociolinguistic theory of language codes, which was developed to explain inequalities based on social class as found in language use. His sociolinguistic concepts of field of production, recontextualisation and educational codes (the elaborated code and the restricted code) may contribute to the researchers on the role and significance of pedagogy in development research and evaluation activities (Atkinson, 1985). Bernstein's sociology of education offers to create a pedagogy which would weaken the relation between social class and educational achievement by variously strengthening and weakening classification and framing as they relate to different classroom practices and relationships.

In the new millennium, in regard to the nature of sociology of education, a point of issue is whether it is a branch of learning under sociology or under pedagogy. Whatever may it be, it is evident that the sociologists of France, Germany, England, Canada, America, Australia, Brazil, Japan and India determined the various aspects of education according to educational sociology. This educational sociology reinforced the already substantial foundations of sociological tendency in the field of educational studies and tried to incorporate the philosophical aspects of educational processes in social life. This breaking point helped social scientists to develop the sociology of education as a discipline that studies the basic relations between education and society.

Some scholars study sociology of education from the perspective of education. Some scholars carry out research in this field by using the theory and method of sociology. Some educators hold that sociology of education is a branch of pedagogies. Some scholars tried to deal with the influences of educational processes on social relationship and the effects of sociological processes on education (Arce-Trigatti, Chukhray and López-Turley, 2018). With educational theory being combined with the study of society, the research and investigation must carry out a useful and realistic study of the issues of education, with an eye to resolving concrete educational problems.

Standing on this point, it is not an exaggeration that the agenda of educational sociology or sociology of education vary on the basis of the contextual philosophical background, the time frame and the nature of social problem. Indeed, towards the end of the nineteenth century, in opposition to an individualistic theory, a pedagogy emerged which held that the nature of education should be considered from a social perspective. In conceiving of the nature of educational sociology or sociology of education in a nutshell, the stage based change in the academic field is to be gauged. As this change occurred in a varied time frame in different philosophical arenas, there may be included the fallacies of oversimplification and overlapping. Still, this may be beneficial in understanding the nature of educational sociology or sociology of education.

Michiya Shimbori (1972: 7) proposed this stage based explation as: In the first stage (1900-1910) educational sociology consisted of the compilation of sociological findings useful for teachers; in the 1920s, it was a sociology of education from the essentialist point of view as against the psychological "Measurement Movement"; and in the third stage (1930-1950) it became a sociology of educational problems, what is called the functional school of educational sociology by some, a scientific base for the "Community School Movement" or for the diagnosis of youth problems. A quantitative methodology was deeply employed in several studies.

Cengiz Aslan (2020) identified a stage, what we may consider as the fourth one (the 1960s): the interactionists' orientation phase, wherein the position of education amid the changes in society and culture and the relations between social mobility and accessibility to education should be accounted. In this stage, the nature of sociology of education had turned its interest to the influence of education upon society, including the role of education in economic development, in the recruitment and training of manpower, and in achieving national independence, unity or revolution. This may be referred to as "demonstrative sociology of education," with the emphasis on establishing complete, objective theories to facilitate the understanding of practical and also possible problems of society.

The fifth stage (the 1970s) depicted the new nature of sociology of education, where a conscious effort to question both school practices and the structure of knowledge and curricula had emerged. Critical of previous conventional sociological and educational analysis which took for granted what happens in schools, the new sociology of education sought explicitly to expose the power relations embedded within educational practices. While this approach drew inspiration from emergent critical sociological analyses, its orientation to research problems and methodologies was primarily interpretative.

Sociology of education of the late 1970s and 1980s from the Marxist perspective and the post-modernist variants that came then, seem to have a basic principle to regard knowledge as "socially constructed." Thus, the nature of sociology of education in this sixth stage (the 1980s) was an external ideological attack. It is said that since the 1980s, the "new sociology of education" has become closely and highly distinguished from "radical" or "critical" sociology of education. The researches were grounded in linguistics and anthropology, and they employed ethnographic methodology in study.

The 1990s is considered as a transitional decade that led in increasing awareness of and resources for national assessment of education. We may consider this seventh stage (1990-2010) as "knowledge transfer" phase, where the nature of sociology of education is very much associated with the inclusive models of educational research. It is a "state of the art" of knowledge utilisation procedure in education and it recognises the proliferation of centers, laboratories, intermediate units, museums and collaborative enterprises as a sign and the process of "knowledge transfer." Effective global policies, programmes, gender orientations, and environments in schools provide some technology based global aims for future empirical research.

The eighth stage (2010 to present day) conveys a new nature of sociology of education. Here occurs "shifts in learning modalities," in which we are learning how adaptable and resilient educational systems, policy-makers, teachers, students and families can be. The pandemic has changed the nature of sociology of education in early 2020s. Two crucial factors have shifted due to the pandemic. First, pedagogical adaptations have proven to be pivotal as the traditional lecturing in-person models and translate it to a remote learning environment with virtual control. Second, the pandemic has recalibrated how teachers divide their time between teaching, engaging with students, and administrative tasks.

## Concluding Remarks

A defining characteristic of the human species is the transference of knowledge and tradition from one generation to the next. The process of transferring accumulated knowledge, skills, and cultures across generations is fundamentally a social process, requiring communication and interaction among people who exchange ideas, skills, attitudes, and feelings. Schools have been developed and have evolved to enhance and systematise this transfer. The transfer is conducted not by computers, teaching machines, textbooks, laboratory equipment, and videotapes; rather it is the direct result of interaction between human beings—between teachers and students, and students themselves.

Education appears as a powerful resource which both affects society and also affected by it. There is a close relationship among needs of societies ideal and values of them and educational systems. There is now enough available evidence on the role structure and relationships in school and classroom. The classroom still contains much unexplored research territory. A fresh approach to the analysis of school impact also is offered by the techniques of systems analysis and simulation gaming, both relatively new to behavioural science and educational research. Sociologists could help in the evaluation of educational innovations and in the development of new learning environment. Research on student peer groups, an agent of socialisation operated both inside and outside the school, has already indicated that many young people will not apply their best efforts to learning tasks unless this is consistent with the norms of their informal friendship groups.

Durkheim's premise is certainly supported by the substantial body of evidence showing that the strongest predictors of a school's academic productivity are the background characteristics of the students' parents and the characteristics of the neighbourhood or community in which it is located. Mostly sociology of education has focused on the local level resources to which students have access and the equitable distribution of those resources. To be sure, such resources as family education and income contribute directly to the opportunities students have to learn in the home and school. But a key aspect of the family resource determines the school the children attend. And a critical resource of the school is the quality of teaching. As a direct result, differences among teachers within and between schools contribute to inequities in opportunities within and between schools.

Schools are considered as social organisations, which are units that partly necessitate continuity in terms of the presence of society and achieving its objectives. The school like other social organisations is part of the society. The schools have become obligatory educational institutes in almost all the societies. Schools are complex social structures in which students, teachers and school administrators interact with each other and educational experiences of the child are shaped. The organisational climate, in sociology of education, does not just define the organisation in structural terms; rather, how members of a school community perceive the routines, practices, and policies influencing their beliefs and practices.

For the progress and development of the individual and society, it is important that educational system, schools and teaching activities to be carried out in a critical approach providing changes and developments. Sociologists of education have given emphasis on the most critical relationship between the teachers and pupils in educational organisations. Although other relationships in educational organisations undoubtedly have important latent functions, their manifest function is to maximize the educational outcome of the teacher-pupil relationship in the classroom, considered as a social system.

The specific role of the sociology of education is assumed once, it has established itself as the science of the relations between cultural reproduction and social reproduction. "This occurs when it endeavours to determine the contribution made by the educational system to the reproduction of the structure of power relationships and symbolic relationships between classes, by contributing to the reproduction of the structure of the distribution of cultural capital among these classes" (Bourdieu, 1973: 71).

As a marginal discipline, sociology of education should have the following special features: First, the combination of theoretical objectives and practical objectives. Second, in the application of concepts, sociology of education applies in a mutually penetrating way the basic concepts of pedagogy and sociology. Third, assimilating and making use of new study methods (Yixian, 1987: 14). The strength of the sociology of education is its ability not only to bring the schooling process to the centre of educational research, but also to challenge many of the prevailing assumptions about the content of schooling. Knowledge is produced, defined, and given meaning and importance through the social contexts in which it appears.

Consequently, much of the research in the new sociology of education, like other forms of interpretative analysis, is devoted in providing detailed descriptions and outlines of the significance of everyday occurrences, such as patterns of joking and teasing in the classroom or the hidden meanings contained within school text-books. Whereas other forms of analysis tend to overlook or trivialise day-to-day activities, interpretative sociology brings these to the forefront as crucial components of social life. Jerome Karabel and A. H. Halsey (1977: 47-8) observe that the new sociology of education was predominantly a British phenomenon that paid little heed to previous, mostly North American classroom research, such as the studies referred to above. However, the attention given by contemporary policy-makers and educators to priorities associated with the emergence of knowledge-based societies has rekindled interest in the kinds of questions posed within new sociology of education explorations concerning what is meant by knowledge and whose knowledge counts the most.

In 21st century, we can view the sociology of education from a more scientific perspective, where the discipline is seen to produce scientific knowledge about the relationship between education and society, and about the causes and effects of schooling. Thus, the label "sociology of education" has its roots in the sociological tradition which attempted to create a "science of society," and emulate the natural sciences. The sociology of education leads to the conclusion that education is a relatively unexplored but potentially rich area for sociological inquiry.

# Chapter - 3

# The Scope of Sociology of Education

The objective of this chapter is to provide a clear understanding of the ways in which educational systems, structures, and processes connect with various aspects of society. Schooling processes, practices are the prime foci in sociology of education. In this new discipline, the terms and concepts have been derived directly from sociology. This endeavour hopes to lead to more efforts in clarifying the nature of sociology of education and thus becomes much wider in its scope and application.

On the relationship of and outcomes to the organisation of society as a whole, the sociology of education also focuses on the social groups and the relations between them. These groups include the teachers, students, parents, officers of the ministry of education, school administrators, school inspectors, community representatives, and others. As an academic path of social sciences, it includes the manner in which students come to abide by the norms and values of society at large, and the role the educational process plays in recreating or changing the social structure as this relates in particular to a system of differentiation, gender segregation and hierarchy of power.

Education is the way through which one generation transmits the wisdom, knowledge and experience with a purpose to prepare the next generation for life duties and pleasure. These processes pave the hierarchy of power structure. Philosophically, education is a condition of human survival. Sociologists have defined education as one of the major social institutions. It "provides knowledge about knowledge" (Manton and Moore, 2010:1). The most important function of education remains that of socialising people with survival skills to become productive members of society. Through a formalised and standardised procedure, i.e. the institutional framing, human beings not only acquire new skills and knowledge, but also restructure the social settings.

Education prepares individuals to do things, which is their responsibility. In our everyday experience, we see that a society has a set of aims, mores and values to which all members pledge and they are to, some extent conscious of the direction in which they want them to change. Thus, every society seeks to produce a particular type of person. It is the role of education to develop the personality of the child not only for this purpose but also to prepare him to be the member of his society. Human personality is not doomed to struggle forever seriatim with a long list of detached groups of facts, in order to get its psychic and social development. The world of experience is one, not many. Pedagogy and sociology are discovering this unity by different processes, and as a consequence of their perception that educational material is essentially one, not many; pedagogy and sociology are bound to combine their demands for a complete change of front in social education.

Education is sociological "because it is part of a network of interrelated societal institutions, because it is a *social process* and because of its *functions*, both intended and unintended" (Abdi and Cleghorn, 2005:5). The "intended functions" are generally referred to as the prescribed curriculum. These functions refer to those aspects of education that come immediately to mind when we ask ourselves what do that schools do. The sociology of education involves human beings and requires them to interact so that the intended knowledge, skills, and values to be transmitted. On the other side, the "unintended functions" are sometimes referred to as the "hidden curriculum," a term coined by Philip W. Jackson (1968), and it refers to the implicit messages students receive about such matters as punctuality, neatness, achievement, deference toward teachers (authority relations), and the like. It also includes the subtle ways in which schooling inculcates in students the values of the society's dominant group.

Thus, the scope of sociology of education is vast. It is concerned with general concepts such as society itself, culture, community, class, environment, socialisation, internalisation, accommodation, assimilation, cultural lag, sub-culture, status, role etc. It further involves the cases of education and social class, state, social force, cultural change, various problems of role structure, role analysis in relation to the total social system and the micro society of the school such as authority, selection, and the organisation of learning, streaming, curriculum and so forth. It deals with analysis of educational situations in various geographical and ethnological contexts with the background of different races, cultures etc. For example, the educational situations in rural, urban and tribal areas are also included in the research of sociology of education. It helps us to understand the effectiveness of different educational methods in teaching students with varied intelligence.

The primary scope of sociology of education is related to socialisation. This provides a deep study of the role and structure of schools and peer groups, and their impact on the personality development of the students. It also helps us to understand the effect of various social agencies like family, religion, police and rules on the students. It studies the relationship between social class, culture, language, parental education, occupation and the levels of achievements of the students. It also investigates the effect of economy upon the type of education provided to the students. It confers an understanding of the problems such as racism, communalism, gender discrimination etc. It suggests ways to develop national integration, international understanding, the spirit of scientific temper, globalisation among the students. It promotes research studies related to planning, organisation and application of various theories in education. All these are the concerns of education and sociology as inseparable discipline focusing on the problems of the society.

## Pedagogy and Conventionalised Abstractions from Reality

The proper educator is reality, not conventionalised abstractions from reality. Hence the demand of the new pedagogy, which is simply not a curriculum, or an act like "teaching," rather it informs both. It is not a nebulous concept and it is "both act and discourse" (Alexander, 2001: 540). Indeed, the term pedagogy derives from the Greek word *pais*, meaning "child," and *ago*, meaning "to lead." Very literally then, *pedagog* means "to lead a child." It is essentially a combination of knowledge and skills required for effective teaching.

Pedagogy is about learning, teaching and development, influenced by cultural, social and political values and principles we have for children in society and is underpinned by a strong theoretical and practical base. This new pedagogy, supported heartily by the new sociology, states that schooling, particularly in its preliminary stages, shall be changed from an afflictive imposition upon life to rationally concentrated accomplishment of a portion of life itself. Here education prepares individuals to do things as their responsibility to do them. For example, Freire's (1970) pedagogy is grounded in a fully developed philosophical anthropology, that is, a theory of human nature; one might say a secular liberation theology, containing its own categories that are virtually irreducible to any other philosophy.

Pedagogy considers how man is developed through his total environment of narrator and nature; while sociology considers only the relation of the individual to his social environment. While pedagogy is based on the relation of the individual to his objective and universal self, sociology is based on the relation of the individual to the institutions of society as the projected realisation of the self. Sociology has to consider the adjustment of the tension between man's social environment and his individual welfare. Sociology, thus, furnishes a means which pedagogy must recognise, while pedagogy furnishes to sociology the laws of individual development by which sociology must regulate itself.

Pedagogy is defined as "a controllable input rather than as a process whose dynamic reflects the unique circumstances of each classroom and which is therefore variable and unpredictable; and the only aspects of pedagogy which are admitted as 'inputs' are those which can be measured. The whole exercise becomes impossibly reductionist, and the educational endeavour itself is as a consequence trivialised" (Alexander, 2008: 7-8).

Pedagogy has the broader scope, in that it considers man in relation to his whole environment, but on the other hand, it must be observed that sociology takes into account all instrumentalities of education as a part and function of the social structure (Sriprakash, 2012). Hence, the distinction is not in the breadth of subject-matter, but in the point of emphasis. While pedagogy considers how the individual lives in and through the entire thought and life of his environment, sociology considers the best organisation of social agencies to further the foregoing life process. On one hand, sociology seeks the best social structure through which pedagogic theories may realise themselves, and on the other, it investigates one realm of the environment through which the individual is educated.

Modern societies differ from their earlier counterparts in term of their heavy reliance on impersonal pedagogical procedures of macro-level system integration. Moreover, these macro-mechanisms gradually detached from the micro-level processes whereby people's everyday life worlds are integrated through open communication leading to mutual understandings and the possibility of well-informed consensus. This discrepancy between system integration and life world is based on impersonal "steering mechanisms" and social integration which is on communication results in large part from the growing size and complexity of society.

This foregoing debate suggests a more immediate connection between these two subjects, in the fact that sociology deals with the subjective side of the individual as externalised in institutions – with the objective fact of the individual which is the substantial foundation to the subject of pedagogy. Thus, the sociology of pedagogy deals with man, who projects many sides of his life world into the forms of institution, in order to be a component of more liquid and complex living with a highly developed division of labour and high levels of individualism.

## From Pedagogical Model to Educational Sociology

It is historical fact that Durkheim's position at the University of Bordeaux in 1887 in pedagogy and social science reflected the first academic recognition of social science in the French university system. When he was promoted at the level of full professor, the name of his professorship was changed to science of education and sociology. The nature of sociology of pedagogical model allocates full responsibility to the teacher for what subject will be learned, how it will be learned, and ultimately has the concept been learned by the learner. Based on assumptions of learning and teaching evolved in European monastic and cathedral schools between the seventh and twelfth centuries, pedagogy is the educational model from which most U.S. schools, including higher education, have been derived.

Last decade of nineteenth century demanded for educational sociology. As Dr. William T. Harris (1893:84), whose training and interests were psychological rather than sociological, wrote: "... but no philosophy of education is fundamental until it is based upon sociology not on physiology, not even on psychology, but in sociology. The evolution of civilisation is the key to education in all its varieties and phases as found in family, civil society, State, and Church, as well as in the school. Once placed on this basis it is easy to connect any one theory of education, that of Froebel, for example, with another that of Chinese verbal memorising, or that of the study of Latin and Greek in American colleges, and to show their rationale and the amount and kind of positive help given to the pupil by each."

A few years later Professor George E. Vincent (1897:v) stated: "the thought of social philosophy which sees in the development of society the growth of a vast psychic organism to which individuals are intrinsically related, in which alone they find self-realisation, is of the highest significance to the teacher, to whom it suggests both aim and method."

Still later Professor Charles A. Ellwood (1911) declared: "now, the science of education has evidently two chief problems, the problem of the aim of education and the problem of organising a curriculum which shall be in harmony with that aim. It is the contention of this paper that both of these problems are essentially problems in an applied sociology, and that the science of education, in so far as it concerns these two fundamental problems in education, is essentially an applied science resting upon sociology."

In "after-dinner address" at the annual dinner of the Harvard Teachers' Association, Harvard Union, March 7, 1908, Dr. Henry Suzzallo (1908: 340) declared: "as we have school hygiene and an educational psychology, so we must have what is basic, an educational sociology." Then, as Walter Robinson Smith proposed, educational sociology was defined: as the application of the scientific spirit, methods, and principles of sociology to the study of education. By such study the social laws governing education may be obtained and applied in such ways as will improve our educational practice" (All these quotes are cited in Smith, 1917a: 15-17).

Twentieth century searches the nature and scope of educational sociology. In its primary disquiet "educational sociology is chiefly concerned with the generic facts and sociological principles and laws revealed in such study of past events" (Snedden, 1922: 350). In analyzing education and its factors as major social process, educational sociology has been frequently informative and helpful to refer to educative processes found among primitive or earlier historic peoples. For educational sociologists, it is therefore, necessary and expedient to introduce any considerable count of the evolution of education and evolution of human civilisation.

Donald Francis Swift (1969: 2) proposed the name of Emile Durkheim as the father of modern "educational sociology." Educational sociology "was deeply distributed by the developing trends in modern industrial society." In Swift's view Durkheim "sought a way out from approaching disaster by reorganising social life, and education was to provide the solution."

Educational sociology must aid in accounting for the large differences among social groups due to heredity, skills, environment, and opportunities. From these differences, there flows a divergence in educational programmes, where pedagogy prevails. Pedagogy also exists in many social relationships where visible forms of oppression and repression are deployed (i.e. workplaces, prisons, etc.) as well as in the sphere of benevolent services where individual care based on specific skills is carried out (i.e. general medicine, social work, psychological support, etc.) (Queiroz, 2011: 56). Pedagogy prevails everywhere, where human beings strive to cure minds, souls and their bodies.

## From Educational Sociology to Sociology of Education

In *Education et sociologie* or *Education and Sociology* (1956 [1922]), and *L'education morale,* or *Moral Education* (1961 [1925]), Durkheim established a clear connection of representation with action. For him the only alternative to rationalism is mysticism. The source of moral evaluation is the collective utility. He wrote: "We must repeat this representation, but in repeating it, give the idea enough colour, form and life to stimulate action. It must warm the heart and set the will in motion" (1961 [1925]: 229).

Here Durkheim sets out his idea of how children can be taught to adopt a set of shared moral values based on self-discipline, freedom, and order. In keeping with his rational, secular, scientific view of society, Durkheim believed that every society had its own education system which was shaped by the society-cultural needs. He also believed that education was the influence exerted on the young generation by the old generation and this influence was a changing process. He said that changes in education practice have a relationship with changes in societal beliefs and practice. Hence, he believed that education was a social control mechanism and an apparatus of transmission of knowledge.

The central idea of Durkheim's sociology of education is that education is about establishing the basis for a shared morality within a given society. Durkheim viewed a system of morality as the lynchpin to society. It is now becoming customary to refer to the sociology of education rather than the old and now suspect terminology of educational sociology. This sociology of education is not the educational sociology in its strict sense. There are, indeed, some differences between them when they come to the subjects of their study.

The interest of educationalists like John Dewey ensured the subject an early start, and it soon became a popular subject in colleges and universities in the U.S.A. "Between 1910 and 1926 the number of colleges offering a course in educational sociology increased from 40 to 194, and

25 textbooks were published between 1916 and 1936" (Corwin, 1965: 56). Yet by 1940s the number of colleges offering it had declined and the subject generally had fallen into disrepute (Banks, 1971). There were different reasons behind this descend status. Three of them were crucial in nature. Firstly, educational sociologists gave a strong emphasis on a programmatic and polemic approach. Secondly, educational sociologists had primordial research techniques. And thirdly, educational sociologists focused on a limited area of problems of interest to the practising teacher. In 1963, James Conant, by making a plea that educational sociology should be taught by sociologists, was able to write: "As to whether the present group of professors who consider themselves educational sociologists, should perpetuate themselves, I have the gravest doubts. I would wish that all who claim to be working in sociology would get together in the graduate training and appointment of professors who claim to use sociological methods in discussing school and youth problems" (Conant, 1963: 131).

In *The Sociology of Education,* William Taylor (1967) had suggested that separate use of two terms, "educational sociology" and "the sociology of education" might be maintained in order to preserve the distinction between an emphasis upon educational or social problems and an emphasis upon sociological problems. According to Tylor (1967: 191), "although in its more rigorous forms it [educational sociology] has brought a good deal of sociological insight to bear upon educational problems, it has tended to be hortatory rather than empirical, inspirational rather than objective, and synoptic rather than analytic."

In a new way sociology of education emphasises sociological aspects of educational phenomena and institutions. The problems encountered are regarded as essentially problems of sociology and not problems of educational practice. This view of sociology of education is different from the concept of educational sociology which is seen as the application of general principles and findings of sociology to the administration and/or processes of education. This approach attempts to apply principles of sociology to the institutions of education as a separate societal unit. The problems of educational sociology are derived from the field of education.

Sociologists of education must abide by certain specific standards in conducting research, called a code of ethics (Bernstein, 1996). The sociologists of education must respect the human dignity of their subjects, and must respect free and informed consent, vulnerable persons, privacy and confidentiality, justice and inclusiveness. In addition they must balance harms and benefits to subjects, minimising any harm. In reality, sociology of education researches on more ethical issues which are related to personal finance and classroom application, highlighting socio-historic connections and moral elements in financial literacy.

The sociologists of education are helpful in illuminating the role of schooling in constructing social problems, where education is effectively carried out in alignment with certain class practices on a daily basis and where the school is conceived as an institution responsible for shaping and diffusing values and conceptions of social subjects, knowledge and learning (Bautier, 2011). Thus, the content of the sociology of education includes general concepts as the society itself, assimilation, accommodation, dominance, social inequality, equity, sub-culture, cultural lag, status, class position, socio-cultural reproduction, socialisation, order and control, teacher's occupational role, etc. Some other considered issues are as (1) the effect of the polity and economy on education; (2) the social forces and determinants that effect educational and cultural change; (3) the social institutions, which involved in the educational process, such as the family, the school and the church, and their various problems in role structure and their role analysis in relation to the total social system; (4) the micro-society of the interaction, communication, link or network and other connectivity are viewed as a formal and informal organisational structure, involving such problems as authority, selection, the organisation of learning and streaming; (5) the relationship between social class, culture and language, and between education and occupation; and (6) problems of democratisation and elitism. These all fall within the purview of sociology of education.

## The Functional Scope of Sociology of Education

Within the general framework of a structural functionalist approach of Durkheim and others, the sociology of education has been developed as a largely macrocosmic study of educational institutions. But in the contemporary field of research, there are two levels of analysis in sociology of education. Firstly, the macrosociology of education that focuses on broad features of social structures in society, like social classes and the relations of groups to one other. Secondly, the microsociology of education that focuses on processes and patterns of social interaction on a smaller scale. Thus, the sociology of education is not directly associated with the branch of applied sociology, rather makes it as a field of specialised discipline. It attempts to develop necessary principles and laws considering education as a system of society. It is concerned with both the construction of a theory and its application.

On the other hand, the educational sociology attempts to apply the innovated principles of sociology to the field of education as a branch of applied sociology. It does not apply any principle that evolves somewhere in the field of sociology of education. As a discipline of social sciences, it uses the results of sociological researches in planning educational activities and in developing effective methods of realising these plans. Its main aim is to study social interaction and it focuses on the importance of the interactions of different elements of the society with an individual.

The functional nature of sociology of education is both to provide analytical tools and to promote practice in education likely to follow societal progress. The failure of sociology of education to influence policymakers in many countries is not just for its unpopular critique of government but also its perceived lack of immediate practicality in the face of huge global shifts in the social and political power order. Sociologists of education have two immediate tasks: (a) to locate the power of the individual, group or country within the new global order; and (b) to find a value position which is internationally valid and transparent. By considering these tasks, the sociologists of education may persuasively engage in critique of educational policies and educational action oriented programmes in the era of globalisation.

Glocally, financial literacy is not merely the process of acquiring and accumulating money for oneself, one's family or one's business. It has a more sophisticated core. It is a citizenship issue. It deals with the justice and social structures that justify wealth distribution through merit-founded argumentations within a global-local nexus. This is a key-point in the sociology of education now, especially for scholars adopting a conflict approach to define and redefine the concept of financial knowledge that focuses on the role of economic, social, and cultural capital in inequalities. The knowledge now holds forms and it "'bits' fit together in a time and space not given by a specific context" (Hoadley and Muller, 2010: 75).

## The Institutional Location of the Sociology of Education

As far as the education of the individual is concerned, now sociology of education focuses on the influence of social life and social relationships on the development of personality. At this point social psychology links up with the sociology of education. Here social psychology as an academic effort tries to understand how the thought, feeling, and behaviour of individuals are influenced by the actual, imagined, or implied presence of others and becomes a scientific study of the principal relations of individuals to one another or to groups, collectivities, or institutions, insofar as they substantially influence, or are substantially influenced by, social forces.

The considerable majority of sociologists, interested in education, utilise social psychology in the sense that they analyze the social organisation of schooling as antecedent to individual aspiration or achievement. This is demonstrated in the particular perspective used for the study of a given problem. Specifically in American sociology researchers are spotting on individual psychological states and behaviour, treated primarily as consequences of social influence (Conant, 1963). They may give emphasis on primary social relationships as the immediate sources of this influence and, therefore, as mediating institutional or collective influences, and by strong implication, the idea that the person's cognitive and emotional states in some way link social context and individual behaviour.

The institutional location of the sociology of education is its view of teachers. This varies considerably across different approaches in this discipline. In some accounts, teachers have been seen as mere fiddles of the system and they unwittingly act as social agents and arbiters of children's careers and are powerless to do anything to change it. On some other accounts, they are seen almost as the shock troops of the revolution to be brought about by means of the education system, or at least as the critical sociologists of education who have the power to demystify the world, to undermine the hegemony perpetuated through schooling.

An approach can consider the position of teachers from a consistently related antagonistic way to the students. It has an adverse effect to the development of students' moral judgment. Some approaches may stress the nature of teaching as passion, or as a profession. Others focus on who become teachers, on their class or caste background. One major strand of work in the sociology of education, classroom ethnography, has teachers as its central focus.

## Gender Dimension of Sociology of Education

The inclusive reality which sociology of education finds comprehending both the processes and the products of these reactions is society, i.e., individuals in association within the conditions imposed by the material environment and modified by human achievement. From this perspective, in the 1950s and 1960s, the British sociology focused on the contribution of education to culture, social mobility, social-class differences in educational attainment, life-chance, gendered position in educational aspiration, and the explanation of these dimensions. Since then the subject has developed in several ways "as a distinct field of study" (Moore, 2013: 10). Firstly, empirical research into teaching methods attempts to identify the effectiveness of different teaching styles. Secondly, reflecting the interest within mainstream sociology in accounts of ideologies, sociologists of education perceive schools as agencies of cultural reproduction and purveyors of a hidden curriculum. Thirdly, school and classroom ethnographies provide descriptions of the social systems of schools, and draw attention to the significance of pupil-teacher interactions for educational attainment. Here sociologists of education promote a direct observation of the activities of the members of specific social group and the description and evaluation of such activities. The last but not least scope of sociology of education is one of the richest veins for feminist sociologists, who investigate the role of the school in reinforcing gender stereotypes among children.

Feminist sociology of education contributes to analyze the gender relations in education. It adds critical views to an understanding of the broader relationship between education, society, and inequality. It was only towards the end of the 1960s that the focus of the debate moved from questions of the organisation of schooling to the content of education and therefore to the curriculum itself (Young, 1998). The typologies of curriculum based positions in the "hierarchies of abstraction" are studied by the concept-rich disciplines. Nonetheless, the sociology of education continues to be marked by theoretical fissures, discontinuities and sometimes-acrimonious paradigm disputes. In 1977, Michael Apple recognised that the women's movement had a particular politics. He observed that the movement had appropriated liberal notions of rights in order to be treated as "full functioning citizens" in the home and workplace and in the state (Arnot, 2006).

The feminist and postmodernist traditions, on one hand, force educationalists and sociologists to engage in critical reflexivity about their own research thereby making the social relations of research production in education itself a subject of critique and investigation. On the other hand, critical analysis plays an important role in highlighting questions of value in research, and in introducing debates about the transformative potential of research in education (Lynch, 2006: 91). Since 1980s the sociology of education has been frequently linked to feminist and anti-racist critiques of public schooling. The critical tradition which persisted within sociology of education in 1990s was very different in its intellectual orientation from what was defined as critical thought in the 1970s and early 1980s. First, it began to challenge the simple correspondence models of reproduction exemplified in the work of Bowles and Gintis in the 1970s by incorporating notions of agency and resistance into debates. Second, it recognised the importance of non-class forms of social exclusion (gender, ethnicity, race, etc.) for understanding the patterning of domination and inequality in education (Morrow & Torres, 1995).

Here the task set for each researcher is to accommodate herself/himself with the prevailing conditions in such manner that she/he may both accomplish and enjoy a maximum share of the development by which the micro stage in social change is empowered to accomplish. This life task of a participant researcher consequently sets the pedagogical task of teachers. Thus, the prime problem of education, in a sociologist views, is how to promote adaptation of an individual to the social conditions, natural and artificial, within which individuals live, and move, and have their being. It would not be in point to discuss here the relative place of action and information in progress toward this end that belongs to the sociology of pedagogical technology.

## Concluding Remarks

Knowledge can be used as a tool for transforming or changing the situation that may natural or social. In any social setting, knowledge helps to alleviate oppression. This knowledge and human experience are politically charged and interrelated -- this recognition accelerates the formation of critical pedagogy. This critical pedagogy followed in the wake of the human potential movement as a way of fostering a more oppositional position toward education and schooling practices. Critical pedagogy is a way of thinking about, negotiating, and transforming the relationship among classroom teaching, the production of knowledge, the institutional structures of the school, and the social and material relations of the wider community, society, and nation-state (McLaren, 2000: 35). The main purpose of critical pedagogy is to prepare citizens for democracy and teach courses that "speak to" that purpose (Breuing, 2011:8).

Critical pedagogy became an issue of interest to feminist pedagogy. On a way, like critical pedagogy, feminist pedagogy is based on those assumptions of the power of consciousness which try to end the events of oppression and work toward a vision of social change and transformation (Abdi and Cleghorn, 2005:18; Gore, 1993). All educators, who plan education, have always been forced to think of their purposes in terms of social well-being. But the problems remain. Problems of whom to educate and to what specific purposes to educate have, therefore, for thousands of years linked up intimately with political, religious, moral, economic, and cultural thinking. Educational sociology is chiefly concerned with this generic facts and sociological principles and laws revealed in its study.

Using "field" theory of French sociologist Pierre Bourdieu and "code" theory of British sociologist Basil Bernstein empirically, in order to capture education as an emergent and irreducible social structure, the sociology of education may participate in financial education projects that contribute to the creation of different economic "habitus" for children, which in turn lead to social disparities, or can highlight the socially constructed codified nature of curriculum and describe subjects as resulting from struggles for status and resources among subgroups, which showed how mother-child and school language influenced the achievement of students and sustained a social class. Thus, the scope of sociology of education identifies its limit in sky.

# Chapter - 4

# Subject Matter of Sociology of Education

The sociology of education is a relatively autonomous subject, because it conducts teaching and research. It is also relatively autonomous in relation to theories and about other fields of investigation. Contemplating present state of thinking, one of the persistent problems of sociology of education is on what grounds sociologists of education can claim that they have a field of their own, distinct from that of general sociologists, anthropologists, psychologists, historians, economists and other groups of specialists.

The subject matter of sociology of education is "societal space," which is after all nothing, but a composite unit in which individual human beings form the component parts of social milieu. It is therefore, necessary for sociologists of education to rely in the first instance on the findings of all those other disciplines which, like human biology, social geography, psychology or history, study individual human beings – the component parts of societies as such – and then to see whether they as sociologists of education have anything to add to these findings.

Sociology of education thus is not only mere an interdisciplinary subject among others, but a subject which encompasses, updates, and transforms all others. It is a subject that stems from, and attempts to satisfy the contemporary needs to articulate different kinds of human knowledge into one whole. It is ordered perspective both for the sake of interpreting, understanding in itself, and to provide a basis for sane and sensible social reform.

Though it is interdisciplinary, but it holds its methods of enquiry, as well as subject matter, as a relatively autonomous scientific type of knowledge. It is often thought that the transition to scientific types of knowledge depends primarily on a changeover to the use of a particular method of investigation. In its precise sense, the sociology of education is methodical. The methodology of research is a tool of thought in which the investigator wants to gain more scientific knowledge by using the theoretical base of the philosophical imagination. It is also assumed here in this context that the image of nature as a self-regulating process has always been prevalent, and the discovery of some new ways by focusing on the individual examples of regular relationships should be gained by the researcher.

In reality, the theoretical conception of a nexus of events and the method of investigation contain a reciprocal interdependence. In that condition, it is particularly difficult to develop a relatively autonomous conception of society, which can served as a key to scientific discovery. The reason is that, in such a conception, the conflicts are not only tied to pre-scientific conceptions of society but also with prevailing scientific conceptions of nature. Practical interconnections in the social order are not identical with those at the lower level of integration represented by physical nature. This is not recognised universally. All our ideas about impersonal nexuses of events stem directly from the level of physical nature, or from a realm of experience, which are derived all categorically.

Furthermore, the professional groups involved in research in the natural sciences possess particularly great social power and, in consequence, social status. Social scientists, like all upwardly mobile groups, are only too eager to bask in the reflected glory of the older sciences by adopting their prestigious models. Unless this is borne in mind, it is impossible to appreciate why it has taken sociology so long to develop as a relatively autonomous field of investigation.

The development of people's conception of the subject matter is found to be inseparable from their conception of the method appropriate to its investigation. It is the science that based on methods and techniques on one hand, and on a good deal of pseudo-specialisation, on the other. The sociology of education thus deals with relative autonomy of scientific theory about its subject matter.

Here the quantitative research produces fact-like conclusions and law-like generalisations about human behaviour and social interaction. In contrast, qualitative research grounds in a dual commitment to realism and constructivism. The primary concern of the quantitative study of social life is to understand the causal relationship among individual actions and the actions of those others who share their social world. The qualitative understanding is best achieved through intimate and prolonged participation in the social settings under study.

If we turn away from the restrictive rules of the philosophical study of science, and take the sciences as objects for theoretical and empirical investigation, it will then soon become apparent that the conception of the subject matter, as it emerges in the course of scientific work, is meaningfully interreliant with the conception of the method used to investigate it. So, the sociologists of education apply social network methodologies in their study of teacher communities, classroom conduct and learning (McFarland et al, 2011: 87). Quite a number of sociologists of education, in fact, proceed in this manner. They investigate the behaviour of learners, views and experience of individual member and process their results statistically.

By means of inquiries of this type, focused on the "component parts" of societies, they endeavour to bring to light the systemic characteristics of the "composite units," of the societies themselves. And as some of their findings in fact indicate social connections and regularities beyond the reach of other disciplines concerned with the study of human beings singly, these sociological findings are often implicitly treated as the solution to the problem of whether or not sociology of education can claim some kind of autonomy in relation to these other individual-centered social sciences.

## The Paths to Understand the Subject Matter

The intellectual climate in which the sociology of education is currently taught is one where there is a debate about the identity and subject matter of the discipline in terms of content (debates about theory and about fragmentation), of purpose (the public-sociology debate) and of inflection (the critique of gloomy sociology considers that things are seriously wrong and getting worse) (Marshall et al., 2009). Considering these three debatable points, there are three main paths for delineating the subject matter of sociology of education.

Firstly, the historical path, whereby we seek through study of the works of founding fathers of the sociology of education. This path considers five thinkers, Karl Marx, Emile Durkheim, John Dewey, Max Weber and Karl Mannheim, as the central figures in the development of sociology of education. Altogether, they span the whole of the nineteenth and first half of twentieth century, during which modern sociology of education was formed.

Secondly, the empirical path, whereby we study current works of theorists in sociology of education to discover the perspectives to which the discipline gives most attention. Here, in sociology of education, contemporary thinkers are incorporated. Mostly, Paulo Freire, Basil Bernstein, Michel Foucault, Pierre Bourdieu, and John Wilfred Meyer and some other name are included at the time of discussion. The focus is given on the interdisciplinary research they undertake, the reports they present or the perspective they reflect in their scholarly articles.

Thirdly, the analytical path, whereby we randomly and frequently partition and fulfill the process of compartmentalisation in larger subject matter and allocate them as an indispensable part of specific disciplines. Here the unit of analysis is society as a whole. And the aspects of social processes which link one to any other are its characters which depict an interlocking system of action.

## The Historical Path: What the Founding Fathers of Sociology of Education Said?

The sociology of education is not merely a collection of sub-disciplines on all realm of life, but rather is the study of those aspects of social life, present in all knowledge forms (Wexler, 2009). Throughout the world, education has become a vast and complex social institution that prepares citizens for the roles demanded by other social institutions, such as the family, government, and the economy.

In fact education has always varied greatly from one society to another, and in the same society it has taken different forms at different times in its history. French sociologist Emile Durkheim (1858-1917) rejects the idea that these differences are due to a series of mistakes in apprehending the true nature of man, or failures to adapt education to its real purpose. He speaks of education as a sociologist and considers education as a social fact.

The core of Durkheim's sociology of education is the idea that education is about establishing the basis for a shared morality within a given society. He considers education, a system of morality, as the lynchpin to society. Without a shared sense of morality, a society would crumble; and education is the principle means to secure this shared sense of norms and values. In *Moral Education* (1925), Durkheim sets out his idea of how children can be taught to adopt a set of shared moral values based on self-discipline, freedom, and order. From this point of view, in usage, he clearly distinguishes the term *éducation* from that of *pédagogie*. To him, *éducation* is the active process to educate the young, while *pédagogie* is that methodical thought, which is applied to the process of education.

Emile Durkheim theorised educational systems as a social construct, used for the replication of social norms and values, and Karl Marx (1818-1883) also believed that education as a part of superstructural element was shaped to maintain the economic system. For example, the part played by education in occupational and social selection will be much less pronounced in pre-industrial as against advanced-industrial societies, where the selective functions of education tend to predominate. Similarly, while it was reasonable for Marx and Engels (1969: 79-81) to observe the early stages of industrialism that "a general prohibition of child labour," on which compulsory universal education depended, "is incompatible with the existence of large-scale industry," it can with equal truth be asserted of present-day technological society that such a prohibition is essential to the continuance of the economy.

His dialectical methodological approach focuses on the problems relating to the interaction between the education system and society. Thus, the Marxist contribution to the research in sociology of education establishes the conditions and connections of education as a component part of the generative social process and also treats the education system as a societal organisation that functions in all levels of interaction between social forces. Like Marx, Max Weber (1864-1920) was concerned with educational institutions becoming an increasingly limiting force on academic freedom.

Weber becomes unique when he identifies education as a differentiating agency, socialising individuals into the total lifestyle of the strata for which they are destined. In this sense higher education has been essentially a phenomenon of status rather than class, a process directed "against the market." He perceives the university as a corporate structure in process of adaptation to industrial society. His general definitional view of status is, in the long run, determined by access to market opportunities. He points out that, "'the cultivated man,' rather than the 'specialist' has been the end sought by education and has formed the basis of social esteem in such various systems as the feudal theocratic and patrimonial structures of domination: in the English notable administration, in the old Chinese patrimonial bureaucracy as well as under the rule of demagogues in the so-called Hellenic democracy" (Gerth and Mills, 1948: 242).

In sociology of education, the studies from a Weberian perspective also explore and explain the changes in educational systems as an outcome of conflicts between rival status groups aspiring to control education and access to certain benefits. Additionally, the term status is employed to explain advantage or underachievement in education. Currently, however, status is mostly employed descriptively as shorthand for social position, as for instance women's status, or indicating a current state of affairs, as in the term health status.

John Dewey (1859-1952) strongly believed that a democratic form of life in which a community is made up of individuals who interact with and respond to society's need through cooperation and a sense of public spirit, was the ideal social context. He viewed knowledge as the "instrument" that guided and controlled the interactions, an approach he called "instrumentalism." Indeed he saw a direct link between instrumentalism and social theory. He contended that humans are, from the outset social beings and that the individual can only achieve success and satisfaction, existing in an educative environment that promotes these interactions. Thus, Dewey affirms his conviction that education must be a process of living and not a preparation for future living.

Dewey (1997[1938]) considers education to be one of the social techniques, a general category of methods for influencing human behaviour so that it fits into the prevailing patterns of social intention and organisation. He glimpses this technique of education as an instrument of social reconstruction. Karl Mannheim (1893-1947) was much influenced by this view of American education, which was under the influence of John Dewey's pragmatism. Like Dewey, he places less emphasis on the conservative social function of education and more on the part that education plays in social change. Mannheim, more than the other classical theorists, visualises education as an essential tool for the social reconstruction of mass society which he views as composed of disconnected groups of atomized individuals with no social ties.

Mannheim's formal treatise on the sociology of education, which was published posthumously from his lecture notes (Mannheim and Stewart, 1969), reflects his ongoing concern with education as a broad social process, that is, the reflection of a society's social and philosophical values. He made the distinction between the "school in society" and the "school and society" in an effort to emphasize the existence of what he called the "educative society." Mannheim's primary concern with knowledge and ways of knowing meant that he directed attention not only to formal education and schooling, but also to other educative processes.

Like Emile Durkheim, Mannheim initiates a tradition (the sociology of knowledge) within which asking questions about the roots of knowledge have been central in UK. He certainly proposes that future teachers should think about epistemological questions. It is worth reflecting, but the sociology of education at his time (after the WW-II) was dominated by the "political arithmetic" tradition established by Charles Booth and Seebohm Rowntree which saw it as a kind of neutral "science for government."

Thus, research on the way of education affects other social behaviours, and the factors which determine education outcomes, that is, educational attainment, achievement, and performance, are incorporated in the sociology of education. The sociologists of education have been at the forefront of theoretical and methodological developments from these classical perspectives. It is generally acknowledged that the modern sociology of education began with the work of Emile Durkheim. Because Durkheim was both a sociologist and a pedagogist, and his approach to the study of education was eminently sociological. His work on moral education, on the sociological forces, which affect educational development, and his focus on the link between education and society have produced a body of sociological literature which has influenced several sociologists of education.

In considering education as conflict, the Marxist view of schooling, and particularly of school processes, shares much with its functionalist counterpart. The Weberian perspective explores a causal explanation of courses and effects of social actions with an absence of a unified theory of society. Albeit of this, the teacher expectations and the process and implications of labeling have been a focal point of a sociological study of education based on Weberian perspective. Dilthey, and late existential philosophers such as Martin Heidegger and Hans Georg Gadamer, consider the philosophical position of hermeneutics as the theoretical foundation for the investigation and interpretation of social life. Mannheim, a renowned figure of "new generation" classical sociologist, has indirectly exercised an impact on thinking about education by and large through his writings about ideology and knowledge, and his sociology of knowledge. Late-twentieth century sociologists of education who take sociology of knowledge perspective or who see the curriculums as negotiated epistemai are the followers of the pioneering work of Mannheim in this area.

From this classic context, the sociology of education has become one of the most vibrant and respected areas of sociological research. Because of the theoretical developments, that have taken place within the sociology of education, there are few areas within sociology which do not treat education as an important variable. In social stratification, or in class research, or in the research on race, ethnicity, crime, deviance, formal organisations, exchange relations and others, all use education as either independent or dependent variable.

Thus, the sociology of education cuts across disciplinary boundaries, and includes important work in curriculum studies, history, gender studies, cultural studies, postcolonial studies, critical race theory, and so on. The legacy of the classical theorists is apparent, which traces the development of theoretical paradigms in the sociology of education, for example, functionalism, conflict theorising, including the Marxian and Weberian inspired conflict theories, and finally forms of interactionist theories.

## The Empirical Path: What Sociologists of Education Do?

If we take "what sociologists of education do" as our guide to what the sociology of education is about, we should then examine two main sources: (1) the perspectives of social scientists to explore the field, and (2) the research they undertake and the reports they publish in books and in their scholarly-journals to identify themselves with one or another branch of sociology. If we observe these two sources, it will be easy for us to understand the empirical paths of the subject matter of sociology of education.

It is evident that conventional sociology of education has resorted to statistical probabilistic models rather than generalisation of laws or law-like explanations. Laws, and law-like models of explanations, should be differentiated from merely empirical generalisations which address the issue of how to move from empirical observations to definitions of causality (Banks, 1971). The problem of identification of causal explanations without relying on interpretations becomes non-problematic when we think of theoretical statements as hypothetical deductive postulations, that is, "logical constructions rather than real entities" (Bredo and Feinberg, 1982: 21). A logical distinction between theory and observation, or construction of a principle to differentiate theory from method, becomes easy in considering a great deal of the empirical work that is being developed in the recent perspectives in sociology of education. This is theory driven research, relying on case studies.

The empirical models in sociology of education do not consider scientific work as separated from its theoretical foundations and universally applicable. The debates among paradigms and approaches, ranging from modernist to postmodernist perspectives and structuralists to poststructuralist models, indicate that any pretension to establish a sense of certainty and analytical precision in a world, which is increasingly unpredictable and imprecise, may be pompous and even naive (Morrow and Torres, 1995). Indeed, Carlos Alberto C. Torres and Theodore R. Mitchell (1998) propose that the new perspectives in sociology of education address the understanding of reality as a concrete totality with a great degree of variability and volatility. Hence, the challenge is to traditional notions of linear and evolutionary concepts of knowledge, around which not only deterministic inferences and deductive conclusions are based, but also empirical foundations are organised. This organising force does not embellish the normative distinction between value judgments and empirical judgments; rather it tries to explore more open-ended scientific models.

After WW-II, the teaching of the sociology of education was categorised as "service sociology", a complex area mainly inhabited by "invisible sociologists". For example, the concept of order in sociology of education becomes multi-dimensional. The focus stresses on the ways of some schools with homogenous populations to secure a moral order of sorts, while others with more heterogeneous intakes seek an order suitable for different groups. But within an "interaction order" (Goffman, 1982) the focus is on the extent to which a school can hold students to the content and pace of high cognitive demand subjects (maths, science, languages) and where a school has to "deregulate" its interaction order by bringing in less demanding subjects. From this, patterns of curriculum hierarchy in different schools can be represented in a concrete visual form, to the extent to which some schools can "export failure" to others forced to "import" poor results, and so on.

Thus, the theory about education and empirically based sociology was expanded and education drew attention in sociology through Freire (1970) in Brazil, Bernstein (1973; 1990; 1996) in Britain, Bowles and Gintis (1976) in the United States and Foucault (1975; 1976), Bourdieu and Passeron (1979) in France. In the same period, qualitative and ethnographic research was established in sociology and carried into the school-based ethnographies through Paul Willis' *Learning to Labor* (1977) in Britain; and then R. W. Connell, D. Ashenden, S. Kessler and G. Dowsett's work on *Making the Difference* (1982) in Australia. In India, sociology of education was initiated with the efforts of scholars like M.S. Gore, Suma Chitnis, I.P. Desai, S.C. Dube, A.R. Desai, M.S.A. Rao, Yogendra Singh, Y.B. Damle and others. They jointly conducted an all-India field survey on the social and economic background of students, teachers and parents, their values, attitudes and aspirations in various educational institutions. Together, they published their findings as *Field Studies in the Sociology of Education* in 1970.

Only after a gap of two decades, N. Jayaram published *Sociology of Education in India* in 1990 from Rawat Publications, Jaipur. This was the second attempt to look at the contemporary emerging issues such as the impact of colonialism on our education – growth of urban education, the education-employment mismatch, reservation policy and the role of teacher and student unions (Nambissan and Rao, 2012; Pathania, 2013). Simultaneously, sociology of education has been defined and redefined by a set of theoretical and methodological disputes. Debates among sociologists and educationists regarding the concern of educational sociology and sociology of education and their respective approaches have characterised the dispute. As a result, no serious attempt was made in India to look inside the school system.

### A General Outline of the Subject Matter of Sociology of Education

I. Basic Focus
   Culture and Society
   Multiple Perspectives of Ordered and Disordered Forms
   Scientific Methods and Explorations in Science
II. Primary Units of Social Life
   Social Acts and Social Relationship
   Individual Personality and Collective Behaviour
   Groups (Including Ethnic and Class)
   Communities (including Urban-Rural, and White-Black)
   Associations and Organisations
   Populations and Pollution
III. Principal Social Institutions
   Economic and Primal (including Family)
   Scientific and Networked
   Spiritual and Technological
   Political and Legal

Recreational and Reformative
Aesthetic and Expressive

IV. Fundamental Social Processes
Inequality and Stratification
Socialisation and Gendered Leadership
Social Conflict (including Social Movements) and Change
Socialisation and Social Control
Dominance and Deviance
Inclusion and Globalisation

Sociology of education sees these aspects in its different forms of investigation. The subject matter of sociology of education becomes quite important specifically when sharing knowledge happens to be a process of initiation of the young into the culture of the particular society. It is that process by which the society, through schools, colleges and other institutions, deliberately transmit its cultural heritage (Wexler, 1992). From this adaptive and latency pattern maintenance American functionalist Talcott Parsons saw education as a force to maintain equilibrium and social order. Empirical evidences suggest that educational institutions, by embracing the dominant group's cultural capital, play a significant role in the process of social reproduction.

In these empirical studies, sociologists sometimes include basic data analysis, such as reporting relevant population-level statistics. Their works are largely theoretical and all emphasise education as an organising process that leads to particular outcomes for individuals who are in some way a part of it. In the 1960s, James Coleman and his co-authors' report titled as *Equality of Educational Opportunity* (also known as *The Coleman Report*) moved large-scale data analysis into the field of sociology using basic regression techniques.

In the field of sociology of education, researchers have applied the concept to critique functionalist assumptions on the role of schools in social stratification. Research on stratification within schools further confirmed the results of Coleman's earlier analysis on equity in education – schools are more effective at educating students from privileged family backgrounds. Because schools have been idealised as a great equalising force by understanding why family background is linked strongly to education. This quest becomes the next important goal of sociology of education.

In 1960s the study of oppression in education became central in empirical study of sociology of education and it was concerned about oppression in general, but oppression of the deprived within the framework of educational system in particular. Paulo Freire (1921-1997), a Brazilian educator and philosopher, inspired by Marxist critical theory and other radical philosophies, first described a praxis-oriented teaching approach, which is commonly known as critical pedagogy (Wink, 2005; Kincheloe, 2008). Critical pedagogy is both descriptive and prescriptive, and as an act of analyzing a dehumanising reality, it is context-specific formulation of a scientific humanist conception that finds its expression in a dialogical praxis, with praxis constituting "action and reflection" (Freire, 1985: 155).

Freire's *Pedagogy of the Oppressed* (2005[1970]) wants to transform reality of oppression by a dialectical process, which is a form of learning through questioning. In this educational model, both teacher and students will question and their questions will be contextualised with their social problems. Among its leading figures are Bell Hooks, Michael W. Apple, Peter McLaren, Joe L. Kincheloe, Henry Giroux, and Patti Lather, who propose that without questioning individual cannot become human being, as questioning equips us with the ability to interact with each other and then only we can act and get emancipated.

In the same decade, Peter Blau and Otis Dudley Duncan's work on status attainment (illustrating the critical role of education) provided another important example of the use of large-scale datasets in their case using path analytic models. Since then, quantitative work in sociology regarding education has been operated through various changes both methodologically and data-wise. However, in contrast to Coleman, who believed in the economists' view of free markets modified by social structure, French sociologist Pierre Bourdieu (1930-2002), influenced by the Marxian view of class conflict, suggested that the upper-class is always in a convenient position.

Bourdieu's concept of cultural capital, with its distinctive focus on the social value of cultural habits, dispositions, and skills, is likely to be an important part of the discussions in theories of inequality, the sociology of culture, and the sociology of education in the future (Bourdieu, 1974). For Bourdieu, the unequal opportunity structures of society "determine aspirations by determining the extent to which they can be satisfied" (Bourdieu, 1973: 83). The cutting edge of research in the sociology of education then shifted toward studies of institutional and demographic effects on educational achievement and attainment, as researchers generally sought to avoid debates over whether social psychological models unnecessarily blame the victims of a constrained opportunity structure.

The sociology of education and culture, therefore, has focused some attention on the conditions under which a bond is established between the state and sports organisations in order to impose a sporting culture in school. Indeed, Bourdieu's work emphasises structural constraints and unequal access to institutional resources based on class, gender, and race. These Bourdieusian theoretical and methodological principles influence Loïc Wacquant, who is famous for his concept of "carnal sociology."

Like the relational theories of Pierre Bourdieu, the British sociologist Basil Bernstein (1924-2000), who was well-known for his work in the sociology of education, creates a working conceptual framework for the empirical study in higher education. Higher education becomes, to adapt Bernstein (1990: 166), "no more than a relay for power relations external to itself; a relay whose form has no consequences for what is relayed." Where internalist studies often emphasise infinite heterogeneity, externalist approaches tend to treat higher education as a homogeneous system and neglect its institutional and disciplinary specificities. From an epistemic position, externalism thereby cannot fully address the methodical question of why cultural studies emerged in certain institutions and from particular disciplines denying others.

The methodological curriculum of our education should therefore be adapted to suit our peculiar environment, culture and needs. It may be falsified and thus, education becomes the only agent that works for the process of socialisation, social control and social change. In its formal and informal aspects, it helps to locate one's self. Construction of self and its reconstructed forms craft man's social identity. Sociologists of education see education as an institution, and consider its social impact as multi-paradigmatic. This has lead to confusion for those, whose explanations of social phenomena are based on different paradigms that focus on different modes of inquiry. For example, the French philosopher Michel Foucault (1926-1984) always presents his notion of self-formation as a struggle for freedom within the confines of a historical situation.

The self is a regulated, but not determined set of practices. Foucault defines the care of the self in terms of "those intentional and voluntary actions by which men not only set themselves in rules of conduct, but also seek to transform themselves, to change themselves in their singular being, and to make their life into an oeuvre that carries certain aesthetic values and meets certain stylistic criteria" (1986[1984]; 1990[1984]: 10-11). Surveillance, re-education and training are essential to enhance the visibility of a new architecture of power. Obviously there are some new anxieties. In education, the midst of these new anxieties about children, Foucault espied a "pedagogisation of children's sex": at home, parents, siblings, tutors, and servants, and at school, teachers and fellow pupils, constituted in relation to the child potential sources of danger, contagion, perversion and bad influence. Childhood sexuality was thus the premise around which great battles were fought in the schools, and also the pretext for the reciprocal surveillance of, and the reorganisation of the relations between, parents, priests, police, pedagogues, and physicians (Foucault, 1981[1976]: 110; 104).

It consequently became more pressing, and more justifiable, to separate children from adults, younger children from older children and middle class from lower class children, and for certain categories of children to be "rescued" from "inappropriate" institutions like workhouses, poorhouses, prisons, and guilds (Popkewitz, 1998). Schools began to develop, first, functionally differentiated spaces, and later, separate classrooms; and pupils were distributed spatially and serially, not only according to progress, age, or level of achievement but also character, cleanliness, even morality. Schools' putative control of all aspects of existence extended well beyond the formal school gates, fostering a whole margin of lateral controls which permitted the indirect supervision of parents and families and, ultimately, society as a whole (Foucault, 1986[1975]: 211).

Schools also exercised what Foucault called "epistemological power" — a power to extract a knowledge of individuals from individuals. This functioned in two ways. On one hand, pupils' or teachers' personal understandings of and functional adaptations to school mechanisms could be recorded, accumulated, and used to subject individuals in new ways; on the other hand, epistemological power generates a kind of clinical knowledge, which underpins current discourses from educational psychology through teacher appraisal to whole school evaluation, and out of which emerged the idea of education as a science.

The learner himself changes visibly almost every day. The reality with which the scholar can have conscious contact is defined, therefore, by the pupil's own powers and opportunities. At each stage, however, himself on the one hand, and nature, men, institutions, on the other hand, are the subject and object of adjustment. A changing self has the task of adaptation to a surrounding frame of things which daily displays new mysteries and complexities. The teacher's task is to help the individual understand this environment, of which the student for a long time seems to be the center himself. It is the teacher's business to help the beginner to understand this whole environment as it is related to their social life.

Research on how the intersection of race, class, and gender shapes educational experiences and outcomes is an important direction for the future of the sociology of education. Emerging from the sociology of education in the 1970s, "New Institutional Theory" (NIT) has become one of the foremost positions within the mainstream of American management studies. It seeks to explain the ways in which institutions are created, sustained, and diffused. NIT's antecedents lay in the institutional theorising of writers like Philip Selznick a generation before. Adherents of NIT are keen to draw a distinction between "new" and "old" institutionalism.

While old institutionalism emphasised politics and the role of conflict, NIT took legitimacy as its master concept. The old institutionalism focused on the existence of a negotiated order between different interest groups, while in its place NIT sought to understand the way in which the quest for legitimacy is a driving force behind the isomorphism of organisations. NIT is interested in understanding the means through which the socially constructed external environment enters the organisation by "creating the lens through which actors view the world and the very categories of structure, action, and thought" (DiMaggio and Powell, 1991).

The critique of naturalism and the empirical tradition in the sociology of education began in earnest in the 1970s from three very different directions which were unified briefly in relation to their object of opposition – the three being; neo-Marxism, interactionism and the sociology of knowledge. These are often rendered together as "the new sociology of education" (Whitty, 1985; Wexler, 1987). At the centre of the new sociology of education (NSOE), there was a focus upon the processes of educational transmission.

The neo-Marxist sociology of education seeks to analyze the reproduction of capitalist socio-economic structures through curricula, as well as the forms of resistance and conflict that accompany these processes. With some simplification, neo-Marxism provides attention to the relationships between forms of schooling experience and the labour process and the reproduction of class relations within schools and classrooms (Bowles and Gintis, 1976). Interactionism, via school-based ethnography, offers a way of exploring the construction of students' and teachers' social identities and generating descriptive accounts of the realisation of social control and social selection in classrooms. The sociology of knowledge problematised subject and school knowledge attending in particular to the underlying rules shaping the social construction of the curriculum and pedagogic practices and later to the historical and political struggles over subject status and content.

Philip Wexler (1982: 275) puts, "[I]n the early 1970s we applied the sociology of knowledge to education and attacked the surface of liberal knowledge." These analyses and critiques of liberal knowledge and liberal pedagogies, and their links to inequalities and oppressions, also laid the theoretical groundwork for a new "possibilitarian" sociology of schooling; critical pedagogy and the teacher as transformative intellectual – a new form of cultural politics or what Giroux (2005[1992]) terms "border crossings." The new sociology of education (NSOE) was, to variable extents, "radical," in contrast to the "reformism" of the empirical tradition. This empirical tradition with the role of reflexivity opens some new analytical possibilities. The new sociology of education (NSOE) laid the groundwork for "rejecting the positivist view of social reality" (Goodman, 1992: 118). Social scientists are facing with an expansive propagation of contending ideas that raise serious questions about the legitimacy and authority of scholarly practice.

## The Analytical Path: What Reason Suggests?

Sociology of education prepares a man to perform nimbly, strategically, dexterously and magnanimously all the efforts either at war or in peace in a given society. Sociologists of education study all aspects and levels of society. A society is a group of people whose members interact, reside in a definable area, and share a culture. A culture includes the group's shared practices, values, and beliefs. One sociologist of education might analyze video of people from different societies as they carry on everyday dialects to study the rules of polite conversation from different world cultures crossed by their education. Another sociologist of education might interview a representative sample of people to see how texting has changed the way they communicate. Yet another sociologist of education might study how migration determines the way in which lingo and innovative ideas spread and changed over time. A fourth sociologist of education might be part of a team developing ways to stay away from nuclear waste.

These examples follow a notion that we, the sociologists of education might reasonably argue that neither what the founding fathers proposed, nor what sociologists today do is most appropriate for determining the proper subject matter of sociology of education. "It should perhaps be decided by a process of logical analysis" (Inkeles, 1964: 13). Yet, as we will soon discover, just what is the most "logical" ground for allocating responsibility for the study of human social affairs is far from self-evident.

From the above point of view, it is clear that the development of subject matter of sociology of education is dependent on the intermingling of different cultural elements of the society for its content. Thus, it is through the educative process that man is equipped to live in his society through the transmission of cultural variables. This cultural transmission is the practice by which the way of life is passed from one generation to the next. It is also a part of the socialisation process where the family takes initiative as an agent, but in most cultures relinquishes some responsibility to the schools early in a child's life. The educational institutions assume primary responsibility for transmitting cognitive culture (thoughts, ideas, and knowledge) and play an important role in teaching normative culture (norms, values, attitudes, and beliefs).

For sociologists of education, culture is not merely transmitted, it is made. It is not just a historical fact and related to past; it is functional and vitally concerned with the present. It is not the collective catalogue of discrete objects, ideas, morals and pieces of knowledge; it is a configuration of the total social inheritance and way of life. Thus, the important function of education is the transmission of culture, which includes teaching norms and values so as to promote patriotism, nationalism, and cultural integration. It is the function of education not merely to preserve and transmit the best of the past, it must demonstrate its function in the present as well as its possibilities for the future, and ultimately it must seek to provide a total view of society and its purposes.

School helps in this intermingling process. The intermingling in the school of youth of different races, various religions, and unlike customs creates for all a new and broader environment. Common subject matter accustoms all to a unity of outlook upon a broader horizon than visible to the members of any group while it is isolated. Home schooling prevents this. Home schooling is not a new idea or practice. For centuries, children have learned outside formal school settings.

Sociology of education provides multiple forms of institutional settings in society. Against the formal structural setting of education there also exists home schooling system. Home schooling is emerging as one of the most significant social trends in education. It is an alternative to traditional schooling in which parents assume the primary responsibility for the education of their children. This contemporary trend which is in fact an old practice, has occurred for a distinctly modern reason: a desire to wrest control from public education and reestablish the family as central to a child's learning. The contemporary home-schooling trend began as a liberal political policy, not a conservative, alternative to the public school.

Conservative and religious families joined the home-schooling trend in the 1980s when they realised in their own way, public schools were undermining their values. Some believed religious duty required them to teach their own children; others sought to integrate religion, learning, and family life. Joining the liberal and conservative wings of the home-schooling movement are families who simply seek the highest quality education for their child, which they believe public and even private schools can no longer provide.

This alternative Western model of schooling changes the institutional nature of education. The sociologists of education consider learning as a process that is influenced not only by the teacher, the techniques used, the classroom setting, and the formal or informal material being taught, but also by the child's ability, motivation, interest in the subject matter, readiness to learn, retentiveness, values and attitudes, relationship with the teacher, feelings about self, relationships with peers, background experiences, and a myriad of other factors.

This compulsory schooling is relatively new. The onus then is on the educators in a society to ensure that educational systems transmit our cultural heritage. Western education should be adapted to our own environment and not adopted wholesale. In the past, most educated elites could not fit into their own society well. This is true even today for the most educated "Third Worldians." To solve this problem, the sociology of education, logically try to apply the sociological perspectives to understand the major institutions of society, and for this reason no special justification is needed as the subject matter of a text for sociology students. This emphasises a way to introduce sociological causality to teachers and students, rather than to explore the sociological dimensions of educational institutions.

Central to the sociology of education, there is a logical question about how schools operate to produce learning. Sociological models of schooling recognise that school systems are complex organisations, with a technical core consisting of classrooms in which teaching and learning – the core technology of schooling – take place. The concept of opportunities for learning provides a key to answering questions about how schools and classrooms can produce higher rates of learning (educational productivity), and about why some students learn more than others (educational inequality).

It is conceivable that a sociology of higher education would have developed sooner and with greater theoretic grounding had a boundary between it and the sociology of education – where concept and theory development have proceeded more swiftly –not been drawn so heavily. But the division developed and has become institutionalised, largely for intellectual than political reasons. Sociological theorists turned their attention in the early twentieth century – to the extent they turned to education – to early schooling, since from this particular point of time, in Durkheim's terms, "real life began." Higher education involves and affects the masses, and thereby inspires interest in its systematic study, reach that stage roughly a half century later.

It is argued that much of the subject matter, theoretical inclinations, meta-theoretical assumptions and methodologies that characterise the sociology of education emerged from the operation referred by Durkheim as a "selection principle." During the period from the end of the Second World War, three factors - context, purpose and location - combined to create the "selection principle" that framed the focus and approaches of the sociology of education. This selection of logical principle took different forms at different periods of time as the relative weight and the relationship of the component parts altered. All sociologists of education are similarly affected by changes in the selection principle. The selection principle is just that, it is a principle, not a formula. It acts as a filter, rather than moulds, still less determines. It does not have any homogenising effect on the discipline because its impact varies according to the precise local valuations of its component parts.

## Concluding Remarks

In this analysis, we have explored three different paths leading to a delineation of the subject matter of sociology of education, considering in turn: "What the founding fathers of sociology of education said," "what sociologists of education do," and "what logic requires." All three approaches indicate that sociology of education deals with a wide range of institutions and social processes. This field of study is growing into an accepted discipline with its own concepts and methodology. The sociology of education, in contemporary global citizenship, could contribute to a theoretical work by exploring the relationship between localised politics and global neoliberalism in terms of the effect on education. Release from the moral position that ties the discipline to seeing all cultural political movements as progressive would enable a more critical analysis of the crisis complexities of local initiatives, including the ways in which cultural identity movements may assist in localising neoliberalism.

Sociology of education has thus come a long way from the Durkheimian foundational suggestion that education, as a tool, helps in studying the knowledge transmission. It has also moved beyond the new sociology of education approach inspired by the reception of Karl Mannehim's critique of knowledge as "a tool in the struggle for status and power" (Wexler, 1987: 26). This new perspectives are promoting the researcher's own politics, progressive as they may be, but weakened by the ambiguities of the underpinning moral imperative. This sociology *of* or *for* education frames a movement that goes beyond the question of school knowledge, and links the sociology of knowledge tradition with the classroom based "pedagogical interest of the curricularists, in both classroom interaction and school knowledge" (Wexler, 1987: 35).

The task has been magnified. The functions traditionally assigned to education—particularly to the schooling of promoting skills, cognitive training, and preparation for citizenship—are either becoming obsolete in the view of some scholars or at least put into question by changes in the process of work and key dynamics in educational environments (Aronowitz and DiFazio, 1994). Regarding the research orientation in education, Krishna Kumar (1989: 9) has remarked that the sociology of education in India can "...hardly boast of a research environment without straining credulity." Such an environment can come about in a one-sided fashion. Notwithstanding the importance of caste, class and other environmental factors, the influence of curricular knowledge and its transmission as well as the experience of pupils in educational settings seen from their own perspective, need closer attention of the researchers.

In twenty-first century, sociological research in education has been focusing more on causality, or causal inference. Now the attention of researchers has been shifted from issues like role of education in society, or from survey based educational studies to the study of educational knowledge, or the ethnographic description of life, as well as pedagogical and social interaction in educational settings. Instead of being interested in finding correlations, or ways in which variables might relate to each other, causality implies that certain variables are in some way responsible for certain outcomes.

A longstanding complication in quantitative analyses in educational research is the lack of random assignment of people in society. Experimental methods rely largely on participants being randomly assigned to a specific group within the study. In sociological studies, people are rarely randomly given different social factors. In education, there are sometimes experiments in which programmes or services are randomly assigned. Since participants are assigned randomly to treatments, this makes it easier to believe that results from treated participants can be compared to results from non-treated or non-controlled participants to see what the treatment effects are.

However, when considering substantive questions within the sociology of education, many social factors are intertwined with others, including education. Individual factors can be added into the data analysis to attempt to ensure that correlations or causal connections are not being wrongly attributed, as in regression. Even so, determining which factors actually cause outcomes remains a complex undertaking. Yet we must recognise that even when educational institutions are the subject of specialised and independent branches of scholarship, they nevertheless continue to be objects of sociological investigation. This is not mere redundancy, nor an example of scholarly imperialism. The aspect of any institution or social process which links it to any other has its character in an interlocking "system" of action.

# Chapter - 5

# The Theoretical Foundations of Sociology of Education

If you are actively concerned about your world that you live in and want to do something constructive and useful in it – may it be law, business, education, medicine, urban or rural planning, or else – sociology provides you the best means for understanding how "the system" works. There are so many perspectives in sociology by which we can understand the inner dynamics of our world in which we live.

We can consider education as an institutional process, or as a system with structured roles and relationships, or as a manifestation of perfection already persists in an individual. The way we consider it, for the sociological theories in education, the investigation of social factors or the significance of the social environment for education, is important in two ways. Firstly, it is necessary to know as exactly as possible the kind of world in which the new generation will be expected to live. We should be able to awaken and cultivate all those capacities in the individual which he is likely to need in that environment. We must take into account the fact that to a large extent we live today in a global village, which in both its upper and lower reaches needs special types of men with special skills which they cannot acquire naturally in the required form and to the necessary extent.

The second way in which such an investigation would be important, already borders on politics. What we just saw was the importance of the knowledge of social factors for training men in such a way that they will be most suited to perform the tasks that fall to them, thus preventing the rapid social, economic and environmental development of our society from making the world unmanageable for present man. That knowledge, however, can have a wider function. Education becomes a way of acquiring knowledge. Here it is not merely a question of adapting men to a certain given level of development; it is a process of producing individuals' capability to develop the existing form of society beyond itself to a further stage.

Much of the sociological materials presented so far have been concerned with how some early thinkers viewed society and internalisation of ways in social life. The sociological interpretations, proposed by different groups of sociologists, had identified different fundamental questions for their different views that they had of man, of society and of the interaction between the two. From their particular position, each group of thinkers observed society and determined how they interpreted it and what would they regard as the most important aspects of social life. This position from which the thinkers approached the study of social life is called perspective.

A perspective can thus be defined, in the line of Roland Meighan and Iram Siraj-Blatchford (1986: 227), as "a frame of reference, a series of working rules by which a person is able to make sense of complex and puzzling phenomena." As they further explicated, for the sociologist, the phenomenon referred to in this definition is social life, and in taking a particular position towards its study, he or she makes a set of assumptions upon which analysis can be structured and which, typically include ideas about the nature of human beings, of society and of the interaction between the individual and society. This interactive space where education rests, indicates a consolidation of knowledge acquiring and shaking processes.

No sociologist would approach the study of social life without making a choice from the pool of available perspectives. Sociological study of education differs on the basis of these perspectives, and as an interdisciplinary field of scientific enquiry, the sociology of education provides a unique look at the social variables, which affects the body of knowledge in a given society. As a study of the relation between education and society, the sociology of education also illustrates the interconnectivity among the major institutions in society.

From the beginning days, the founding fathers of sociology like Auguste Comte and Emile Durkheim in France, or Karl Marx, Max Weber and Georg Simmel in Germany, and other sociologists have struggled with the question of interpreting social life and social phenomena. There is no avoiding the fact that in the years since Durkheim (1895[1964]) published his *The Rules of Sociological Method*, commitment to the development of sociological theories of society has become new scholastic orthodoxy. On one hand, there are thinkers like Parsons and Merton who, with Durkheim, assert the primacy of society over an individual. They stress the paramount necessity of external constraint for both societal and individual well being hence, the notion of a social system which, though created by people, nonetheless, enjoys an independent and external existence while at the same time acting as a constraining and conditioning influence upon individuals (Dawe, 1970; Meighan and Siraj-Blatchford, 1986).

On the opposite side, and at every level in conflict with the system theorists, thinkers like Max Weber, Mead, Cooley and Blumer reject the notion of a social system or the view that human action is a response to that system. The key notion of the action theorists is that of "autonomous man" who is able "to realise his full potential and to create a truly human social order only when freed from external constraint" (Dawe, 1970: 214). These latter genre of thinkers have tended to emphasise the ability of individuals to create meanings, constitute social situations and, in effect, control the social and natural world (Meighan and Siraj-Blatchford, 1986).

In the middle, stood thinkers like Karl Marx, Georg Simmel and Ralf Dahrendorf who combined the study of social structures and institutions and critical theory. Considered also as system theorists because of a number of other characteristics, they have in common with the earlier system theorists their acceptance of the notion of society as a social system and human behaviour as being shaped by that system, they are still recognised by many as having provided an alternative critical approach which, in the main, challenges the conservative notion of social order and control of the earlier social theorists.

Herbert Marcuse, Theodor Adorno, Erich Fromm, Max Horkheimer and others had focused on reflective assessment with a critique of society and culture in order to reveal and challenge existing power structures of society. Thus, this "critical" perspective differs from the earlier "conflict" perspective. Unlike the Durkheimian view that stresses the primacy of society over the individual, conflict theorists view social order as being achieved "through a continual process of disputed interaction between men, of sectional struggles and of the imposition of order by those who win power" (Meighan and Siraj-Blatchford, 1986: 261).

The main sociological perspectives which are represented by these three groups of theorists enumerated above as consensus, action and conflict. These sociological perspectives persist today along with some new perspectives. Each perspective with its extension affects not only the way on which the researcher seeks to explain the problem under study, which radically separates him or her from the others, but also the recommendations that he or she makes for redress. As an extension of feminist theory, the queer theoretical perspective challenges whatever is at odds with the normal, the legitimate and the dominant. It is an attempt to redefine sexual identities in the institutionalised structure of our society. Sociological researches are approached from these different theoretical perspectives ranging from structural functionalism, Marxism, interactionism, feminism, poststructuralism to postmodernism.

The structuration and postmodern perspectives would be examined in order to see what it is about these sociological theories that have made them so different from each other. In doing so, we must also look at the meaning and scope of sociological perspectives to understand sociology of education. We must clarify - what are the sociological perspectives and the assumptions on which a given perception grounds its analysis and interpretation of social life. From that point we must further ask what conclusions about the nature of sociological perspective follow from our definition, and how the different perspectives enumerated above can intersect with the study of education.

## Functionalists' Perspectives of Sociology of Education

The main sociological perspective under the consensus model is functionalism, which views society as a system of interrelated parts. In the functionalists' view, the basic unit of analysis is society and the various parts that make up the society, are understood mainly in terms of their relationship to the whole (Haralambos, et al., 2004). The early sociologists viewed society as an organism like the human body, which is made up of several important parts that work harmoniously together towards the survival and maintenance of the whole. Hence, an understanding of any part of the society would require an analysis of that part's relationship to other parts and most importantly, its contribution to the maintenance of society. In furtherance of this analogy, the functionalists argued that, just as the human body (to which it is likened) has certain basic needs that must be satisfied if it is to survive, society, too has its own basic needs that must be met if it is to continue to exist. Within such understanding, social institutions such as the family, religion, polity, education and the economy are regarded as indispensable parts of the social system rather than as isolated units. In particular, they are understood in the light of the contributions they make to the system as a whole (Haralambos, et al., 2004).

**Classical Functional Analysis**

Auguste Comte begins with the nature of positive philosophy and he avers that it brings all phenomena under unchanging laws. Therefore, the primary purpose he sets for himself is to search appropriately for these laws. He gives the instance of gravitation. To reach the positive stage, knowledge has passed through many stages and this development has occurred on the basis of simplicity, generality, and independence. The most notable development in positive philosophy is the emergence of a new science called sociology. The functionality of positive philosophy could be seen in the following dimensions:

1. It helps us in discovering rational laws of the evolution of the human mind.
2. The educational structure of Europe, which Comte thought to be theological and metaphysical, could be changed with the help of positive philosophy.
3. Combination among various sciences contributes towards their progress.
4. Only positive philosophy can help in the reorganisation of society. Comte was critical of political instability during the 19th century. Positivism can play an important role in the maintenance of social order.

In a way, to reiterate, Comte's positivism is a theory which aims at rejecting the contradiction between order and progress and tries to establish that after reaching the highest stage of human mind, this contradiction would disappear. The society of man, Comte taught, must be studied in the same scientific manner as the world of nature.

Another French pioneer, Emile Durkheim showed that social forces are at work. "If society is to be considered as the normal goal of moral conduct, then it must be possible to see in it something other than a sum of individuals; it must constitute a being *sui generis,* which has its own special character distinct from that of its members and its own individuality different from that of its constituent individuals. In a word, there must exist, in the full meaning of the word, a social being. On this condition only society is able to perform the moral function that the individual cannot" (Durkheim, 1961: 60).

Though, there are other perspectives in social sciences that focus on some unique aspects of the society, the central concern of sociology is the social relationships of mankind. Sociology also uses scientific method in its study. Methodically, Durkheim points out, the educator must foresee and prepare for the development of the new sentiments. Here, science is an accumulated body of systemised knowledge and widely accepted processes dedicated to the discovery of generalisations and theories for refining and building on the existing knowledge. The scientific method which is universal (though now objected to by some scientists), consists of formulating a problem to be investigated, formulating some hypotheses and conducting a research which must be public, systematic and replicable.

Emile Durkheim (1956) proposed that the society, as a whole, in a particular social milieu, determines the ideals, which education realises. Education perpetuates and reinforces those elements, which maintain homogeneity and diversity at a time with a balancing condition. For example, education plays an important role in socialisation and social control by embedding social norms, values, customs, rules, etc. On the other hand education helps human beings to acquire new knowledge and to quake past knowledge to reproduce new ways. This practice exposes the status of education as ignite of revolution and change.

All of the major institutions, including education, are studied by Durkheim through the first way and convinced that the complexity of division of labour helps to develop education system that could pass on the skills required in filling the various specialised roles. In the traditional society, where repressive laws prevail, occupational skills could be learnt within the group and social life. Durkheim did admit social change, where education, by no exception, performs its special task as "the methodical socialisation of the young generation." By this he destined the development within the child of certain values and certain intellectual and physical skills "which are demanded of him by both the political society as a whole and the special milieu for which he is specifically destined" (Durkheim, 1956: 71). Only in this way, as he anticipated, the cohesion and survival of the society be assured.

Durkheim saw education as a means of organising the individual self and the social self. The internalisation of values and discipline represents the child's initiation into the society. This is why it is very important to study and analyze education using sociological approaches. For the sociology of education, he depicted a theoretical view to analyze how education becomes embodied in subjects, to explore the consequences of this embodiment for the moral health of society, and to recognise that embodied beings are not simply a location for society, but possess creative capacities which can also revitalise and begin to change the social space in which they exist. To explore it, he identified a correlation between education and suicide rates. Suicide rate is high among the professional and higher classes. Durkheim regarded this high rate as a consequence of loosening of values in such societies. It is interesting to note that lesser number of women commit suicide than men.

Moreover, the percentage of Catholics in higher education was lower in proportion to their population, whereas the number of Protestants getting education was higher. Durkheim concluded that suicide rates are higher among Protestants than Catholics and Jews. Max Weber, German sociologist, proceeded on to identify another difference between Protestant and Catholics, namely, the occupational pursuits.

Martin Offenbacher's statistical analysis, comparing the school enrollment of German Protestants to Catholics, had played a significant role in the articulation of the functional perspective in the field of sociology of education. With the help of these data, Weber goes on to argue that Catholic workers have a tendency not to pursue promotions, whereas Protestant workers are more oriented towards taking up the skilled or administrative jobs: the main reason for this orientation being the religious environment at home.

After concluding on the basis of data on Baden-Baden, Weber describes similar conditions prevailing in many European countries. He made a general comment on Jews. He pointed out that minority communities that are directly or indirectly excluded from political influence, work very hard in the economic action, e.g. Poles living in Russia and Eastern Prussia, Huguenots and Jews in France, and some religious sects in England. However, such a tendency is absent among the Catholics of Germany (Judge, 2012: 160). Weber identified the role of ethical socialisation on an institutional view of informal education. Throughout his work, he kept it by arguing that his theory could be established historically and empirically by simultaneously emphasising primacy of the economic factor.

Weber tried to examine education as central to an understanding of his notions of "religion" and "politics," which, as Bendix and Roth (1971) argued, were his dominant intellectual interests. Weber (1978: 305) wrote that "The unfinished last part of Karl Marx's Capital apparently was intended to deal with the issue of class unity in the face of skill differentials." Weber made the above comment after he identified three kinds of classes: propertied class, commercial class, and social class. Among the social classes, Weber included working class, the petty bourgeoisie, propertyless intelligentsia, and "classes privileged through property and education" (*ibid.*: 305). Weber became disillusioned with the kind of culture emerging in the newly developed political party. Some of these experiences form the basis of his explanation of complex social phenomena such as inequality, power, authority, leadership, bureaucracy, rationality and organisations, and all of these elements also appeared in his interpretation of modern educational systems as well (Rao and Singh, 2018).

As an alternative explanation to Marx's theory of classes, Weber's theory of inequality explained power through a group of intelligentsia. These intellectuals or highly educated people are imposed and interpreted by men outside their class. This notion is widely used in the social sciences in analyzing the influence of modern capitalistic social stratification systems on the life chances of individuals and groups, including education.

Weber's examination of the sociological foundations of education systems was largely a result of his exploration of Chinese society. His methodological idea is important here. Once he outlined it as *Verstehen,* the sympathetic introspection. He also emphasised that empathy is only possible if the researcher shares cultural variables or meanings with the objects of study. Weber showed equal interest in both causation and consciousness. Therefore, it is found that Weber's epistemology is both praxis and process—something quite similar to Marx. The difference between the two is in terms of the unit of analysis. Weber seemed to be suggesting that individual is capable of thinking and acting, whereas Marx's unit is man but his analysis of both praxis and process is collectivity manifested through class.

From this capability perspective, Weber then differentiated between cultivating education (general) and expert education. "Cultivating education (i.e., imparting a "cultural" qualification in general terms) seeks to polish an individual while expert education is aimed at shaping eligible individuals into aspirants for office." "General education," he argued, "has been monopolised by political authorities. The two are usually not mutually exclusive, and both are seen as essential—cultivating education is regarded as crucial for belonging to a status group while expert education is tied to eligibility for office" (Rao and Singh, 2018: 79).

## Modern Functional Analysis

The elements of the conversion of educational advantage into social and economic advantage in Weberian thinking are subsequently found in the writings on the convertibility notion of capitals (social, economic and cultural) by Pierre Bourdieu (2004). This new dimension helped later functionalists to search the basic needs or necessary conditions of existence, which are generally referred to, in sociological literature, as the functional prerequisites of society. Various approaches have been used to identify these functional prerequisites of society that cut across all societies.

Like classical tradition, modern analysis has mainly concerned itself with the central question of how social system is maintained. The theory of functionalism in education might look like and a fuller expression of the implications of viewing education by examining the relationship between the structures of society. Basic to the functionalist approach is a concern for maintenance, legitimation, transmission and internalisation of the "collective conscience" that, in the functionalist's view is so central to the society's integration and survival (Haralambos et al., 2004). Here, the system of education is seen as a means of perpetuating and reinforcing the much-desired societal homogeneity by inculcating in the child, from the beginning, the essential similarities that collective life demands. Thus, the object of education is to legitimise rather than challenge the status quo of the existing social arrangements in a given society.

The term "function" in this analysis refers to the contribution of the part to the whole. From Hobbes (1951) to Levy (1952), or from Davis and Moore (1945) to Murdock (1949), or from Parsons (1955) to Merton (1968), these functional prerequisites are in a larger way, inferred than identified. If we quote Ritzer (1996: 240) on Parsons' functional analysis through an organisational system of education, we can find that Talcott Parsons proposed seven assumptions that govern structural functional perspective in education system:

(i) Educational systems have the property of order and interdependence of parts;

(ii) Educational systems tend towards self-maintaining order, or equilibrium;

(iii) The educational system may be static or involved in an ordered process of change;

(iv) The nature of one part of the educational system has an impact on the form that the other parts can take;

(v) Educational systems maintain boundaries with their environments;

(vi) Allocation and integration are two fundamental processes necessary for a given state of equilibrium of an educational system; and

(vii) Educational systems tend toward self-maintenance involving the maintenance of boundaries and of the relationships of parts to the whole, control of environmental variations, and control of tendencies to change the system from within.

From above seven assumptions, two points become important to illustrate the consequence of viewing education from a functionalist perspective. First, any question about the organisation and process of education will have to be observed in terms of education's role in providing space for the adequate socialisation of the individual. Second, if education is to succeed in fulfilling its cultural transmission, behavioural socialisation and personality development functions, then its nature and purpose must be manipulated by society.

The implications of these two views are many. First, education must be viewed as having a conservative and integrative function – that of transmitting the cultural heritage of older generation to younger generation and maintaining the social order. The main function of education in this regard would be to work towards solidarity and integration rather than differentiation or managed pluralism. In this sense, the education system becomes an important part of the process of achieving unity, cohesion and consensus in society. Secondly, the functionalist view would influence interpretations of three key areas of schooling, namely, the curriculum, the roles of teachers and pupils and interpersonal relations with a flow of economy and environment. In all three areas, the functionalist would find a common pattern of maintaining social order. The task of designing the curriculum involves selecting only those contents that can be demonstrated as a part of the common collective culture.

Similarly, this same dominance of social needs over those of the individual prevails in the expected role of the teachers who must ensure the inculcation of group values, allegiance and sense of responsibility in their pupils. The pupils on their parts are seen as passive recipients of the rules of society from their teachers. They must be passive and restrained because they lack knowledge and skills and are sometimes motivated by selfish desires which need to be controlled. In this definition of roles three distinct elements characterising interpersonal relations in the school are distinguished: (i) by virtue of their knowledge, experience and authority, teachers enjoy superior position over their pupils, (ii) teacher-pupil relations are structured in such a way as to mediate conflict or disharmony in the social order and (iii) within this arrangement, neither the teacher's authority nor the pupil's passivity is to be defined by personal need or interest, rather, both are to be governed by the collective culture on which the entire functionalist perspective rests.

In an anti-Marxist point of view, or standing against conflict and social change, Parsons identified the unit act to analyze social structure. Education as a selective process is genuinely assortative social act. As virtually in all comparable processes, ascriptive as well as achieved factors influence the outcome. In this case the ascriptive factor is the socio-economic status of the child's family, and the factor underlying the opportunity for achievement is his individual ability. Education helps individual in goal achievement, thus it is individual capability, not class background that determines position in role structure.

At this point it will be seen that application of the functionalist model to education or indeed any social institution, even at the level of simple analysis, requires a measure of understanding of the fit between the parts of the social system and their functional contribution to the smooth running of the whole. Functionalist analysis aims to uncover the "deep structures" operating in the consciousness of the whole by focusing on what can be regarded as the cardinal functions of its various parts on which the entire social structure rests. Like Durkheim, Parsons argued that the school represents society in miniature form. Modern industrial society is increasingly based on achievement rather than ascription, on meritocratic principles which are applied to all its members.

The institution of education via schools is a significant agent of socialisation, i.e. inculcation of values and attitudes acceptable to the society. Education reflects the general pattern of society. This means to say that the school curriculum for education is determined by the socio-cultural pattern or needs and aspirations of the society. Schools bring together people from diverse social backgrounds so that they share common social experiences and develop commonly held norms, attitudes, and beliefs.

Thus, as Merton (1968: 191) proposed "that education leads to intelligence and consequently to job and money success." This functional aspect considers individual's autonomy within the society. In a specific social system, the individual is treated and judged in terms of universalistic standards, which are applied to all members, regardless of their caste, creeds or kinship ties. Merton's functional analysis depicted that like other social institutions, education has both manifest (open, stated) and latent (hidden) functions. The most basic *manifest* function of education is the transmission of knowledge. Schools teach students how to read, speak other languages, and repair automobiles. Another important manifest function is the bestowal of status. Because many believe this function is performed inequitably, we will consider it later, in the section on the conflict view of education. In addition to these manifest functions, schools perform a number of *latent* functions: transmitting culture, promoting social and political integration, maintaining social control, and serving as an agent of change.

## Action Theories in Education

From a consideration of the functionalist perspective which places primacy of society or the whole over the individual, we move onto another which holds just the opposite view known as action perspective. This perspective emphasises rather the role of the individual and how he interprets reality as an entity not really governed by the group. This difference in emphasis has brought as well a new methodology, quite different from that adopted by functionalists. A key difference in their methodologies will of course be highlighted. Thus, whereas functionalism claims objectivity in its methods, issues are more or less static, and predetermined in ways essential to the individual. In the action perspective, the main stress is given on individual's subjective interpretation of the reality. The great implication of this perspective and its accompanying methodology are then applied to the institution of education as a unit. The sociological study in action perspective can also revolve around the school goers, school teachers and the school culture that they engender.

Basic to the action perspective is a concern for the individual-level rather than the social-level approach. Whereas functionalist perspective has attempted to answer questions about the process by which order is achieved in social life, including both-the way interpersonal relations are regulated and how individual affairs are constrained using a social system model, action perspective looks for another dimension. The society is viewed as the product of man, a human creation which does not merely reflect the product of its members' construction of meaning, but at a deeper level conveys the actions and relationships through which they attempt to impose that meaning on their historical situation (Meighan and Siraj-Blatchford, 1986).

Thus, the object of action perspective is to discover how the actions of men help to produce society rather than how the society regulates and constrains their affairs. The action theorists, as we have seen earlier, reject the notion of a social system that is "ontologically and methodologically prior to its participants", a notion that puts society above and external to the individual. Here the progression works in direct opposition to the functionalists' view, where the single unit of analysis is the society, which is regarded as a system that shapes human behaviour. Action perspective goes from the smaller unit of social action to the more comprehensive, focusing on small scale interactions rather than society as a whole.

An action theorist with a strongly antilarge-scale unit of analysis bias, Weber for example, shows the tendency most clearly in his preference for the "individualist" method over the collectivist notions, as he maintains, it is in the action of one or more, few or many individuals that collective notions find their meaning. Whether such an approach can ever be reconciled or viewed as complementary to the functionalist's large-scale macro-level analysis remains an open question. However, some major interpreters of Weber's work notably, Susan Hekman (1983), Walter Garrison Runciman (1972), Ludwig M. Lachman (1971) and Murray Wax (1967), who espouse macro-structural methods in their study admit that, Weber's theory involves both approaches.

To describe the kind of individual-level approach which operates without the functionalist theoretical presuppositions, Weber developed the concept of *Verstehen* (German for understanding), an idea derived from a field known as Hermeneutics devoted to the study of the meaning and interpretation of published writings. Hermeneutics aims at understanding the thinking of the author and the basic structure of the text. Weber sought to extend this idea to the understanding of society by focusing on actors and interaction with a view to identify the meaning behind observable behaviour and events (Ritzer, 1996).

This approach is far removed from that of Durkheim or Parsons both of whom stress the importance of macro-level analysis. Weber's method, as noted by Meighan and Siraj-Blatchford (1986), requires the user: (i) to define the ways in which members of society create the social order within which they live through both their individual and collective actions, and (ii) to comprehend and assess the structural and internal arrangements employed by members of society to both act socially and to impose some form of control over their existential conditions. A stress on the creative capacity of individual members replaces the constraining framework of functionalism, while the absence of a large-scale theory of structures and their interrelated complementary functions further put this approach in a category different from that of Durkheim or Parsons.

This action perspective goes through a subjective reality where knowledge lies. Before moving to the various schools of thought grouped under this perspective and the main differences between them, we should briefly look at the unifying factor that binds the groups together. At this point in the analysis, it will be apparent that the method of the action theorists seems to be touched by a concern for the subjective dimension of reality, which requires the user to take into analysis the subjective vision of the individual actors and what Meighan and Siraj-Blatchford (1986: 259) describe as the "idiosyncratic and situationally specific features of human behaviour."

The group is thus unified by the fact that its members are willing to make the actions and the subjective interpretations of real people their main concern. Jack D. Douglas (1970), in his edited volume probably speaks for all when he rightly asks if anyone not committed to the subjective reality of social action would ever discover the real meaning of that action: "*Any scientific understanding of human action, at whatever level of ordering of generality, must begin with and be built upon an understanding of the everyday life of the members performing those actions.* (To fail to see this and to act in accord with it is to commit what we might call the *fallacy of abstractionism*, that is the fallacy believing that you can know if a more abstract form what you do not know in the particular form)" (Douglas, 1970: 11).

The action theorists make the basis on subjective reality of action for any sociological analysis, which is derived from their conception of and attitude to what constitutes acceptable forms of sociological knowledge. Actually the available framing of knowledge is included and has cited much deserved attention on educational forms. It is a clear demonstration that a theory of educational systems can be firmly rooted in an analysis of curriculum, pedagogy and evaluation. To do that, from its general rule, the action theorists accept the use of concepts which refer to collective behaviour or general patterns of conduct and notions of whole group of people and the objectified relationships between them. They cautioned that these concepts are but mere images and possible interpretations of the complexity of human life rather than concrete descriptions of actual behaviour.

This act of pointing out possibilities is merely a vehicle for explaining which the real actor wishes to convey. Although the medium is certainly important, the action theorists maintain that it cannot replace or be more accurate than the social actor's own interpretations of his or her actions. The meaning of social action must therefore be sought in the actor's own interpretation of his action. As David Gorbutt (1972) cautioned us about the tension of social scientists between conceptions. On the one hand of social science, it is based on the methodical practices of natural science and on the other hand, it is based on the intersubjectivity of social world. According to his new sociology of education from a teacher's perspective, a teacher is considered as an observer, who must not assume that his or her predetermined interpretation and understanding of a social situation as an intersubjective construction of reality.

If we conceptually consider teaching and learning as an intersubjective construction of reality, three related areas of teaching assume particular importance: (1) the problematic aspects of educational knowledge, (2) the social nature of categories constructed and maintained by educators, and (3) definitions of the situation evolved in classroom interaction (Gorbutt, 1972: 7). When teachers have a priori recognition of the research act as a social act, they are less intimidated by the mystique of the researcher and more able to adopt a positive, critical stance toward research.

Thus, at every stage in the process of sociological inquiry, the observer must avoid, as far as possible, superimposing his or her own premeditated interpretation of the phenomenon under study. In general then, it may be seen how central the stress is on the relativity of knowledge and the subjectivity of meaning to the action perspective. Considerable benefit may clearly be derived from the application of this approach to the study of social reality. When controlled by a subjective methodology, the interpretation of human reality assumes a whole new dimension focusing attention on both the knowledge that people have of their world and the meanings they give to the objects which constitute it.

The interactionist perspective focuses on social interaction in the classroom, on the playground, and in other school venues. Specific research finds that social interaction in schools affects the development of gender roles and that teachers' expectations of pupils' intellectual abilities affect the extent of their learning. Here research can focus on how teachers treat girls and boys (Jones and Dindia, 2004). Certain educational problems have their basis in social interaction and expectations.

An important interactionist perspective of education relates directly to student life: schools provide for students' social and recreational needs. Education helps toddlers and young children to develop interpersonal skills that are essential during adolescence and adulthood. In their high school and college years, students may meet future husbands and wives and establish lifelong friendships.

When people observe high schools, community colleges, or universities from the outside, students appear to constitute a cohesive, uniform group. However, the student subculture is actually quite complex and diverse. High school cliques and social groups may crop up according to race, social class, physical attractiveness, placement in courses, athletic ability, cultural inclination and leadership roles in the school and community.

From this action perspective, we can identify four distinctive subcultures among college students (cited in Schaefer, 2013: 319):

1. The *collegiate* subculture focuses on having fun and socialising. These students define what constitutes a "reasonable" amount of academic work (and what amount of work is "excessive" and leads to "grind"). Members of the collegiate subculture have little commitment to academic pursuits. Athletes often fit into this subculture.
2. The *academic* subculture identifies with the intellectual concerns of the faculty and values knowledge for its own sake.
3. The *vocational* subculture is interested primarily in career prospects and it views college as a means of obtaining degrees that are essential for professional advancement.
4. Finally, the *nonconformist* subculture is hostile to the college environment and seeks ideas that may or may not relate to academic studies. This group may find outlets through campus publications or issue-oriented groups.

Each college student is eventually exposed to these competing subcultures and must determine which (if any) seems most in line with his or her feelings and interests. On the basis of the psychological variables, and freed from the rigid assumptions of the objective methodology, action perspective has taken a variety of directions, namely, interactionism, phenomenology and ethnomethodology.

While acknowledging the considerable variety within the forms of action perspective, Martyn Hammersley and Peter Woods (1976) in the introduction of their edited volume: *The Process of Schooling: A Sociological Reader*, speak of three elements, which are fundamental to the methodological distinctions of these three main branches of the interpretive sociology mentioned above, namely "process", "meaning" and "rules".

Firstly, interactionism aims to uncover the "process" through which people construct their actions. As the name suggests, it is concerned with the interaction between people. Basic to interactionism is the belief that action is meaningful to those partaking in it and so to understand the meaning of a social action would require an interpretation of the meanings the actors in a given context give to their activities (Haralambos, et al., 2004). This means that true meaning of a social action can only be derived from the actors and the context in which the action is taking place. It also means that meanings are not fixed entities but are rather negotiated within the actual process of interaction just as prices of goods in the open market are negotiated between the seller and the buyer. The interactionist seeks to understand this process of negotiating knowledge as it happens in educational contexts.

Secondly, another branch of the action perspective is phenomenology. The phenomenologist's emphasis is on "meaning" rather than "process". The aim is to uncover the knowledge and assumption which individual actors must possess and act upon in order for the social world to exist. These knowledge and assumptions are not always obvious at the conscious level and are more often taken for granted in the course of our everyday lives (Meighan and Siraj-Blatchford, 1986). The task of the phenomenologist is to construct meaning from an analysis of what the actors think they know and the way in which they interpret their actions and the context in which such actions are taking place.

Thirdly, the branch is ethnomethodology that deals with nature and scope of knowledge. Like the interactionists and phenomenologists, the ethnomethodologists are also concerned with the ways in which members of society create and maintain the social world within which they live. However, their main emphasis is on the methods and devices as well as the practical activities which make such construction possible at all. In this sense, the ethnomethodologists are poised to uncover the rules of social interactions: How do members of any given society negotiate a new social order? From an ethnomethodologist's perspective, the construction of social reality proceeds from negotiated meanings that are constructed within ongoing interactive situations. The stress therefore is on the nature, construction and expression of the regular techniques used by social actors to negotiate roles and make their actions rational and comprehensible for others (Meighan and Siraj-Blatchford, 1986). Thus, ethnomethodological studies of converse in educational settings are concerned with the explication of the "routine grounds of everyday life" (Garfinkel, 1967: 35) in classrooms, staff meetings, diagnostic and testing sessions, parent-teacher interviews, and other settings in which the practical work of schooling goes on.

In summary, then, it can be seen how the action perspective has taken a variety of directions. However, although the three groups identified above as representing these directions may differ in methods and conclusions, they all fall squarely within the general theoretical framework of interpretive sociology. Even a casual observer can readily see considerable overlap between these separate branches of the action perspective. Roland Meighan and Iram Siraj-Blatchford (1986) ask doubtfully if anyone could effectively describe the processes of classroom life exclusive of the meaning that the real actors in the classroom take from it and the negotiated roles they partake in order to create and order that life, as well as, render their behaviour accountable to others in the interactive situation.

Because to some extent the works of symbolic interactionists reflect the interface between these concerns. Only that branch is of interest at this point. A brief description of symbolic interactionism, as it evolved from its beginning in the work of George Herbert Mead (1863-1931) in the 19th century to its present day modification, as a tool for sociological research can create an edge in educational research.

Symbolic interactionism owes its beginning to the developments in sociological theory which followed the publication of G.H. Mead's *Mind, Self, and Society: From the Standpoint of a Social Behaviorist* in 1934/1962. Mead and those who follow this perspective argue that human beings are unique in their ability to use symbolic communication (use of ideas and concepts as distinct from mere gestures) in their social interactions. In this sense, language, which represents the symbol system in use, reflects certain universal symbols or structures, which in turn reflect universal orders within the human mind. All communications in some way are expressions or exchanges of these symbols and the tasks of the interactionist are to discover or uncover the nature of these patterns of exchanges (Ritzer, 1996; see also Meighan and Siraj-Blatchford, 1986).

Mead argues that human beings, unlike lower animals, are endowed with the capacity for thought. This thinking capacity is shaped by social interaction, where people learn the meanings and the symbols that allow them to exercise their distinctively human capacity for thought. Thus, the individual becomes an active participant in his social world as actor and being acted upon within and towards situations. The meanings and symbols allow people to carry on distinctively human action and interaction. People are able to modify or alter the meanings and symbols that they use in action and interaction on the basis of their interpretation of the situation. These modifications and alterations allow them to examine possible course of actions by assessing their relative advantages and disadvantages in choosing one. The intertwined patterns of action and interaction make up groups and societies (Ritzer, 1996: 347).

Individuals respond to situations on the basis of how they perceive and define them and these definitions refer to the meanings individuals attach to the ongoing events in which they find themselves. So to arrive at an adequate interpretation of an event, the investigator must understand both the various definitions of the situations by the actors in the event and the ways in which these different definitions intersect with each other resulting in series of negotiations of roles which act in concert to produce the totality of the interactional setting (Meighan and Siraj-Blatchford, 1986). Thus, in the sociology of education, symbolic interactionism focuses on social interaction in the classroom, on school playgrounds, and at other school-related venues. Social interactionism contributes to gender-role socialisation, and teachers' expectations may affect their students' performance.

From a micro-sociological perspective, symbolic interactionism is at the centre of the exchanges between administrators and staff when it comes to develop faculty capacity through an evaluation system that seeks to truly change instructional practices. Through this sociological lens, researchers view the interactions of school leaders as a critical component of school success. In this role, administrators help to establish social reality by shaping the ways in which administrators work with teachers in an evaluation system and translate that work to changing classroom practice. Thus, the use of symbolic interactionism as a means to monitor teacher performance and increase student achievement is a historical shift in the paradigmatic view of the teacher evaluation system.

A new conceptual model for teacher evaluation systems, thus, is built on the sociological perspective of symbolic interactionism and includes a supervisory process that aims to influence "school processes that are directly linked to student learning" (DiPaola and Hoy, 2008). The processes, directly linked to student learning, are the processes which impact teacher knowledge and skills. They start and end in a cyclical evaluation system of effective communication and action between leaders and teachers. Therefore, the conceptual model of today's supervisory cycle is one of symbolic interactionism whereby the leader engages teachers in observational techniques, conversations, and actions that truly lead to improved teaching practice, and accordingly, increased learning outcomes.

As a prime part of micro-sociological theory, the symbolic interactionism depends on interaction process, which has enlivened the reciprocal meaning and values with the aid of the symbols in the mind. From this micro aspect, sociologist like Anthony Giddens (1984; 1990) has developed a micro-macro link model of structuration theory, which describes the capacity of human action as being constrained by powerful stable societal structures, such as education. It is the idea of structuring social relations across time-space, in virtue of the duality of structure. It offers perspectives on human behaviour based on a synthesis of structure and agency effects known as the "duality of structure."

The concept of "the duality of structure" is important for library information professionals because it suggests that everyday professional activities are not merely the performances of certain skills or the accomplishments of certain tasks, but also the production and reproduction of structure. In social reality, these professional activities are influenced by and have some implications for professional standards, practices, and policies of educational institutions.

Following Giddens' work on "structuration," which argued that structure and action could not form a dualism, and that structure was inherently transformable by agency at any point of time, have emerged concerns to be able to retain analytical dualism (Archer, 1995; Willmott, 1999). Without a reification of structure, or returning to determinist

Marxist accounts, this means being able to see structure as having a degree of relative autonomy which exists regardless of how actors construe or behave within it. In order to explain how structures act differentially on different actors (sometimes more constraining than others) we have to see a structure as having some independent properties persisting over time and space. For this the structuration theory can make a valuable contribution to the field of institutional education and it also provides the necessary concepts for the study of the interrelationship between the everyday work of information professionals and "the social" that provokes critical and reflective thinking.

## Actor-Network Theory

Network theory is a sociological perspective that focuses on the structural analysis of social networks, and views individual behaviour as constrained by such networks. Wellman Berkowitz (1988) indicates that the network theory characterises interlinked structures in terms of nodes (individual actors, people, or things within the network) and the ties, edges, or links (relationships or interactions) that connect them. The ties in such networks may result from individuals' membership in several clusters or because certain persons have "foreign relations" with other portions of the network. The nodes in a network do not have to be only individual persons; there can be sets of nodes, groups, nation-states, or other discriminable units. This focus has narrowed down the functionalist's search for an answer to value consensus – a collective conscience consisting of common values, norms, beliefs and sentiments without which social solidarity and cohesion would be impossible.

Particularly to science and technology studies, this network theory added the concept of actor from structure-functional theory of sociology. Then the micro-macro linkages in sociological theory try to understand the area where sociologists and computer scientists try to transfer methods and theories from one discipline to the other. This paradigm shift emphasises the importance of the functional point of an agent and explores the sociologically founded theories applied in artificial intelligence research. The problem of how individual action and structural rules in a set of agents interact is a foundational issue for both everyday life technology and sociology.

Like organisation sociology, sociology of education deals with meso-level analyses. Here sociology, as a science of social institutions and organisations, studies the network principles that have been deployed in discourses of educational governance reforms to signal the decentralisation of performance management to local education authorities and schools. The depoliticised consensus and empty promises are embedded in network discourses of educational policy. The actor-network theory (ANT) approaches in the sociology of education to offer useful theoretical resources for policy studies.

From functional structure analysis, firstly the ANTists re-examine the latent and manifest functions of education in everyday life structure. The manifest functions of education consist of the basic and obvious functions of education. According to Swift (1969), there are at least four manifest functions of education in society. Inculcation of values and standards of the society is determined by scientific education. And it is a manifest function like the maintenance of social solidarity by developing in children a sense of belongingness to the society together with a commitment to its way of life, as they understand it. Transmission of knowledge from one generation to another comprises the social heritage and by shaking processes the creation and development of new knowledge are also manifested.

The provision of literacy and numeracy, and the specialised training for occupational competence jointly help individual to fulfill personal and social contribution. Another important manifest function of education is its encouraging factor. The democratic participation through the learning of verbal skills and the development of individual's ability for rational thinking become concrete evidence in intellectual horizons. For example, the production of patriotic citizens through lessons by illustrating and demonstrating the nation's greatness and glory is important in school curriculum. On the other way, education is an agent of upward social mobility in society and it also works as an agent of socio-cultural change and reform.

The institutional frame of education not only manifests some functions for which it was intended, but also performs some latent functions with unintended, and sometimes unrecognised, social consequences. The policy-makers through actor-network theory must consider these latent functions of education. Education serves the latent function of promoting social and political integration by transforming a population composed of diverse racial, ethnic, and religious groups into a society whose members share—to some extent—a common identity. These latent functions of education refer to the functions of education, which are not obvious but are implied.

The institutional structure of education performs its function as a care giver. It is a easy baby-sitting service, separating children from their parents for regular and reasonably prolonged periods of the day and year. It provides opportunities for children to become acquainted with a wider and more diverse circle of friends than they would otherwise reach. College and university campuses also serve as large dating and marriage markets. The campus becomes a useful marriage market because young adults sometimes choose their mates from amongst their educational peers. People usually choose marriage partners of similar educational attainment and background, and many college graduates meet their spouses while attending school (Mare, 1991). It is also a means by which the supply of labour is reduced.

A number of important social networks are created in college. Lifelong friendships are formed, and fraternity and sorority affiliations often pay off later in securing employment, promotions, raises, and other occupational opportunities. As a social institution, education performs a rather conservative function—transmitting the dominant culture. Schooling exposes each generation of young people to the existing beliefs, norms, and values of their culture. In our society, we learn respect for social control and reverence for established institutions, such as religion, the family, and the presidency. Of course, this statement is true in many other cultures as well.

In performing the manifest function of transmitting knowledge, schools go far beyond teaching skills like reading, writing, and mathematics. Like other social institutions, such as the family and religion, education prepares young people to lead productive and orderly lives as adults by introducing them to the norms, values, and sanctions of the larger society. Otherwise teachers and guidance counsellors may encourage male students to pursue careers in the sciences but steer female students into careers as early childhood teachers. Such socialisation into traditional gender roles can be viewed as a form of social control.

Through the exercise of social control, schools teach students various skills and values essential to their future positions in the labour force. They learn punctuality, discipline, scheduling, and responsible work habits, as well as how to negotiate the complexities of a bureaucratic organisation. As a social institution, education reflects the interests of both the family and another social institution, the economy. Educational programmes can and have transformed people's lives. For example, continued formal education has had a positive effect on the income of people; median earnings rise significantly with each step up in the educational ladder. Consider the significance of those increased earnings when they stretch over an entire lifetime. Obviously, racial, ethnic, and gender differences in income are also significant.

So far, we have focused on the conservative functions of education—on its role in transmitting the existing culture, promoting social and political integration, and maintaining social control. Yet education can also stimulate or bring about desired social change. Sex education classes were introduced to public schools in response to the soaring pregnancy rate among teenagers. Affirmative action in admissions—giving priority to females or minorities—has been endorsed as a means of countering racial and sexual discrimination. In response to a high pregnancy rate among adolescent girls, many schools now offer sex education courses that promote abstinence as well as safe sex. When schools attempt remedy to negative social trends, they serve as agent of social change.

This functionalist perspective portrays contemporary education as basically a benign institution. For example, it argues that schools rationally sort and select students for future high-status positions, thereby meeting society's need for talented and expert personnel. The actor-network theory becomes most promising in its contributions to open new understandings of policy processes, through "(1) a propensity to cause trouble, provoke, be awkward; (2) a tendency to work through difficult conceptual issues in relation to specific empirical cases, deflating grandiose theoretical concepts and claims (and even some ordinary ones); (3) an emphasis on the local, specific and contingent…; (4) caution about the unreflexive adoption and deployment of standard social science lexicons (e.g. power, culture, meaning, value); (5) reflexive attention to the (frequently unexplicated) notions of our audiences, value and utility… etc." (Woolgar, Coopmans and Neyland, 2009: 21-22).

Universality is always local universality in the ANT. Further, in practice a standard functions not as one professional's strict performance of a standard, but as the outcome of negotiation processes among various actors. The ANT accounts of standardisation attempts in education make this abundantly clear. The concept of an "immutable mobile" of standards travelling around different regions and insinuating itself into different messy negotiations among actors in ways that translate all into an extended network is inadequate to describe educational practice, or arguably any practice.

In analyzing the Personalised Education Plan (PEP) with virtual media, ANT explores a wide connectivity with its limitations. ANT was originated in Paris in the late 1970s, and does not focus on the meanings constructed by texts and objects, but sets its lens on what things do. ANT can be used to explore how things or "entities" come together to form assemblages or networks of associations and connections. ANT is relational rather than representational, in that it accepts that reality is performatively achieved. Therefore, until something is enacted it does not exist. By taking a more than social approach (Latour, 2005), ANT provides us with a descriptive tool through which we can examine the associations that constantly make, unmake and remake phenomena that we may label as "societies." By positioning non-human objects as equally important to humans within networks, ANT extends and redefines the domain of the social and may, therefore, be a useful way of exploring the entanglement of human and non-human entities enrolled into networks of change for LAC, while considering the relative strengths and weaknesses of these associations within a network.

In contrast, the conflict perspective views education as an instrument of elite domination. Conflict theorists point out the sharp inequalities that exist in the educational opportunities available to different racial and ethnic groups. Conflict theorists also argue that the educational system socialises students into values dictated by the powerful, schools stifle individualism and creativity in the name of maintaining order, and the level of change they promote is relatively insignificant. From a conflict perspective, the inhibiting effects of education are particularly apparent in the "hidden curriculum" and the differential way in which status is bestowed. The term hidden curriculum refers to standards of behaviour that are deemed proper by society and are taught subtly in schools. According to this curriculum, children must not speak until the teacher calls on them and must regulate their activities according to the clock or bells. In addition, they are expected to concentrate on their own work rather than to assist other students who learn relatively slower to them.

## Conflict Theory

Conflict sociological perspective was developed essentially as a reaction against functionalism. This perspective rejects the ideas of consensus and asserts that our society is a condition of perpetual conflict between individuals. The central ideas in this perspective are competition, and exploitation. Notwithstanding this basic difference, the conflict sociological theory shares something in common with functionalism – their concern for the whole society in their analysis. And like the preceding perspectives we will be examining the different varieties of the conflict perspective, namely Marxism, neo-Marxism and feminism.

Conflict theory posits that conflict is a fundamental part of the social order. Conflict theorists observe that credentialism may reinforce social inequality, and that schools are a critical site in the reproduction of social inequality, particularly class conflict and racial stratification. Applicants from poor and minority backgrounds are especially likely to suffer from the escalation of qualifications, since they lack the financial resources needed to obtain degrees succesively. Schools are not meritocratic; individual talent and hard work do not necessarily guarantee success. Larger social forces produce unequal outcomes that favour the power and inequality within and among schools and thus help in reproduction of the status quo. In addition, upgrading of credentials serves the self-interest of the two groups mostly responsible for this trend. Educational institutions profit from prolonging the investment of time and money by people while staying in school. Now it may be said that the education is a crucial type of investment for the exploitation of modern technology and thus, conflict theorists see education as maintaining existing power structures while creating a docile workforce or underclass.

Sociologists of conflict school have long recognised that schooling is central to social stratification. Both functionalist and conflict theorists agree that education performs the important function of bestowing status. From a functionalist perspective, this widening bestowal of status is beneficial not only to particular recipients but to society as a whole. According to Kingsley Davis and Wilbert E. Moore (1945), society must distribute its members among a variety of social positions. Education can contribute to this process by sorting people into appropriate levels and courses of study that will prepare them for positions in the labour force. Capitalism requires a skilled, disciplined labour force, hence the educational system of any country is structured with that objective in mind. Citing numerous studies, they offer support for what they call the correspondence principle. According to this approach, schools promote the values expected of individuals in each social class and perpetuate social class divisions from one generation to the next. Thus, conflict theorists hold that the educational inequalities produced by tracking are designed to meet the needs of modern capitalist societies.

Conflict theorists are far more critical of the *differential* way in which education bestows status. They stress that schools sort pupils according to their social class backgrounds. Although the educational system helps certain poor children to move into middle-class professional positions, it denies most disadvantaged children the same educational opportunities afforded by children of the affluent. In this way, schools tend to preserve social class inequalities in each new generation. Higher education in particular acts more like a sieve that sorts people out of the educated classes than a social ladder that helps all with ambition to rise.

Conflict theorists do not believe that educational institutions reduce social inequality. Rather, they believe that the educational system reinforces and perpetuates social inequalities that arise from differences in class, gender, race, and ethnicity. From functionalist standpoints, a number of studies have shown that the number of years of education is a strong determinant of occupational achievement. The concept of achievement, the existence of systematic social arrangements and some interactional social situations, which seem to favour some groups more than others, are never questioned. Social inequities in terms of access to and ability to use and control resources in society are accepted as given and unproblematic (Meighan and Siraj-Blatchford, 1986). But even the conservative functionalists accept that social groups can have differences of interest resulting in conflict as a valid and necessary part of social discourse even though they undermine the significance of such conflict in disrupting the social order.

The failure of both consensus and action perspectives to provide satisfactory answers to the question of uneven distribution of resources or the exploitative relationships prevalent in the society gave rise over the years to an alternative theory of how societies hold together and developed as a way of demonstration as how order and coherence in society are founded on conflict and the domination of some over others. This relatively new theory emerged from the writings of Karl Marx (1818-1883). Marxian perspective had broken the notion of education to increase class exploitation and developed educational theory as an essence of tool of practice. The elements of a Marxist conception of education appear, from the 1840s, in many works of Marx and Engels (e.g. *Capital* 1, ch. 13; *German Ideology,* Vol. I, pt. 1; *Critique of the Gotha Programme,* sect. IV) and includes *Principles of Communism* (Engels, 1847).

On the basis of these analytical parts, a more coherent theory of education has been gradually built up. A major impetus was given to it by the Bolshevik Revolution and its need for a Marxist educational praxis. The main components of the theory are: Firstly, free public education, compulsory and uniform for all children, assuring the abolition of cultural or knowledge monopolies and of privileged forms of schooling. In this way education becomes a weapon as a knowledge tool to weaken the role of the family in social reproduction. Secondly, Marx's formulations helped sociologists in combining education with material production. The objective implied here is neither a better vocational training, nor the inculcation of a work ethic, rather the closing of the historical gap between manual and mental work, between conception and execution, by assuring to all a full understanding of the productive process. Thirdly, Marxist points of education germinate an alternative form of capitalist division of labour. Here education has to assure the all-round development of the personality. With re-united science and production, the human being can become a producer in the full sense by unfolding all his or her potentialities. With the Durkheimian view of the primacy of society over the individual by focusing on the notion of power as the mediating factor in its concept of binary opposition, but it opened the door to a number of other theories, particularly where the concept of binary opposition and the notion of power lent support.

For Marx, the basic aspect of social order is to be found in the concept of binary opposition. Social order is achieved through a continual process of disputed interaction between issues, of sectional struggles and of the imposition of order by those who win power (Meighan and Siraj-Blatchford, 1986). Using this Marxian binary model, the conflict theorists demonstrate that although the "haves" and the "have-nots" or the owners of the means of production and the forces of production are binary opposites, the notion of power mediates between each pair of opposites.

This mediation operates at two levels. First, it empowers certain individuals within a group to shape, direct and define the rules governing the conduct of other members of the group as a way of managing intra-group conflict and maintaining order. At the second level, it enables one group of people to successfully overcome opposition from other groups or even other individuals. In this way, all social arrangements governing the interrelationships between individuals' actions and the structure of society and all interactional situations are subjected to a pervasive Hagelian dialectical analysis. As noted by Haralambos, Holborn and Heald (2004), although there are many varieties of the conflict perspective within sociology, all: (i) view society as a whole, (ii) adopt a structural approach;

(iii) use the notion of the existence of different groups that have different interests in society resulting in conflict, and (iv) submit that social arrangements will tend to favour some groups at the expense of others.

Conflict theorists at least with reference to their emphasis on the existence of competing groups and interests in society, would agree that conflict is in some way central to the maintenance of social order. Finding the ways in which these competing differences and interests are either resolved or controlled is the true goal of analysis. This does not mean however, that conflict is a permanent feature in our social arrangements as there are periods of truce and compromises resulting in harmonious co-existence of the competing groups. But even these periods of harmony do not last forever, and new forms of conflict may eventually erupt (Haralambos et al., 2004).

From this it can be seen that like the functionalists, the conflict theorists are also inclined to the study of social structures and institutions. However, as noted by Ritzer (1996), the conflict theory represents largely a series of contentions that often contradict the views of the functionalists about social reality. Ritzer follows Dahrendorf (1958, 1959) in juxtaposing the tenets of the two theorists. Whereas the functionalists view society as static or in a state of moving equilibrium, the conflict theorists regard society at every point, as being affected by the processes of change. Furthermore, whereas functionalists emphasise the orderliness of society, conflict theorists in contrast, direct attention to the existence of dissent and conflict at every point in the social system.

Again, where functionalists explain social order in terms of value consensus and a common morality, the conflict theorists perceive order as resulting from coercion of some members by those at the top. Thus, where functionalists regard shared social values as the main factor in social cohesion, the conflict theorists stress the role of power in bringing about order in society. The ruling class uses educational institutions, along with the media and other means of communication, to disseminate ideas that will support its continued rule. Given this assumption, the conflict perspective often focuses on the role school systems in influencing public opinion, or implementing social control. Although there are many varieties of conflict theories, the focus in this unit will be on only three namely, Marxism, Neo-Marxism and Feminism.

The Marxian theory presents itself as a major alternative to structural functionalism. However, we have seen that, in spite of this claim, Marxism merely affirms a modified macro-structural theory as a means of explaining how societies hold together. The main difference between the two being Marxism's rejection of the notion of the primacy of consensus in the dialectical process. Emphasising on the contradictions and conflict in the economic system, Marx developed a new theory of conflict for explaining the dynamics of social reality.

The neo-Marxian theory emerged as a reaction against the poor version of Marxian theory, which characterised the works of early conflict theorists, such as, Ralf Dahrendorf. Nevertheless, we have also seen that though all the neo-Marxists begin with a dialectical disavowal of the economic determinism of the early Marxists, they often go in separate directions, and in spite of their differences, they all align themselves and base their dialectical structure on Marxian analysis. Both among Marxists, and between Marxists and non-Marxists there are also current debates about the theory of personality; the "nature-nurture" controversy; the role of school and education in social reproduction, and their innovative potential within prevailing social determinisms; and the relative importance of the contents, the methods and the structuring of education in promoting social change.

## Critical Theories

Critical theory was developed by a group of German neo-Marxists notably, Max Horkheimer, Theodore Adorno and Herbert Marcuse who were based at the Institute of Social Research (or simply, the "Frankfurt School") in Frankfurt. The main contribution of this theory is in its efforts to steer Marxian theory in a subjective direction at both individual and cultural levels. At the cultural level, the critical theorists argue that the economic determinists have over emphasised the prominence of economic structures at the expense of other aspects of social reality such as the culture.

The thinkers of the Frankfurt School criticise Modernity by emphasising the two-fold scheme that lies at its core: technology – civilisation/culture, i.e. the relation which essentially affects the development of modern societies. In the educational sphere, which is intertwined with social changes, we are living in a period of severe questioning regarding the introduction of new technologies to the teaching / learning process. It is claimed here that the critical pedagogic approach is an important weapon for the essential understanding of the new facts of social reality and can be a decisive factor for the healthy transition to an integrated student-oriented educational practice (Kokkinos, 2007).

The central argument of critical theory is that all knowledge, even the most scientific or "commonsensical," is historical and broadly political in nature. Critical theorists argue that knowledge is shaped by human interests of different kinds, rather than standing "objectively" independent from these interests. This is the turning point from where the educational principles start to take shape. This is inclined to produce a narrative what Hegel would call the "unhappy consciousness"—"unhappy" because the too elevated, too abstract premises inculcated by its artificial education render its owner incapable of mastering the conflicts which are the stuff of real life; he tends to feel at home only when dealing with the possible, the potential, and to discount all reality as *a priori* "bad" (Mannheim, 1952: 232). The true meaning and function of the "idea" is to carry reality forward a stage beyond itself; but such an artificially cultivated "idealist consciousness" leads on instead to a second "ideal world", which in so far has any relation to the concrete historical and social present, really only exists to hide from us the unmastered reality of the "primary" world and to conduct us out of the realm of genuine idealism into that of its dangerous opposite, Romanticism.

The Hegelian Marxists are not alone in focusing their interest in subjective factors. As noted by Ritzer (1996), this initial interest laid the basis for the subsequent development of critical theory, which concerns itself almost exclusively with subjective factors. Put simply, critical theory consists largely of criticisms of various aspects of social and intellectual life ranging from the economic determinism of Marxian theory from which it draws its inspiration, scientism of the discipline of sociology, the cultural repression of the individual in modern society, to the absolutism of the positivist methodology (Ritzer, 1996).

Education as a praxis helps man to form critical knowledge from traditional knowledge (Mannheim and Stewart, 1962). Horkheimer's critical theory does not continue tradition's effort to establish an innate philosophical discourse but attempts a meta-critique of the traditional philosophical discourse. For Max Horkheimer (1947) any theory which claims that man can cognize only what is offered to his senses, his perception, is condemnable. What defines critical theory is its purpose, its social function, which is not the pursuit of pure knowledge but action, the contribution to the making of a transformed society which will conceive of man as a subject of this new social reality.

From an ideological frame of cultural practice, critical theorists attack on music educational shows as "pseudo-democratic". This critical aspect complicates any straightforward elaboration of a postwar public pedagogy. For Adorno, music education should be focused on the music itself and the education of musically critical and self-determined students. He was very critical about the misuse of music education for ideological purposes. Adorno (2000: 127-28) believes that "the sociology of education gives far too little attention to such matters – to say something about the concept of fetishism in science." In this context he tries to understand fetishism in science to mean that science, with its specific form of argumentation and its immanent methods, becomes an end in itself, without any relation to its subject matter.

Jürgen Habermas understands knowledge as corresponding to human interests that are "instrumental," "practical" and "emancipator" in nature. Instrumental knowledge corresponds to technical human interests that are associated with work, labour, or production and with the natural sciences. Practical knowledge refers to interpretive ways of knowing through which everyday life actions and social human activities are coordinated and given meaning. Emancipatory knowledge, finally, is the kind that critical theory itself seeks to generate, and it is articulated in terms of power, control and emancipation.

In particular, the critical theorists have concerned themselves with what Habermas (1975) described as "legitimations", which are simply defined as systems of ideas developed by the political system or any other system to legitimise its continued existence. Such systems are designed to manipulate the masses in accepting the legitimacy of the prevailing political system and the status quo of the existing social arrangements in society. At the individual level, the critical theorists are concerned with actors and their consciousness as well as what happens to them in the modern world (Ritzer, 1996). Through legitimating the consciousness of the masses, the control mechanism reaches to the extent that they no longer perceive domination as a problem to liberate themselves.

A second aspect of the critical theorists' main contribution lies in their dialectical approach, which stresses the importance of social totality. A hint of this notion of social totality may be found in Connerton's (1980: 30) statement: "No partial aspect of social life and no isolated phenomenon may be comprehended without relating it to the conceptual whole, the social structure of production in its entirety." As pointed out by Ritzer (1996), this approach rejects a focus on a single aspect of social life outside of its broader context such as that promoted by the economic determinists.

This view also has methodological implications. Basic to the critical theorists' method is a concern for both diachronic and synchronic approaches. Whereas the synchronic approach focuses attention on the interrelationship of the different parts of society within the social totality, the diachronic approach concerns itself with "the historical roots of today's society" as well as its future direction (Ritzer, 1996). While examples could be multiplied, the preceding might serve to illustrate a wide range of approaches that can be grouped under the more general term, neo-Marxian theory. We have seen that although all begin with a dialectical disavowal of the economic determinism of the early Marxists, they often go in separate directions and inspite of their differences they all align themselves and base their dialectical structure on Marxian analysis.

When education produces a more social-minded leadership, social progress will be less often retarded by a division among the social leaders and their varied thoughts make each step in advance a process of conflict and conquest rather than intelligent cooperation. It is never to be expected that human society will be led forward with no struggles and antagonisms in the ranks of the leaders, but to the degree that those having social influence acquire the attitude of the scientist in dealing with social experience. Progress through violence will be replaced by advancement on the means of deliberation and design.

To the critical theorist, the function of school "is to produce the kind of people the system needs, to train people for the jobs the corporations require and to instill in them the proper attitudes and values necessary for the proper fulfillment of one's social role" (Szymanski and Goertzel, 1979). Critical theorists would also argue that we have become a credentialised society (Collins, 1979). A degree or certificate has become necessary to perform a vast variety of jobs. This credential may not necessarily compel the recipient to perform the job better. Even in professions like medicine, engineering, and law, most knowledge is acquired by performing tasks on the job. However, credentials have become a rite of passage and a sign that a certain process of indoctrination and socialisation has taken place. It is recognised that the individual has gone through a process of educational socialisation that constitutes adequate preparation to hold the occupational status.

## Feminist Theory of Education

Another brand of the conflict perspective is the feminist theory, which has been aptly described by George Ritzer, (1996: 444) as "that system of general ideas designed to describe and explain human social experiences from a women-centred vantage point." There are, as noted by Ritzer, many different versions of feminism but most share common elements. Ritzer (1996: 444) cites three questions that govern and unite all the varieties of contemporary feminist theory: (i) "the descriptive question, and what about women?"; (ii) "the explanatory question, why then is all these as it is?"; and (iii) "the qualifying question, what about the differences among women?". Using the response pattern to the first of these three questions, i.e.: and what about the women? Ritzer went further to categorise feminist theory into four types as follows:

(a) **Gender Difference:** This category emphasises the differences between men and women in terms of their location in, and experience of, most situations.

(b) **Gender Inequality:** This category stresses that women's location in most situations is not only different from that of man, but is also less privileged and unequal.

(c) **Gender Oppression:** This category promotes the view that women are, in addition to being different from and unequal to, oppressed and actively restrained, subjugated, moulded as well as used and abused by men.

(d) **Third-wave Feminism:** The fourth category argues that women's experience of difference, inequality and oppression varies by their social location.

The fundamental presupposition of feminist sociology of education is that gender is a social category, hence a social construction. Ann Oakley (1972), an anthropologist, argued that if gender (rather than sex) could be used as a theoretical construct, then it could be applied to the study of socialisation and society. The concept of "gender" therefore, became analytically, as well as politically, preferable to the concept of "sex" (that is, biological distinctions between men and women) in sociological studies of education. Through the critical application of the social category of gender to the study of education, gender patterns in schooling were linked to broader social inequalities.

The sociology of education has been concerned primarily with examining class inequalities in educational achievement, and especially the relative failure of working-class children in obtaining educational qualifications. Until recently, sociologists have overlooked other important dimensions of educational differentiation – for example, gender and racial differences in achievement. Feminists have argued that girls are not only disadvantaged in the educational system, but they learn to be subordinated and to accept dominant ideologies of femininity and masculinity. Girls are gendered; they come to see themselves as less important than boys.

Today, dominance in gendered society becomes a cult, myth that prevails in individuals' social settings. Violence against women is rightly abhorred. But we may address violence against men as entertainment. Think of football, boxing, wrestling, or ice hockey, rodeos, and auto racing. All are games used to sugarcoat violence against men, originally in need of sugarcoating so our team - or our society - could bribe its best protectors to sacrifice themselves. Yet even today the violence against men in sports is still financed by our public education system, and by public subsidies of the stadiums in which sports teams play. Violence against men is not just called entertainment, it is also called education. We all support it in our everyday life beliefs.

In a racially segregated gendered society more black males are in the prison system than are in the college system. In the United States, "436,000 black males of all ages are in college; 609,690 young black men are under the control of the criminal justice system." On the other hand, Marc Mauer (1990: 3) writes, "white males, are more than four times as likely to be in college as in the criminal justice system." It is incredible that one out of four black males is either in jail, prison, on probation, or on parole. That is almost 50 percent greater than the number in college. This does not even come close to being true of black women. If it is, imagine the number of job training, education, and rehabilitation programmes we would be sponsoring for black women. The black male does not face double jeopardy, he faces quadruple jeopardy: racism, sexism, antagonism, and neglect.

Like the Marxists, feminists concern themselves with the divisions within society, but they differ from the Marxists in the way they explain these divisions. Whereas the Marxists focus on class differences, the feminists see the major division as being between men and women (Haralambos et al., 2004). Likewise, although they share with Marxists the view that society is characterised by exploitation, they differ in terms of the nature of exploitation they concern themselves with: Whereas, the Marxists concentrate on the exploitation of the working class by the ruling class, the feminist tend to emphasise the exploitation of women by men as the most important source of exploitation. For these reasons the feminists describe contemporary societies as patriarchal, a man's world in which women are dominated and relegated to lower status positions, poor-paid jobs and restricted access to political power. The ultimate objective of these varieties of feminism therefore, is to end men's domination and rid society of male chauvinism and its resultant undesirable and unjust exploitation of women.

Finally, the implications of the Marxian analysis for the study of education are drawn. The application of the Marxian analysis to the study of education has taken two directions. These are those like, Samuel Bowles and Herbert Gintis (1976), who examined the structural "fit" between the education system and the economy; and other like Willis (1977) and Apple (1980) whose main attention focused on the way in which the education system is manipulated and used to legitimise and perpetuate the cultural beliefs and practices of the capitalists society (Meighan and Siraj-Blatchford, 1986).

The educational system of any country, like many other social institutions, has long been characterised by discriminatory treatment of women. In 18th century or in 19th century more men's colleges were established. Patriarchy believes that women should aspire to become wives and mothers, not lawyers and intellectuals. In addition to attending classes, female students washed men's clothing, cared for their rooms, and served them at meals. In first half of 20th century female students refused to write a commencement address because it would have been read to the audience by a male student. In the last half of 20th century, sexism in education showed up in many ways—in textbooks with negative stereotypes of women, counsellors' pressure on female students to prepare for "women's work," and unequal funding for women's and men's athletic programmes. But perhaps nowhere was educational discrimination more evident than in the employment of teachers. The positions of university professor and college administrator, which hold relatively high status in the modern practices, were generally filled by men. Kindergarten school teachers, who earn much lower salaries, were largely female.

A single school can reinforce class differences by putting students in tracks. The term tracking refers to the practice of placing students in specific curriculum groups on the basis of their test scores and other criteria. Tracking begins very early, often in reading groups during first grade. The practice can reinforce the disadvantages that children from less affluent families may face if they have not been exposed to reading materials, computers, and other forms of educational stimulation during their early childhood years. To ignore this connection between tracking and students' race and social class is to fundamentally misunderstand how schools perpetuate the existing social structure.

The sociology of education in the 1960s and 1970s was gender-blind – either no consideration was given to the different experiences of boys and girls in the education system, or research focused exclusively on boys, or girls' experience was interpreted through the boys' eyes. This meant that boys were constructed as the norm and girls as different from the norm. Thus, sociology failed to challenge the commonly held view that if men/boys were not naturally superior to girls/women, they necessarily became so, both because of their role as breadwinners and also because boys/men needed to be constructed by the work and other demands placed on them (Abbott, Wallace and Tyler, 2005: 114).

Feminist sociology was concerned with studying the experiences of girls/women and challenging assumptions of male "natural" superiority in education. In doing so they studied not girls/women in isolation but the relationship between men and women, highlighting the ways in which patriarchal power structured masculine and feminine identities. In the 1980s and 1990s two male perspectives developed which were concerned with understanding the construction of masculinity. The first, associated with "men's studies," was concerned with men's rights and argued that it was necessary to study men in the same way as feminists had studied women – to bring men in. This perspective ignored both the fact that much research had been accomplished by men and about men and that feminist research had been concerned with the relationship between men and women. Some researchers from this perspective have been concerned to argue that schools are "anti-boy" or "pro-girl" (e.g. Moir and Moir, 1999) – a position rejected by feminists. The alternative position is the study of men in the terms devised by feminists – "pro-feminist" studies.

Who is at greater risk of failing in our schools these days—girls or boys? On gender bias in classroom, some researchers, like Myra Sadker and David Sadker (1994), believe that sitting in the same classrooms, reading the same textbooks, and listening to the same teachers, boys and girls receive very different educations. A body of research, including most prominently a 1992 study sponsored by the American Association of University Women, *How Schools Shortchange Girls,* has held that girls face much deeper difficulties in school, whereas boys get the lion's share of educational resources and teachers' attention. Over the course of years, the uneven distribution of teacher time, energy, attention, and talent, takes its toll on girls.

A recent set of studies has considered how masculinity is constructed through schooling. Taking their lead from feminist studies of schools that have explored how femininity is constructed and perpetuated through education, these studies have considered masculinity as problematic. Beverley Skeggs (1995), for example, argues that masculinity is part of a set of codes and expectations found within the school system. The social and educational theorists Mairtin Mac an Ghaill (1994), in an empirical study as how masculinity is created within a school setting, found that the male peer group (with which the male teachers colluded) encouraged an atmosphere of hostility, homophobia and misogyny – in other terms, peer groups of male members were created out of a resentment of gay men and hostility towards women. He suggests that rather than such peer groups being supportive, they tended to ridicule and intimidate boys who did not conform. In this way masculine culture and peer groups within the school served to create and police the boundaries of masculinity and ensure a heterosexual dominance.

## Queer Theory in Education

Why in the field of education, the unusual and unconventional "queer" is becoming relevant at present? Is there a queer pedagogy? How the queer pedagogy is pertinent in academic discipline today? Is due to sexual metaphor queer has its own theoretical significance in the post-adolescence phase of human life? What is the present position of queerness in political discourse or in the question of identity? How are sexual identities theorised according to queer theory? Why queer is gaining popularity in Indian higher education? What does queer theory imply for classroom practice? How does it differentiate between a normal classroom position from its queer variety? Is the weakness in the Marxist Critical Theory or in Radical Theory responsible for the surging popularity of queer? Which view does queer uphold in social change perspectives? Exploring the queer world, we will gradually understand its comparative theoretical analyses in the contemporary phase of academics.

Queer theory portrays post-structuralism, postmodernism and propose implications for teaching. The central argument is that a queer theoretical construction may be more valuable pedagogically than a lesbian and gay one, because it shifts the focus from inclusion to inquiry, that is, from including sexual identities, which are minority to examining how society, politics and culture work regarding all sexual identities. Educational sociologists have viewed that homophobia (a prejudice) and heterosexism (systematic discrimination) can adversely affect teaching and learning and therefore need to be addressed within the classroom, in the educational institution/organisation, and in the profession at large. In class and on the ground of higher education, any student or teacher – not just those who identify themselves as straight – should be free to decide how open they wish to be about their own sexual identity without fear of incrimination.

The founders of queer theory include Gayle Rubin, Judith Butler, and Eve Kosofsky Sedgwick. They drew significantly on the work of Michel Foucault and his concept of biopower – the power of scientific (biological) discourses. Unfortunately, they seem to have missed the point that biologically legitimising sex, gender, and sexuality statuses tends to lead people to become more accepting, rather than less. Queer theory sees the concepts of sex – male and female – and gender – masculine and feminine- as oppressive. The main objective of queer theory is to subvert these concepts and to break them down. Rejecting the possibility of there being a knowable objective reality, queer theory asserts that language creates the categories, enforces them, and scripts people into them. The boundaries are arbitrary and oppressive according to queer theory.

Moreover, while queer's rapid expansion in the academy can be explained largely in terms of an older and more slowly established model of lesbian and gay studies, queer theory is often represented as having a greater investment in the institutions than in the politics. The professionalisation of queer has mostly benefited those relatively few individuals who are making academic careers as queer scholars (Malinowitz, 1993: 172). This suspicion is often registered disquiet in queer theory's increasingly specialised vocabulary and analytical models, both of which are taken as evidence that queer theorists are not accountable to any community outside the universities.

A tenet of queer theory is that the social body negotiates multiple identities through multiple social spaces, creating complex intersections between self, perception of others' self, and perception of selves. It challenges the heterosexual bias in a society. Actually, the emergence of queer theory during the past decade represents a huge leap in our understanding of lesbian, gay, bisexual, and transgendered identities. Identities are complex to begin with and become more complicated when relating them to the nation and sexuality. Contemporary Indian sexual identities are constructed out of the multiplicitious effects and perceptions of tradition, modernity, colonisation and globalisation that are more often not in conflict with each other.

Of course, queer theory's assertion that identity is liquid and performative, works against the understanding of social construction. It has opened up new approaches for treating sexuality and gender inequality as subjects worthy of consideration in their own right, rather than as offshoots of general cultural identity (Stanley, 1983-1984). Education programmes are now commonly privileged acts over identities. Educational strategies demonstrate the limits of that paradigm shift which is widely understood to distinguish modern from premodern or from postmodern sexualities (Spargo, 1999; Huffer, 2009). Gay and lesbian studies, along with medical sociology advocated an assimilationist line, insisting that homosexuals were people like everyone else and that it was more productive for them to co-operate with experts in the fields of medicine, law and education in order to effect social change. Indeed, queer theory goes beyond exploring aspects of gay and lesbian identity and experience.

Thus far, calls for gay-friendly pedagogies have drawn on a lesbian and gay identity framework, which aims to legitimate subordinate sexual identities. Although a lesbian and gay identity construction has been very useful politically in mobilising for civil rights, it may be less useful pedagogically (Luhmann, 1998). Queer theory shifts the focus from gaining social rights to analyzing discursive and cultural practices, from affirming alternative sexual identities to create turbulence in all sexual identities. Pedagogies of inclusion thus become pedagogies of inquiry.

Like cultural, postcolonial, and critical race studies, queer studies have been a privileged site for the explicit reconsideration of disciplinarity and knowledge production. In a conditional reality, pedagogy produces social relations as much as knowledge. Queer epistemology insists social science researchers to embark on extended investigations of normalisation and intersectionality. Queer is understood as a challenge to traditional understandings of sexual identity by deconstructing the categories, the binaries, and language that supports them. This epistemological and pedagogical effects help in the emergence of queer theory that disrupts and challenges traditional modes of social thought (Luhmann, 1998). In reality, queer pedagogues have continued to build on the ideals of critical theory and feminism, but moved them further into the realm of the postmodern. Today, we find ourselves in an ironic historical moment of "queer liberalism." Liberalism, in a sense of queer, indicates liberal queer ideology in a lesbian plot, and demands "all sex education curricula must include lesbianism as a valid, legitimate form of sexual expression and love" (quoted in Marotta, 1981: 244-5). In recent years sexual politics in particular have become polarised. Not surprisingly, where sex education is concerned, public and even many private schools are becoming sites of controversies.

In the academic context queer theory emerged where radical social critiques had become passé. The flaws of critical theory help postmodern encounters to explain social reality. This is in part due to popular attacks on the academy, which have portrayed colleges and universities as enclaves promoting elitist conceptions and students who are, at best, unmarketable, and it is also a result of the present conservatism in the culture at large. Particularly in the liberal arts, the idea of the academic world as a practical endeavour has seemed to some to be something of an oxymoron. Liberal education, for many, is no longer regarded as a stepping-stone to career objectives or a practical tool for social integration (Tierney and Dilley, 1998). Urbanisation, communication and modern education allowed people of varied castes and classes and other fragmented groups to intermingle freely and most of the queer literatures around this time depict passionate and erotic interaction amongst men of different strata.

A common feature in developing countries is a steadily increasing population in general and a relatively fast growing number of students searching for higher education opportunities. In countries like India, Pakistan, South Africa, and China, this has resulted in a demand for massification of higher education. This growth is associated with huge diversity and different levels of development. The obvious sequel of population growth and demand for higher education is the focus of higher education on access and equity rather than quality. This has also resulted in a shortage of human capital, which is the key requirement to fuel sustainable development.

In these circumstances, poststructuralist aspect offers educators a lens through which educators can transform their praxis so as to explore and celebrate the tensions and new understandings created by teaching in order to look into the world in new ways. However, poststructuralist pragmatism is much less secure in its ability to separate different parts of experiment or practical knowledge from one another. It is not a matter of revising things piece by piece. They are interconnected and any practical work is a transformation of all of them. Yet some order is still possible because how they are transformed is different, both in terms of the alteration of the parts and their relations, and in terms of spatial and chronological relations. For example, in Indian educational sphere, gender also has a cross-cutting effect: in some poorly represented minority groups of girls are more likely to access higher education, mainly on account of superior performance at school. This is obviously a positive example of resistance when expansion, inclusion and excellence are becoming the three major concerns of Indian higher education.

To be sure, the disintegration of social programmes has also meant the erosion of public primary and secondary schools. This point of intersection relates to educational and public policy related to queer theory.

The central claim of queer theorists is that the categories through which identity is understood, are all social constructs rather than given to us by nature. In this era of globalisation, traditional student mobility patterns have changed. Higher education system, originally designed to serve the elite, will now have to serve the people. Innovation and change are required and understanding that change will be essential. This position opens a number of analytical possibilities. For example, queer theorists examine how fundamental notions of gender and sex, which seem so natural and self-evident to persons in the modern West, are in fact constructed and reinforced through everyday actions, and that this occurs in ways that privilege heterosexuality.

This is a central theme in the work of Judith Butler. It also becomes apparent that gender and class pervade and are produced by these classifications and discourses. If gender attributes are performative (Butler, 1990: 141), pedagogy begins to look like more than just an unruly performance. In its interdisciplinary transdisciplinarity, and its blend of "female" and "male," it appears "androgynous/bisexual/queer" (Windmeyer and Freeman, 2001: xxxii). The consequence is an academic identity which cannot easily (if at all?) be authorised by or as part of existing genderised academic categories and practices, not least because "we regularly punish those who fail to do their gender right" (Butler, 1990: 140). For female students and tutors, pedagogy may therefore prove to be one more route to marginalisation, and not just influence, and grounds for our ambivalence as academics. Thus, queer theory refers not to identity per se but to a body of theories that "critically analyzes the meaning of identity, focusing on intersections of identities and resisting oppressive social constructions of sexual orientation and gender" (Abes and Kasch, 2007: 620).

Queer studies in education depict a social change perspective. There may be four dimensions of change in society for education if observed through a queer lens. The first is heteronormativity in education.

Heteronormativity is an institutionalised ideology that positions heterosexuality, heterosexual identity, and heterosexual practices as normal, natural, and universal. Second dimension is gender performativity that has been drawn on to disrupt normative assumptions as student's gendered behaviours, especially as these take place within the context of social relations with peers and are a consequence of their biological sex. The third dimension significantly recasts the meaning and deployment of the fag epithet within homophobic social interactions, mostly among the post-adolescent males in academic settings. The fourth dimension obviously indicates the queer masculinities in education. Queer masculinities deconstruct the relationship between the politics of social identity formation and critical pedagogical practices (Kincheloe, 2008).

The queer body challenges social science researchers to acknowledge those who do not easily fit in the normative patterns that shape our formal educational institutions, classrooms, and curriculums, including issues of ethnicity, race, and heteronormativity. At the same time, queer theory demands that complicated and intersecting renderings of sexual minority and other marginalised youth are utilised in the theories built, curriculums developed, students taught, and teachers trained.

Queer studies research in education is placed within a broader set of intellectual contexts. In a theoretical context it has effectively re-opened the question of the relations between sexuality and gender, both as analytic categories and as lived experiences; it has created greater opportunities for transgender studies; it has pursued the task (begun long before within the sphere of lesbian/gay studies) of detaching the critique of gender and sexuality from narrowly conceived notions of lesbian and gay identity; it has supported non-normative expressions of gender and sexuality, encouraging both theoretical and political resistance to normalisation; it has underwritten a number of crucial theoretical critiques of homophobia and heterosexism; it has redefined the practice of lesbian, gay, bisexual, and transgendered history; and it has dramatised the far-reaching theoretical promise of work in lesbian and gay studies.

But with the institutionalisation of queer theory, and its acceptance by the academy (and by straight academics), new problems and new challenges have come. There is something odd, suspiciously odd, about the rapidity with which queer theory–whose claim to radical politics derived from its anti-assimilationist posture, from its shocking embrace of the abnormal and the marginal–has been embraced by, canonised by, and absorbed into our (largely heterosexual) institutions of knowledge, as lesbian and gay studies never were.

Despite its implicit (and false) portrayal of lesbian and gay studies as liberal, assimilationist, and accommodating of the status quo, queer theory has proven to be much more congenial to established institutions of the liberal academy. It negates that politics which assumes social change to be oriented toward a confrontation with the very nature of the social structure. Identifying with social movements on the basis of similar patterns of exploitation, rather than mechanistically deconstructing them, queer theory can begin to resolve the stagnation that has dominated attempts to develop coalitions around issues that matter.

## Poststructuralist Perspectives of Sociology of Education

Sociologists may examine how social practices and especially divisions between what is to be done and what is not, corresponding to the dichotomy between "closeted" and "out" structure thought process. This outer world concept within social reality makes moments with a dichotomous network. When we look at dichotomies such as natural/unnatural or masculine/feminine, we find in the background an implicit reliance on connectivity, and an understanding of the sexual world as split into two species. Such binary oppositions as the tolerant and the tolerated and the oppressed and the oppressor, yet still hold[s] onto an analysis of social difference that can account for how dynamics of subordination and subjection work at the level of the historical, the structural, the epistemological, the conceptual, the social, and the psychic realms. Body social, socialisation and cultural knowledge settings (presence of elements) accelerate social practices of uncertainty/risk.

This other sources of meaning, or changing perspective of understanding criticises queer theoretical outlook and develops a poststructuralist dimension in social science and literature. Here, a related criticism is that queer theory cannot make crucial distinctions, since it refuses any essence or reference to standard ideas of normality. For example, queer theorists usually argue that one of the advantages of the term "queer" is that it includes transsexuals, sadomasochists, and others with marginalised sexualities. Critics ask how far this extends. For instance, while some queer theorists specifically disallow pedophilia as permissible in University campus, others overtly refuse to rule out pedophiles as "queer." Furthermore, it has not been cleared that based on which philosophic resources, the theory should rule out pedophilia or more extreme forms of sadomasochism.

Queer theory has recoursed to a very technical jargon. To overcome this problem the poststructuralists had started a new theoretical way to convert concepts. Poststructuralist approach in textual analysis considers that a reader's culture and society share at least an equal part in the interpretation of a piece to the cultural and social circumstances of the author. From this standpoint of conversion, economic capital can be converted into symbolic capital in order to gain sufficient obligation back and create relationships of dependence from lower social classes. This new idea opens a new critical dimension in educational research where Pierre Bourdieu (1984) developed the cultural deprivation theory. This theory implies that higher class cultures are better when compared to working class cultures. Bourdieu (1967) argues that working class failure in schools if measured by exam success. It is the fault of the education system, not of the working class culture. He refers to possession of the dominant culture as cultural capital because with the education system it can be translated into wealth and power. Cultural capital is not evenly distributed throughout the class structure, and this largely accounts for class differences in educational attainment.

This critical pedagogical perspective opened up by a nonqueer approach, although certainly implicit in what has just been referred to, is especially important. Critical pedagogy is a perspective toward education and is concerned with questions of justice, democracy, and ethical claims (Kincheloe, 2008). Since most anti-gay and anti-lesbian arguments rely on the alleged naturalness of heterosexuality, queer theorists attempt to show how these categories are themselves entirely social constructs. The situational tensions among the generally "nonqueer" (Britzman, 1995; Renn, 2010; Taylor and Coia, 2014) context of teacher, education and queer theory are at play in intellectual, pedagogical, academic world, and curriculum theory is a space wherein these tensions can be considered. In fact, queer theory has failed to live up to its potential and must therefore move beyond a declaration of its own intent.

Critical pedagogical studies in sociology are concerned with issues of power, privilege, and oppression. As an academic sub-field it also refers to "critical" analyses of the existing organisation and social meaning of sociability and social identities, rather than merely descriptive accounts of performing function. The criticality of critical thought spaces poststructural theoretical work that can be found across a number of disciplines in the humanities and social sciences, including the field of education, and, hence, has influenced disciplinary knowledge production. This approach argues that to understand an object, one must study both the object itself and the systems of knowledge that produced the object.

According to Bourdieu (1977), agents do not continuously calculate according to explicit rational and economic criteria. Rather, social agents operate according to an implicit practical logic—a practical sense—and bodily dispositions. Instead of confining his analysis of social relations and change to voluntaristic agency or strictly in terms of class as a structural relation, Bourdieu uses the agency-structure bridging concept of "field", which refers to any setting in which agents and their social positions are located. We can identify an educational institution/ department/section as a "field".

Moreover, economic capital can be deferred via symbolic capital. Bourdieu gives the example of the education system in consumer society to establish his idea of symbolic capital. Education and knowledge of higher order can be purchased with money. Thus, for one's offsprings one spends money but is rewarded at a later stage by the process of reproduction as the symbolic value of higher educational possessions ploughs back high status position for the family. Cultural capital, in contrast, works via superior aesthetic tastes which relates to social position. In his empirical study of tastes among different social classes, Bourdieu (1984) demonstrates the importance of cultural and symbolic order in modern consumer society over the material order.

Bourdieu (1973) views culture as a kind of economy or market place. In this marketplace it is the cultural goods/capital which is utilised for social placements rather than economic goods/capital. This capital is expressed symbolically, but is an expression of one's social class origin as well as their educational possessions. While studying differential tastes, Bourdieu asserts that, actual preferences are very much inclined to social status. By examining the different categories and forms of capital and showing their derivative character, he basically confirms that capital is a form of social relation.

Thus, the use of poststructuralist thought in educational research is constrained by a tension between, on the one hand, what is considered to be its emancipatory and empowering potential and, on the other, a reluctance to be distracted from practical concerns and, hence, a fear of alienating the practitioner by speaking in terms of the theoretical.

This tension may lead to a superficial relationship that educational research has to depend on ideas of this kind upon which it draws and of which it makes great claims. Learning is at the heart of most poststructuralist philosophies, for example, in later Foucault, in Deleuze's difference and repetition, in Kristeva's works on writing and learning, in Derrida's works on philosophical education, or in Lyotard's late works on Augustine. Different realms presuppose different senses of space and time and, therefore, any experiment involves long and short effects, and more importantly, effects that are in some sense, outside time in its familiar linear sense. Asymmetry then becomes an opportunity to describe different functions in each realm. This explains why poststructuralism is a philosophy of principles, limits, critical guidelines and radical creativity in the field of educational research.

## Postmodern Perspective of Education

Much of what has been written relative to postmodernism is a critique of modernism (Birden, 2003). Postmodernism includes various groups of philosophers who follow multiplicity (Lyotard, 1992). On this aspect, the philosophers identify postmodern society as more diverse, consumerist, fragmented, media-saturated (hyper-real) and allows individuals much more freedom of choice than its previous counterpart. In this society education has become more individualised. Teachers are expected to use a variety of teaching approaches in their delivery of lesson, to take account of the variety of "learning styles" of students, and where possible "facilitate" lessons so that would be learner centered. With the introduction of marketisation and open enrollment, parents now have more choices over which school to send their child to. For this cosy educational system with a fragmented curriculum, the postmodern perspective does not lend itself in developing a comprehensive philosophy of education. Postmodernism is critiqued as deconstructing the ideals of modernism rather than with laying down principles concerned with the development of knowledge and its relationship to higher education.

One of the criticisms that postmodernists direct at modernism is its reliance on development and maintenance of hierarchies (Bloland, 1995: 526-530). Presidents are higher than deans, deans higher than chairs, chairs higher than instructing faculty, instructors higher than students. This is the manner of things in higher education—and, for that matter, in most modern organisations. Hierarchies also exist in the relationship of higher education disciplines to each other (sciences being higher than arts, and arts being higher than professions), credentials (doctoral degree over baccalaureate degree over associate degree) and institutions (university over university-college over community college).

These hierarchies set up definitions about whom or what qualifies as being "in" or "out" or as "top" or "bottom." The minority student or minority institution is certainly not at the top of the list (Bergquist, 1995). Making space in a hierarchy is making room for someone to be superior and someone to be inferior. Hierarchical institutions are valuable if we believe that anything the hierarchy perpetuates is more important to the well being of society than what individuals might want. We may not have the ability to recognise what is important to the well being of the greater society, the argument goes on, but the hierarchy keeps the society's needs in balance.

Hierarchy may not be such a good thing if those who lead us are unaware of the interweaving of hierarchy, power and knowledge (Broom and Klein, 1999). Who is allowed to ask questions? Who is allowed to generate and disseminate knowledge? Knowledge creation is political. Who in higher education presently asks the questions that promote the generation of new knowledge? It is not the students. It is the professors and the granting bodies who are interested in the creation of questions. Who has defined that we study disciplines as they are presently arranged? Who has equated learning with the granting of the credit?

Modern educational theory attempts to classify and segment learning. The world is taken apart, split into disciplines, objectified, quantified and then repackaged as courses with learner objectives. This model relies on "the sage on stage" to parcel out the information to learners. Learners can utilise strategies to improve learning. A grade is assigned based on the degree to which the learner has achieved these teacher-determined objectives.

Postmodern life is not just about rapid and turbulent change. It is also about fragmentation of old systems and expectations. There are constant disruptions. It is hard to count on any one set of values or any one paradigm. To deal with the fragmentation of the old paradigm, postmodern students apply their own story and experience to the learning environment. They learn to trust not only their own rational processes (housed primarily in their prefrontal cortex), but also their exceptionally-gifted intuition (housed primarily in their much older, larger and more mature limbic brain). (Lehrer, 2009) The postmodern instructor who is engaged with a learner from an appreciative perspective, encourages this person to relate the directions of the course or programme to their personal experiences, instead of viewing this as past baggage that should be left outside the educational experience. Instructor/tutor and student co-create new learning and understandings in the moment.

Postmodern learning is a creative act. It involves ever-changing environments and learning arrangements. Individual plans can be created wherein the learner is an active participant. The postmodern teacher and mature student are partners in learning a body of knowledge within a contemporary context. Other methods are not discarded, but they are used, modified and recreated to suit the situation at hand. The postmodern instructor is a "guide on the side" whose role is more to facilitate learning experiences toward the meaningful aims. Alternate views and content integration are encouraged. Ideas are brought together through a holistic approach to form new ways of knowing the world.

New learning relationships and knowledge creation potential are heightened and become an exciting aspect of the postmodern class. Firstly, knowledge about ways in which to live and learn in an open system in which there is considerable ambiguity and serendipitous development; secondly, information literacy skills for students and awareness by students of their own selection bias; the postmodern instructor leads their students through the data and information to the knowledge that is involved with the purposes of the course of studies and with the meaning relative to the life of each individual student; thirdly, relationships between the course's and programme's directions, and the individual's personal experience; new learning and understandings is co-created in the moment; fourthly, creation of individual plans wherein the learner is an active participant; creation of partnerships between teachers and students in learning a body of knowledge within a contemporary context; fifthly, creation of instructor role as a "guide on the side"—tutor, learning coach and facilitator—of learning experiences toward meaningful aims; sixthly, ideas are brought together through a holistic approach to form new ways of knowing the world; new learning relationships and knowledge creation potential are heightened and are an exciting aspect of the postmodern class; seventhly, meta-strategies (or meta-cognitive strategies) are required; students learn how to learn; eighthly, learners are encouraged to find personal meaning from the learning, as the teacher is allowed to discard the mask of authority and be more themselves, modeling the lifelong learning value of postmodernism; and lastly, learners (living in a postmodern world) are encouraged to formulate and engage a clear, stable, sustaining image of self and identity (Tierney, 1994).

The modern method of instruction fills the minds of students with content; it tries to elicit a specific way of thinking. This modern approach to learning requires that an instructor be firmly in charge of student learning in the classroom. The instructor or department directs the student in their specific learning. By contrast, a postmodern approach allows students to self-direct their learning. They interweave their ongoing work "in the world" with their educational programme—gaining credit not for their prior experience but instead for their current, ongoing experiences. Parameters of a programme are set out for student groups (cohorts) and the student cohorts self-direct their shared programmes. Using dialogue and meta-dialogue (What are we saying by saying this?) the cohort decides what it wants to learn (relative to a course or the programme), how it wants to learn, which directions it will take in the learning process and which steps need to be taken next to achieve the aims of the individual cohort members and the group in this learning process.

## Concluding Remarks

Sociological theories help us to take various pieces of a puzzle and put them together, using a specific framework to help us make sense of it all and to give us the tools we need to talk about the social reality. Each theoretical perspective represents a particular way of understanding the social world. Classical Functionalists view education as one of the important social institutions in a society. Modern structural functionalists contend that education contributes two kinds of functions: manifest functions, which are the intended and visible functions of education; and latent functions, which are the hidden and unintended functions. The perspective of conflict theory, contrary to the structural functionalist perspective, considers the whole education system as an overlain with ideology, which is provided by the dominant group.

Conflict theorists see the purpose of education as a way to maintain social inequality and a way to preserve the power of those who dominate society. Pedagogy of "teaching the conflict" bleaches to the extent that it robs students of the opportunity to access the critical discourses that will enable them not only to deconstruct the colonial and hegemonic paradigms, but will also help them to realise that one cannot teach conflict as if, all of a sudden, it fell from the sky. The conflict must be anchored in those competing histories and ideologies that generated the conflict in the first place (Freire, 2005[1970]).

Education must also perform another function: As various jobs become vacant, they must be filled with the appropriate people. Therefore, the other purpose of education is to sort and rank individuals for placement in the labour market. The micro aspects of sociological theories focus on interactions between individuals. But they cannot deny the "publicness" of the state that has to be strengthened and acknowledges that the private sector will always have a role in public services. This late capitalist societies explore education as a basic weapon to enhance skill within the institutional fragmentation.

Late capitalism is justified by calculation and statistical means. Now the concept of alienation in late capitalism has been replaced with fragmentation (Jameson, 1991: 14). Fragmentation highlights the increased separation of people from one another that is now taking place. Welfare activities must be cut, trade simplified and enhanced, environmental programmes eased, and social programmes eliminated to remain "competitive." While the destruction of education, health programmes, and other social services are lamented, these actions become rationalised as necessary evils to further academic goal of success. In reality, of course, the object is the goal of increased profit.

The increased fragmentation of individuals from communities is reflected in social theory. These developments appear as "natural" and much of academic theories mirror as well as reinforce the society at large. It has become commonplace to assume that concepts that promote the further individuation of the individual are the correct direction for academic development. Unlike India, in the United States, at least, the need for higher education is upheld on one level, while on another, attacks are played out in popular culture with media spins asserting that colleges are overcharging the public and that the employees of higher education are simply intellectuals involved in meaningless debates of their own making. In a post-structuralist and postmodern point, in United States, an author can introduce himself as "I am an anthropologist, a gay man, a white American, a university professor" (Kirsch, 2000: 1), but for an Indian author it is not so media based.

While race, sex, gender, and class have become buzzwords in the postmodern university setting, it is infinitely less dangerous to use them within the contexts of theory than to take on the foundations of the larger socio-political structure. Similarly, it is certainly safer to "deconstruct" and "reconstruct" theories of social being than to "construction" modes of social action. From this perspective, Indian postmodern gay activists and some queer theorists propose that the language of love, like the language of marriage and coupledom, is too heterosexual, too commercialised, too patriarchal, too bourgeois (take your pick) to use by gay people. It is partly as a result of this type of argument that social theorists in their writings overwhelmingly prefer words like "desire" to "love." It also assumes that all lovers, cross-sex or same-sex, who aspire to marry are deluded by notion that orthodox Marxists term as false consciousness.

Now the design of the model curriculum is directly incorporating the inputs that are required to develop practical knowledge. Educational research skills, like any other skill, can be learned. Teaching research skills represents a shift from focusing on the research topic to focusing on learning outcomes. 21$^{st}$ century research requires a spectrum of cognitive abilities, from the simple ability to establish facts to the more complex ability to judge and evaluate. In higher education we might reasonably expect students to be led through this spectrum to the point where they are able to criticize, to analyze, and to reach a deep understanding of knowledge. The theoretical understanding of the sociology of education deals with the study of how public institutions and individual experiences affect education and its outcomes.

Sociological theories, thus, are responsible not just for their substantive discoveries, but for having analyzed the very possibility of socially created reality, in which we spend our daily lives. Sociological truth, as with any other kind, persists only because sociology has generated its own ways of conceding truth in episteme. This truth is not an aggregation of private people sensing individual objects, but a public, rule-guided, and institutionalised canon of socially ingrained habits, skills and dispositions.

# Chapter - 6

# The Peda-, or Andragogical Link with Social Movement and its Theories

The conception of a social movement is linked with the conception of society. It rejects the idea of a fixed and unchanging conception of ethics, values, norms, power and hierarchy in society. Rejecting or altering the past and present forms of norms and values of the society or supplanting the values from the past and transposing them in the imagined structure of the future society, social movement cogitates on an aspirational map and a working design for that desired future.

Education makes consciousness and organises people, resources, and ideas for social change. This "social mobilisation and its resultant social movements, rather than 'representing the interests of dissident groups,' are also an effective vehicle for the attainment of democratic rights for citizens" (Ferguson and Smith, 2012: 992). In any country, social work education takes initiative to broaden the context of its field practice training opportunities to include such movements and progressive organisations.

Conceptually, the term "social movement" has been a difficult task to define. Protests, conflicts, collective actions, agitations, resistances and rebellions, collective mobilisations of all varieties have generally been described as social movements. There is no single definition by which we can easily understand the meaning of social movement, even there is no single method for studying them, nor any consensus on particular types of questions that need to be addressed.

In the *Oxford English Dictionary,* Henry W. Fowler (1965: 569-70) defines a movement as "a course or series of actions and endeavours on the part of a body of persons, moving or tending more or less continuously toward some special end." It, for the sociologist, does not distinguish a social movement from any other form of social behaviour, considered over a period of time. The point is that the regular habit of taking as of equal sociological merit every phenomenon, which somebody or other has named a social movement, results in general debasement of the concept for fruitful sociological purposes.

As an endeavour, social movement is an important form of group behaviour in which large numbers of people are organised or altered to support and bring about or to resist social change (Banks, 1972). From this perspective, we can consider a social movement as a collectivity with a common goal and shared values. The sense of membership suggests that the individual is subject to some discipline. In addition to shared values, a social movement possesses norms. These norms prescribe behaviour that will symbolise the member's loyalty to the social movement, strengthen his commitment to it, and set him apart from non-members.

The process of participation in a social movement is primarily informal. The supporters are loosely organised but sustain campaign in support of a social goal, typically either for the implementation or the prevention of a change in society's structure or values. Although social movements differ in size, they are all essentially collective. That is, they result from the more or less spontaneous coming together of people whose relationships are not defined by rules and procedures, but merely share a common outlook on society. Presently, the scholars have identified the role of formal organisations to form social movements in different parts of our globe. This perspective recognises the social movement organisation (SMO) as a key factor in the study of movements.

One of the defining characteristics of a social movement is that it is relatively long lasting; the activity of the members is sustained over a period of weeks, months, or even years rather than flaring up for a few hours or a few days and then disappears. A social movement is usually large, but, like duration, it is also relative. Some social movements, lasting many decades, may enlist hundreds of thousands of members. Some movements take place within the boundaries of a specific secondary group, such as a religious association or a local community, and may include only a few score or a few hundred members. In contrast to the more sanitised participation advocated by much of the theory and policy of community work, the sociology of education provides opportunities for a more collective pedagogy and andragogy to emerge a critical form of participation in social issues.

## Movements Move People, when Education Helps to Forge a Critical Reason

Sociologists link social movements with education to analyze social change. This perspective offers students the opportunity to examine how education is linked to social movements and change. Students can explore the social, political, pedagogical, and cultural bases of campaigns for educational justice and equity across different regions of our globe. Critically applying the notion of "public pedagogy," students can investigate how social movements use educational practices and ideas to put forward their agenda for justice and freedom (Madan, Sastry and Ramdas, 2019: 45). Using art, historical archives, and campaign materials, students engage with the diversity of voices and movements that contribute to educational change. The inquiry-based pedagogical approach focuses on real-world problems to solve them. This approach helps to equip students with the knowledge and skills to critically analyze policy reform so as to understand the relationship between history, education, and social movements.

Political change can be a catalyst for the transformation of an educational system through the positioning of grass-roots social movements as an alternative to bureaucratic state mechanisms and non-governmental organisations in designing and implementing education reform. Institutions of higher education and journalism, along with the wealth of foundations and individuals, have created an infrastructure on which the andragogical perspectives of social class of intellectuals belong. Portions of this social class function as the continuing culture creators (and elaborators) of many social movements (Crowder and Shaw, 1997: 276). Some educational institutions have been created with the specific interest in supporting educationally the work of social movements - in other words, they have attempted to further the aims of these movements by making the political more educational.

Social scientists claim that the opportunities must be made for students to work in communities where they can spend time with ethnically diverse populations in the context of community activism and participation in progressive social movements. "Students need to move beyond simply knowing about critical, multicultural practice... Critical pedagogy should put ideology-critique at its center of gravity" (Kincheloe, 2000: xii). For example, the "green" living movement, in which many groups focused on nonviolent protests which is a resultant of education, when others resorted to criminal activities called "ecoterrorism".

Movements move people. They provide the impetus, energy and resources which mobilise people for collective action. The carryover from preexisting values and understandings illustrates the importance of what Pierre Bourdieu (1980, 1984) considers "cultural capital." Factors such as participants' education, gender, race, ethnicity, and class background, generally viewed as structural, provide groups with distinct sets of beliefs and skills, or cultural resources, that shape the contours of their resistance (Alexander, 1990). In Pierre Bourdieu's (1980, 1984) terms, this is "habitus," which is "cultural know-how"; in Ann Swidler's (1986) terms, it is the cultural "tool kit" from which movements borrow its vigour.

John Lofland (1995: 208) identified the formal educators, who make a live teaching in educational institutions from kindergarten to the most advanced graduate training, as the creators of social movements. The way, in which these educators earn their livelihood, encourages them to be more than normally sensitive to ideas and ideals, to conceptions of the way the world is, what is wrong with it, and how it might and should be changed. They advocate against the inequalities in education, employment and other social system in any society, where they live in. We ought therefore not to be surprised by discovering the ranks of formal educators, who are disproportionately populated with activists, participants, fellow travellers, and sympathisers for virtually every movement—left, right, or whatever.

Education can help to forge a critical reason, which can be used to understand and change the world. Richard Henry Tawney (1926) claims that social movements have provided the dynamics and interest for radical education and that "...if you want education you must not cut it off from the social interests in which it has its living and perennial sources" (cited in Jackson 1995: 184). Progressive social movements have historically provided the context for popular education; we argue that adult educators and community workers with a commitment to social change need to recognise the potential of social movements and should exploit their own relative autonomy to work with them.

## Concept, Meaning and Definitions of Social Movement

Sociologists draw distinctions between social movements and social movement organisations (SMOs). A social movement organisation is a formally organised component of a social movement. Therefore, it may represent only one part of a particular social movement. SMOs can be defined as formal organisations that take the collective pursuit of social change as a primary goal. Thus, the basic sociological point is that a social movement must evince a minimal degree of organisation, though this may range from a loose, informal or partial level of organisation to the highly institutionalised and bureaucratised movement and the corporate group.

Collective behaviour in crowds, panics, and elementary forms (milling, etc.) are of brief duration or episodic and are guided largely by impulse. When short-lived impulses give way to long-term aims, and when sustained association takes the place of situational groupings of people, the result is a social movement. American sociologist Albion W. Small (1897: 340-341) tries to understand this meaning of social movement. According to him, "the social movement was the growth of the third estate from a name to a power. The social movement was the abolition of political privilege, the enlargement of religious toleration, the extension of industrial opportunity." In its modern sense, "the social movement means that there is a new note in men's purpose to better themselves. It has new force. It has a changed outlook." Social movements primarily take the form of non-institutionalised collective political actions which strive for change in social settings. After French revolution, or specifically after industrial revolution, the cultural institutions like education, media etc. play crucial roles in social movement, where the major components were: issues, ideology, identity, organisation and leadership. Thus, the study on "social movements" cannot be confined by the boundaries of separate academic disciplines.

The primary concern of classical Marxist analysis is to define the preconditions of revolution by examining the structural contradictions of the capitalist system. From this perspective, Werner Sombart (1896: 2-10) defines the movement as "the conception of all the attempts at emancipation on the part of the proletariat...To picture the Social Movement of our day ... we must imagine a huge wave of humanity, from which scarcely one individual stands out, covering the dry land to the distant horizon." Sombart was the first one, who established its study as a legitimate object of research. Actually in the mid-1840s, it was Lorenz von Stein, who coined the German phrase which later translated into the English as "social movement".

Centering its investigation on the logic of the system, it has underestimated the processes by which collective action emerges, as well as the internal articulation of social movements (mobilisation, organisation, leadership, ideology) and the forms through which revolt passes in becoming a class movement (Melucci, 1980: 199). A class movement tends to describe the situation, in the language of its cultural system, as a struggle between he who produces the social resources and he who appropriates them for himself. According to this view, the party, as a centralised organisation emerges, as well as the internal articulation of social expression of collective action, and the conquest of the apparatus of the state remains the first objective of this action. The political processes in social movements give shape to the state structure at the same time that an institutionalised set of knowledge based selectivity rules alter the intensity, degree and level (character) of class consciousness, hence social conflict.

Reform and revolution are thus presented as alternative ways of adjusting the form of government and the legal order to the changing order of society. The social movement, in other words, need not culminate in a revolution. Apart from reformation, revolution is considered as a form of movement in its classical analysis. In modern analysis, a successful revolution requires some kind of group organisations. Unorganised masses, assembled crowds and mobs cannot start or carry out a revolution. Even if the revolution is not the work of a political party, there are usually a fairly large number of more or less secret, more or less intentionally revolutionary circles with strong ideological commitment, armed forces, or committees formed in advance of the outbreak of a revolution. Thus, all social movements are not revolution, as Heberle (1951) argued that each social movement has its peculiar socio-psychic texture that differentiates revolution from an ordinary social movement. He identified four types of social movements: redemptive, reformative, revolutionary and alternative.

There is no precise definition of the term "social movement" accepted by scholars of all disciplines, or even scholars belonging to the same discipline. Some scholars apply this term as a confusion of fussy, fidgety folk, blocking each other and everybody else by their foolishness. On the other side, some scholars use this term "movement" interchangeably with "organisation" or "union." One may utilise it to mean a historical tendency in which development occurs. Another scholar can identify the fashionable trend of social reformers, or the political leaders to call their activities as "movements." In political sense, social movements are a major vehicle for ordinary people's participation in public politics.

Social movements are conceptually defined as a kind of social collective. This definition may cause some difficulty for those who are accustomed to think of movements in social life as processes rather than groups. These processes may identify as trend, but all trends and tendencies are not movements. Rudolf Heberle (1951) regards the belief system that underlies social mobilisations as an expression of collective will of the participants. It is the conscious volition of individuals acting collectively that brings about the embodiment of ideologies in social movements. Social movements are, of course, very important factors in producing tendencies or trends of social change, but not all social change is a result of that kind of concerted social action which we call social movement.

Many trends and tendencies are merely the aggregate effect of many individual actions or the acts of pressure group. A pressure group is distinguished from a genuine social movement by the limitedness of its goal—it does not aim at a general change in the social order—and the fact is, it is an organised group. The main criterion of a social movement, then, is that it aims to bring about fundamental changes in the social order, especially in the basic institutions of property and labour relationships. Heberle (1951: 8) emphasised on conscious volition which was developed in relation to his concept of the "social collective." He conceived of social movements as "a special kind of social group of a particular structure. Although containing among their members certain groups that are formally organised, the movements *as such* are not organised groups." For example, the educational ideas of a social movement were based on the urban and industrial working class during a critical period in the development of American capitalism.

In 1950s, three basic elements were considered essential in identifying a social movement. These were: collective mobilisation, the presence of an ideology and an orientation towards change. C. Wendell King (1956: 27), for example, stressed geographic scope and persistence through time in defining a social movement as "a group venture extending beyond a local community or a single event and involving a systematic effort to inaugurate changes in thought, behaviour, and social relationships". Ralph Turner and Lewis M. Killian (1957: 308) noted the conservative nature of some social movements and proposed as their definition: "a collectivity [which acts] with some continuity to promote or resist a change in the society or group of which it is a part". Hans Toch (1965: 5) placed more emphasis on the psychological dimension: "an effort by a large number of people to solve collectively a problem they feel they have in common".

Thus, the social psychological points of view are incorporated in studying social movements. In this definitional aspect, William Bruce

Cameron (1966: 7) argued that social movements require more than a small clique of concerned individuals, since they occur "when a fairly large number of people band together in order to alter or supplant some portion of the existing culture or social order". Finally, Herbert Blumer (1969: 8) defined social movements as "collective enterprises to establish a new order of life." This classic definition captures what is central in any conception of social movements: group behaviour directed in a concerted way in bringing about social change. To make the definition more precise, however, other authors have emphasised certain aspects of social movements.

Cultural analysis focuses exclusively on culture as a movement characteristic—a product of interaction within a movement. Pornography threatened to change the nature of sex, sex education to undermine paternal power over it (Jasper, 2014). Ethnic and racial characters, religious faith, orientations toward marriage, sex, gender, work and leisure are often incorporated into thinking about man. Even for those, who seek to break the bonds of tradition, the processes of cultural innovation become socially and psychologically difficult. In contrast, "social movement groups, even those who can claim deep and elaborate histories, must reintroduce this material to new recruits and new believers and, in doing so, transform it" (Johnston and Klandermans, 1995: 19).

Definitional precision, however, remains problematic because of the diversity of social movements. They range from religious to secular, from revolutionary to reactionary, from cooperative to schismatic. Yet whatever its nature be, a social movement usually includes among its salient characteristics a shared value system, a sense of community, norms for action, and an organisational structure (Killian, 1964). In addition, the movement usually seeks to influence the social order and is oriented toward definite goals (although the ends and purposes of individual members may vary considerably). Robert H. Lauer (1972: 318) had identified a number of distinguishing characteristics of social movements, including a well-defined objective or goal, an organisation and structure, leadership, membership characterised by a "we-consciousness," a guiding set of values, and normative expectations.

Different aspects of social movements construct a basis of a rank-order or hierarchy of social movements to import, by the back-door, a theory of the relative importance of certain movements. One of the most apparent changes in social movement is a shift in leadership. In its earliest stages the strongest influence on a movement is likely to be the charismatic leader who personally symbolises its values. At some point intellectuals play a leadership role by contributing to the developing ideology of the movement. And if a movement endures and grows for any length of time, administrative leaders arise who are concerned with the practical matters of organisation and strategy.

In 1970s, it was possible to analyze the difficulties encountered in refining the social movement concept under five main headings: the problem of generality, dangers of ambiguity, problems of reification, problems of the "type" concept, and problems of comparison. Paul Wilkinson (1971: 15-27) provided a working concept, which could be adequately deployed and related to empirical phenomena by the combined, and often collaborative efforts of historians, political scientists, sociologists, social anthropologists and psychologists. "A social movement is a deliberate collective endeavour to promote change by any means, not excluding violence, illegality and revolution or withdrawal into 'utopian' community… *and it* must evince a minimal degree of organisation though this may range from a loose, informal or partial level of organisation to the highly institutionalised and bureaucratised movement and the corporate group… A social movement's commitment to change and the *raison d'être* of its organisation are founded upon the conscious volition, normative commitment to the movement's aims or beliefs and active participation on the part of the followers or members."

This definition of movement spells out a collective action through legal means, which are very much within the boundary of institutions as well as violent extra-institutional collective action. Wilkinson's argument, based on a typology of social movement, considers that the movement concept is very closely linked to the concept of culture. The language, ideas and styles of movements inevitably reflect wider cultural changes and can often be found to be important in themselves as agencies of cultural change. Social movement has, therefore, important expressive and aesthetic dimensions revealing both cultural distinctiveness and assimilatory tendencies in the wider society.

## New Millennium and New Social Movement

Social movements are rich in emotions that receive intermittent attention in social science research. In this research, the emotional contents of social movements help in collective mobilisation. The collective behaviour theorists see this emotion as an indication of the fact that movements are composed of somewhat hysterical people. Only in the 1990s, the investigators began to recognise their relevance in cognitive and instrumental processes (Milan, 2013). Patricia O'Gorman (1993) proposes that social movement is a socio-cultural phenomenon and it has a treatment perspective. It is a form of codependency which can be defined as learned helplessness.

New millennium considers social movements as central to modernity. They are central both in the ways that modernity connotes movement and modernity involves new political alliances and allegiances in which mass movements play a significant role. But social movements are more than the spontaneous gathering of masses of individuals. They are distinct in their form as collective behaviour. They are more enduring than other forms of collective behaviour. They are purposive and relatively structured forms of collective behaviour. Crowds, even traffic jams, are made up of masses of individuals, but they are not modern movements. Unlike crowds, social movements are composed of groups of individuals gathered with the common purpose of expressing subjectively felt discontent in a public way and changing the perceived social and political bases of that discontent. What makes social movements modern is not their collective but their distinctly political character.

Charles Tilly and Lesley J. Wood (2009) propose that the social movements are inclusive organisations that comprised of various interest groups. Social movements contain the significant strata of society such as workers, women's groups, students, youth and the intellectual component. These various interest sectors of society will be bound together by one common grievance which, in most of the cases, will be the commonly perceived lack of democracy in a specific political setting. The idea of legitimacy is central to the modern understanding of politics. Political action requires minimally "that an actor or actors make some explicit claim that the *means* of action can be recognised as legitimate *and* the *ends* of action become binding for the wider community" (Offe, 1985: 826–27). Thus, it is possible to make a distinction between socio-cultural and socio-political movements. Socio-cultural movements, for example, religious sects or countercultures, make use of legitimate and accepted forms of collective action—public demonstrations, recruitment, bloc voting, and so on—in their attempts to increase their members and secure the right to practice their beliefs. Yet they usually do not intend by these actions to make these beliefs or practices binding on the entire political community. When they do so, as in the case of many contemporary Islamic movements, they are no longer sects or socio-cultural movements, but they develop full-fledged socio-political movements.

Sociologically, any researcher can distinguish sociopolitical movements from socio-cultural movements and other forms of collective behaviour. To differentiate socio-political movements from ad hoc protest groups, it is further required that socio-political movements have a more or less generally accepted set of shared beliefs. Such a set of beliefs provides for a common understanding and definition of a conflict situation and allows continuity from one specific situation to the next. Socio-political movements must also possess some form of organisation and means of communication to give them stability and continuity.

Socio-political movements, then, are more than masses of people gathered in protest; they require forms of organisation and communication that allow continuity over time and space. The forms these movements take differ in modern societies depending on the specific political culture, but the existence of such organisations and networks of communication is a characteristic of modernity and modern politics. Socio-political movements, in other words, are a defining characteristic of modern politics and modern society.

In pointing out that modern social movements require a degree of organisation and networks of communication in order to ensure their continuity over time, it is necessary to distinguish sociopolitical movements from more highly structured organs such as political parties, which are themselves characteristic of modernity and modern politics. Although they are more structured than crowds and mass mobilisations, socio-political movements are less structured than political parties. They expand and contract, continually taking in and losing participants. They are more flexible in organisation and tolerant in beliefs than political parties because their purpose is less a practical and instrumental one than an expressive one. However, the line between parties and movements cannot be drawn too firmly. Socio-political movements may produce their own political parties or work with and within other parties as tactics for achieving some of their ends. Not all who participate in the movement need to join or even accept the idea of a more formal political party as part of the movement itself.

For many participants, in most cases, even to the majority, the movement may be only a vaguely defined or experienced set of beliefs and emotions through which one may discover and express dissatisfaction without necessarily feeling loyal to any organisation or political programme. To maintain a sense of continuity, socio-political movements require both the fluidity of ideas and emotions, as expressed in public demonstrations, pamphlets, and newsletters, and the stability provided by more formal organisation and leadership. The leadership stands for and speaks for the movements at times when no mass is visible, something that seems necessary and yet that creates problems of its own.

When defined as more-or-less organised forms of collective action aiming at social change, social movements are a distinctly modern phenomenon (Touraine, 2002). They depend on and express our modern political culture, which permits and recognises mass discontent as part of the repertoire of political action and which is based on the awareness that fundamental change is indeed possible. Modernity and modern politics rest on the assumption that society and policies are made by people, not gods or kings. The absence of such awareness, that is, the lack of a political content to mass discontent, distinguishes modern social movements from more traditional forms of popular discontent and rebellion.

In the post-industrial economy, the movements are significantly different from previous social movements of the industrial economy. The primary difference is in their goals, as the new movements focus not on issues of materialistic qualities such as economic well-being, but on issues related to human rights, such as gay rights or pacifism. Social and cultural issues are more attached with these new social movements (NSMs). NSMs act as a platform for collective action in civil society or in the cultural domain, rather than as an instrumental tool for the state. As such, new movements are often considered to be anti-authoritarian. Claus Offe (1985: 828) defined new social movements "as those movements that do make a claim to be recognised as political actors by the wider community - although their forms of action do not enjoy the legitimacy conferred by established political institutions - and who aim at objectives, the achievement of which would have binding effects for society as a whole rather than just for the group itself."

It is common today to distinguish "old" social movements from "new" ones (Melucci, 1980; Singh, 2001). Such a distinction rests on two sets of criteria. The first, associated with Alain Touraine, is built upon the theory of the historical transition from an old industrial society to a new post-industrial society (Touraine, 1981). From this point of view the labour movement is an old social movement because it expresses the conflicts of industrial society and industrialisation, that is, the conflicts between labour and capital. New social movements, such as the women's movement, express conflicts representative of the new post-industrial society.

A second set of criteria differentiating between new and old social movements stems from the issues they raise and the locus of the changes they wish to bring about (Castells, 2010a). In this case the labour movement not only reflects the old struggle between labour and capital but also is rooted in and concerned with the labour process itself in its demands for change and its vision of the future. New social movements are claimed to depart significantly from the conventional economic reductionism of labour process. Here the concerns are primarily non-economic issues, such as gender relations and the meaning of war and peace. Thus, the new social movements express concerns that are more cultural than economic. They aim at changing norms and values rather than productive and distributive relations.

*The Voice and the Eye* is a conceptual work of Alain Touraine (1981) that describes itself as an attempt to move beyond social science determinism in its various nineteenth- and twentieth-century incarnations, namely Parsonsian structural-functionalism and Marxian economism. Touraine's alternative way to the determinist view of humans as automatons mechanistically responding to forces outside their ken or control, is to pronounce action-in particular collective action as the irreducible social fact. Society is a "hierarchized set of *systems of action,* i.e., of social relations between actors who may have conflicting interests but who belong to the same social sphere and therefore share certain cultural orientations." Touraine's actors are class actors who battle for control of "historicity," or the definition of the situation on a large cultural scale. The key to understanding society is to understand: (1) who are the actors? and (2) what is the object of contention? Touraine advocates "interventionism" (the sociologist's directly participating in the social movement under investigation) as the appropriate methodological technique for pursuing knowledge of social action and thus of society. In Touraine's view, social movements are the central collective actors and they can reveal the stakes of the conflicts that are at the heart of society's production of itself.

On the second set, in his *The Information Age Trilogy*, Manuel Castells (2010b) saw identity as a defining principle of social organisation and analysing the importance of cultural, religious, and national identities as sources of meaning for people, and the implications of these identities for social movements. Social movements tend to be fragmented, localistic, single-issue oriented, and ephemeral, either retrenched in their inner worlds, or flaring up for just an instant around a media symbol. In such a world of uncontrolled, confusing change, people tend to regroup around primary identities: religious, ethnic, territorial, national. Religious fundamentalism - Christian, Islamic, Jewish, Hindu, and even Buddhist (in what seems to be a contradiction in terms) - is probably the most formidable force for personal security and collective mobilisation in these troubled times.

These two points focus on a new pattern of explanation that differs from old one. The distinctions between old and new social movements provide a convenient way of categorising various contemporary political conflicts and social movements. This may be considered as a journey from *ideology* to *identity*. For one thing, classes and related class interests, which provided the prime source of collective identity and motivation for collective action in the past (at least in Europe), seem less a factor today, at least for explaining social movements. Contemporary social movements seem motivated by concerns other than those directly associated with income and economic security.

In addition, rather than focusing on the labour process the realm of concern has shifted to what is called the "life-world," which involves issues of personal identity, personal life, neighbourhood, sexuality, and life-style. Finally, the types of demands put forward by the new social movements lie, to some extent, outside the realm of traditional compromise politics, whether that is labour-market politics or representative democracy as it currently exists. Unlike working-class movements, which offer and withdraw their labour power in exchange for concessions from capital, the new social movements have little to offer in exchange. Their demands tend to be made in nonnegotiable terms and are usually expressed negatively: anti-war, anti-nuclear, and so on. Whether this approach represents tactics or is an early stage of movement development remains to be seen.

The literature on social movements includes a long-standing discussion concerning the strategies and tactics of social movements. J. Craig Jenkins (1981: 83) proposed that a movement requires actions as well as change-oriented beliefs. Moreover, these actions must take on a collective character. An individual who hijacks an airplane is not part of a movement unless the act is a part of a larger collective effort to bring about change. In any case the distinction between old and new social movements seems worthwhile from an analytical point of view. From the actor's point of view its validity seems beyond question.

Alberto Melucci (1980: 219) identified the present contexts of social movements which are not oriented toward the conquest of political power or of the state apparatus, but rather toward the control of a field of autonomy or of independence vis-à-vis the system. "The new social movements are struggling, therefore, not only for the reappropriation of the material structure of production, but also for collective control over socio-economic development, i.e., for the reappropriation of time, of space, and of relationships in the individual's daily existence. The new forms of class domination are identified less and less with real social groups and are starting to share the impersonal character of the various institutions. The new conflicts and the new movements are not manifested in the action of a single class, in the sense of a social group identified by a particular culture and way of life."

The lifestyle or the way of life holds power, which is important for the study of social movements. Discourse, not only carries power, it acts as a room for maneuver for social movements thus restricts and enables specific worldviews. Social movements not only observe discourse, they strategically shape their communication accordingly. They are the product of discourse, too (Foucault, 1974b). Such sociology of knowledge approach to discourse regards the communication of social movements, e.g. their leaflets, symbols, not merely as goal-oriented, instrumental action, but as expressing their identity and thus their internal system of knowledge. The epistemai are the historical a priori of discourse (including the grand theories), allowing for a certain structure of knowledge and basic modes of thinking in a certain epoch, e.g. the establishment of science over and against a pre-scientific level. They affect the thinking of subjects, but their impact does not have to be reflected on a conscious level (Foucault, 1974b: 189–192). These concepts remind the social movement researcher of social movements' embeddedness in their time and culture.

Foucault informed us about the heuristic typology of social movement heterotopias. We can understand the heterotopias as spaces where a portion of the social becomes alternatively ordered. Five heterotopia "types" are considered: "contained," "mobile," "cloud," "encounter" and "rhizomic." Each has particular attributes, but all challenge normal, routine politics. They do so by being, from the perspective of state and capital, either in the "wrong" place, moving in the "wrong" way, or involving the "wrong," connections, affinities or organisation. These are "constructed-types," proposed for the purpose of description, comparison and prediction.

These social movement heterotopias are different types of space that facilitate practices of resistance and transgression (Beckett, Bagguley and Campbell, 2016). Foucault's concept of heterotopia is potentially useful for social movement studies (SMS) because it helps us to explore the non-normative aspects of social movements – how they often involve spaces where things are "different" in some way – without construing them as pathological. According to Foucault, contemporary social and technological developments are allowing for social movement an activity which is at variance with, or outside of, known space (heterotopic) and disruptive of conventional time (heterochronic). Thus, new social movements do not push any power for specific changes in public policy, rather they emphasise on social changes in identity, lifestyle and culture. Examples of those new movements include the women's movement, the ecology movement, gay rights movement and various peace movements, among others.

In sociology of education, by a social movement we mean a clearly structured and identifiable organisation which has the explicit goal of grouping members with a view to the defence or promotion of certain precise objectives, generally with a socio-cultural connotation. The main characteristic of a social movement is that it is essentially demanding. It seeks recognition and acceptance of its ideas, interests and values. Thus, a social movement is neither an academic discussion group, nor a religious order. It necessarily occurs in the public view.

## Theories of Social Movements

All definitions of social movement reflect the notion that social movements are intrinsically related to reconstruct a new social order. In their *Communist Manifesto* (1848), Karl Marx and Friedrich Engels identified the working class and the labour movement as the prime historical agents of social change in modern society, but they did not define properly the concept of social movement (Barker, 2013). Max Weber and Emile Durkheim conceptualised social movements in relation to problems of social integration, as forms of behaviour associated with periods of societal transition. They do not encompass the activities of people as members of stable social groups with established, unquestioned structures, norms, and values as social movement. The behaviour of members of social movements does not reflect the assumption that the social order will continue essentially as it is. It reflects, instead, the faith that people collectively can bring about or prevent social change if they will dedicate themselves to the pursuit of a goal.

To achieve that goal, the members of social movements construct a network among them and thus become something, which is not merely a perpetuated crowd. Social movements are more structured than crowds; their members consciously work together to achieve a common objective (Rocher, [1968] 1990; Blumer, 1969). Furthermore, crowd mechanisms cannot be used to achieve communication, motivational mechanisms and coordination of activity over a wide area, such as a nation or continent. A movement is a mixture of organisation and spontaneity. There are usually one or more organisations that give identity, leadership, and coordination to the movement, but the boundaries of the movement are never coterminous with the organisations.

Social movements, then, occur in a wide variety of societies (Tilly and Wood, 2009). They can be local in purpose, such as a movement against the construction of a toxic waste dump in a neighbourhood, or they can be national or even international in focus. Social movements are also broad in their aim. Some may seek to reform an existing political system, while others may aim to halt change. On the other hand, some are not political at all and instead may seek cultural or individual change. Still others may seek revolutionary change on both a political and social/ cultural level.

There is no single, standard typology of social movements. As various scholars focus on different aspects of movements, different schemes of classification emerge. Hence any social movement may be described in terms of several dimensions. Many attempts (Wilkinson, 1971; Shah, [1990] 2004) in categorisation administer attention to the objective of the movement. The social institution in or through which social change is to be brought about provides one basis for categorising social movements as political, religious, economic, educational, tribal and the like. It may be argued that all movements tend to be either political or religious in character, depending upon whether their strategy aims at changing political structures or the moral values of individuals (Oberschall, 1973). The moral philosophy of a social movement is empowered by the institutional level of education of that given society.

The study of social movements as specific social processes with specific patterns emerged from the field of movement's study in sociology. The American sociologist Herbert Blumer identified four stages of social movements' lifecycles. The four stages he described were: "social ferment," "popular excitement," "formalisation," and "institutionalisation" (della Porta and Diani, 2006: 150; Blumer, 1951: 203). According to Blumer

(1969: 12) the first, or "social ferment," stage would be characterised by unorganised, unfocused agitation in which great attention is paid to the propaganda of "agitators." In the second phase, of "popular excitement," the underlying causes of discontent and the objectives of action are more clearly defined. In the third phase, of "formalisation," disciplined participation and coordination of strategies for achieving the movement's aims are arrived at by creating a formal organisation. Finally, in the "institutionalisation" stage the movement becomes an organic part of society and crystallises into a professional structure.

Others have questioned the "necessity" of such an evolution, however. Even organisational sociologists point out that this four stage theory of social movement development can also help scholars to understand the ways through which social movements affect society. While this four stages theory of social movements offers some useful insight into some movements, it has limitations as well. Some of the limitations are consequences of the organisational emphasis and a preoccupation with political change. Some social movements also emerge in response to cultural and social issues, and these movements do not fit easily into these four stages of development. For this crisis, and for other circumstances, social movement theory has increasingly moved toward examining social movements with new elements, or movements that have emerged in the late 1960s around the issues of identity and quality of life (Inglehart, 1990; Melucci, 1995). Many also tend to emphasise social changes in lifestyle instead of specific changes in public policy or for economic change.

Actually, after World War II, American and European sociologists provided important analysis of social movements that helps us to understand both past and present societies, as well as to anticipate changes and trends that may play out in the future. Then the macro-structural explanations of social movements (SMs) became relevant in sociological studies. In 1950s, view was that SMs were outgrowth of particular type of social behaviour, known as collective behaviour. These arose out of a breakdown of traditional order with some underlying shared source of excitement or stress or anxiety or frustration. Breakdown of traditional patterns of order and social control produces elementary forms of collective behaviour which, if persist, may lead to social movement and then may evolve into integrated structures and new established norms. Following very much the functionalist view of order and change in a gradual manner, SMs were viewed from their adaptive responses to strains in transition from traditional to modern mass societies.

Social movements emerge out of spontaneous and amorphous mass discontent. The functionalist perspective viewed it as a sphere of "popular mind." Influenced by theories of crowd behaviour developed by French polymath Gustav Le Bon (1896), social movements were interpreted as a form of collective behaviour and were understood on a scale of rationality, from the irrational behaviour of the crowd to the more rational social movement. In America, functionalist thinkers, like Talcott Parsons, made a significant contribution in the development of the collective behaviour perspective. In *Social Forces* (1942), he had written an article "Some Sociological Aspects of Fascist Movements," which made use of classical social theory to explain the emergence of contentious collective behaviour due to "strains" relating to the rationalisation of society which was accompanied by modernisation. Then, social movements were conceptualised from a macro-perspective as collective behaviour caused by the strain stemming from rapid social change, which initially marginalised and then constituted certain groups. The collective behaviour perspective focused on the strains of societal transition and the alienation and marginalisation of groups in relation to them.

The functions of SMs are considered as a point of contribution to the formation of public opinion. From an organisational point of view, it demands a training ground for leaders of political establishment to understand public opinion and to form social mobilisation processes. The homogeneous crowds, sects, castes, and classes are not discussed in this functional analysis. Robert King Merton (1957) had tried to analyze deviant behaviour from this perspective. In this theoretical development, Blumer first rejected the macro aspects to study SMs. The micro aspect of SMs became important in the field of empirical observations of social movements. Neil J. Smelser (1962) was concerned to explain social movements and other forms of collective behaviour as they take shape within social systems in forms of schools, factories and wider society itself. He linked the macro aspects with the micro positions to form a collective expression. Following Talcott Parsons (1951), he considered social systems as institutionalised patterns of interaction with a set of formal and codified rules or laws, unwritten and informal rules that perform the same function, that is, the coordination and legitimation of specific patterns of individual action.

Smelser saw social movements as the side-effects of over rapid social transformation. According to Smelser, in a system made up of balanced subsystems, collective behaviour reveals tensions which the homoeostatic rebalancing mechanisms cannot absorb in the short term. "[Movements and protests] occur with regularity. They cluster in time; they cluster in certain cultural areas; they occur with greater frequency amongst certain social groupings . . . This skewing in time and place invites explanation: Why do collective episodes occur where they do, when they do, and in what ways they do?" (Smelser, 1962: 1).

Smelser's value-added model of collective behaviour postulates that while a number of determinants are necessary for the occurrence of a social movement, they need not occur in any particular order. It consists of six steps: structural conduciveness, i.e. a certain configuration of social structure can facilitate the emergence of conflicting interests; structural strain, i.e. the fact that at least some trait of the social system is experienced by a collectivity as a source of tension and problems; growth and spread of generalised belief, i.e. the emergence of ideology, or a shared interpretation by social actors of their situation and life hazards; precipitating factors, i.e. stressful events that induce actors to take action; mobilisation, i.e. the network and organisational activities that transform potential for action into real action; operation of social control, i.e. the role of social control agencies and other actors in shaping the evolution of collective behaviour and its forms (Crossley, 2002).

Emphasised on running interaction between movement and society, Smelser said that the idea of the life cycle permits the discovery of conditions that must be present if any movement is to proceed from one stage to another. It may also help to identify the conditions that cause a movement to change direction. Still, it can be said that a social movement has a career; as it endures it always undergoes changes in many of its characteristics, though the sequence of these changes may vary from movement to movement. This value-added model rejects the conflict perspective of social movement that considers social movement as special sorts of interest-group collectivities which attempt to gain benefits for individuals, produce social reforms to gain entry into the established structures of society. Albeit of this newness, value-added model remains more descriptive than explanatory, and unclear about the kinds of structures and strains.

For that weakness questions remain unanswered: why would people instead spend their time promoting a social movement? According to Eric Hoffer's (1966) frustration theory, those who participate in social movements are frustrated and troubled. They use social movements as a diversion, which enables them to hide from themselves their personal problems, such as a sense of inadequacy and inferiority. Furthermore, through a social movement, they can gain a sense of being noble and magnanimous as they fight for a good cause beyond their own self-interest. A social movement can also provide a sense of belonging and a way of identifying oneself. Members are therefore, in Hoffer's view, strongly dedicated to their movement's objective, following their leaders blindly as true believers.

There are also some sociological holes in the frustration theory. The most important is that it effectively blames movement participants rather than society for their frustration (Turner and Killian, 1957). In fact, it is often unpleasant social conditions, such as social injustice or racial discrimination, which have brought about the discontent in the first place, as is obvious in the case of the civil rights movement. Thus, a number of sociologists have developed the breakdown-frustration theory, contending that a social breakdown in the form of, say, racial strife or widespread unemployment can cause a social movement by creating frustration among masses. But such frustration is assumed to be only the first condition necessary for the emergence of a movement. Other factors are also considered important, such as frustrated individuals identifying a common source of discontent, working out a plan to eradicate it, and banding together to carry out that plan (Oberschall, 1992).

In fact, both resource mobilisation and breakdown-frustration can be found in practically all social movements. The importance of each varies from one movement to another. As Harold Kerbo (1982) notes, frustration plays a larger role in "crisis movements" involving African Americans, the unemployed, or poor people, while resource mobilisation figures more in "affluence movements," such as environmental movements and abortion-rights movements, which involve mostly affluent Americans. Some of them had been most active in the study of social movements and came out of a resource mobilisation and political process theory background. Others came out of an organisational studies background, especially in neo-institutional theory and in population ecology. They varied in whether they were more "micro" or "macro" and in their methodological commitments. The conference was loose in its structure; some sessions were devoted to idea sharing, while others were devoted to rough paper outlines.

Indeed, since the early 1970s two new strands of theory and empirical research have arisen –one in the United States and one in Western Europe. The first, called resource mobilisation theory and the second theory is the new social movement theory. With these two strands of theory, there are some other theories, which are as follows: deprivation (or relative deprivation) theory; political process theory; structural strain theory; leadership theory; framing theory; and multi-factor theory.

**Relative Deprivation Theory**

The concept, relative deprivation was formulated by S. A. Stouffer *et al.* (1949) and developed by R. K. Merton (1957) in the fields of social sciences. It suggests that people mainly experience feelings of deprivation when they compare their own situations unfavourably with those of other individuals or groups. Comparisons can be made both with individuals with whom people interact and with outsiders; what matters is which reference group the person or group chooses as the focus of comparison (Runciman, 1966). "Relative deprivation is defined as a perceived discrepancy between men's value expectations and their value capabilities. Value expectations are the goods and conditions of life to which people believe they are rightfully entitled. Value capabilities are the goods and conditions; they think they are capable of attaining or maintaining the given social means available to them" (Gurr, 1970: 13). The emphasis on people's subjective frames of reference is a useful addition to the study of deprivation, but the concept itself does not determine at what point relative deprivation becomes objective and absolute deprivation.

An important task of the student of social movements is to identify those conditions under which social movements are most likely to arise. According to absolute deprivation theory, social movements develop when people are unable to obtain adequate food, shelter, or other basic needs. While the existence of widespread poverty and suffering might seem sufficient to give rise to efforts at reform, it must be emphasised again that some basis for hope must also exist to stir people to make the effort. Paradoxically, partial alleviation of conditions of deprivation may provide such a basis, by serving as the impetus for the formation of a social movement just as things seem to be getting better. The success of other people similarly situated, such as victorious revolutionaries in a neighbouring nation, may be another source of hope.

Social movement scholars were surrounded by earlier empirical work on rumours, panics, crowds, and mobs together with a "smorgasbord" of theoretical perspectives, including the collective behaviour, mass society, and relative deprivation approaches (McAdam, McCarthy, and Zald 1988: 695). But living conditions or political limitations only become intolerable when people come to view them as unacceptable relative to how they think things should be. Gurr (1970: 46) describes three ways that can make a man to a rebel. In any society, "three distinct patterns of disequilibrium can be specified: (1) *decremental deprivation,* in which a group's value expectations remain relatively constant but value capabilities are perceived to decline; (2) *aspirational deprivation,* in which capabilities remain relatively static while expectations increase or intensify; and (3) *progressive deprivation,* in which there is substantial and simultaneous increase in expectations and decrease in capabilities. All three patterns have been cited as causal or predisposing factors for political violence."

Relative deprivation is a feeling unable to achieve relatively high aspirations. In this theory, both individual psychological states and the characteristics of a society at a particular time may be considered as causes of social movements. Individual factors are psychological states that either convince a person to join a movement or weaken his commitment to conventional groups that he is willing to risk their disapproval because of his belief in an unpopular cause.

Deprivation, discontent, and frustration are frequently assumed to be sufficient causes for initiating or joining a social movement. The relationship is not a simple one, however, there is little evidence that the most deprived segments of a population are most likely to participate in social movements. The concept of relative deprivation has been used to explain the fact that persons who could be much worse off than they are but still feel deprived in comparison with even more fortunate groups, often plays a prominent part in social movements.

Relative deprivation theory distinguishes between egoistic deprivation and fraternal deprivation. Egoistic deprivation refers to a single individual's feeling of comparative deprivation. On the other hand, fraternal deprivation, also known as group deprivation, refers to the discontent arising from the status of the entire group as compared to a referent group. Fraternal deprivation may strengthen a group's collective identity (Singer, 1992). People may also experience relative deprivation when they witness a condition or a pattern of behaviour that they find unacceptable in terms of deeply held personal moral standards.

Jungyun Gill and James DeFronzo (2009: 205) explain it from a perspective of *moral relative deprivation* in which many people participate in movements even though they do not personally suffer from the conditions they want to change. Thus, *moral relative deprivation* explains why many college students participate in social movements dealing with issues that may be remote from their personal experiences, as in campus mobilisations against South African apartheid in the 1980s and early 1990s. From this development, it is evident that relative deprivation theory focuses on feelings and actions.

In the field of sociology, relative deprivation theory is used to explain the root causes of social movements and revolutions (Krahn & Harrison, 1992). But the critiques argue that the relative deprivation perspectives focus on the genesis of political violence instead of social movements, per se, there are two points to keep in mind: relative deprivationists examine the genesis of political violence but do not focus on the dynamics of such violence; and they focus on political violence, while not analyzing other forms of political protest. The relative deprivation model of social movement has been also criticised both structurally and conceptually. Critique of this theory has pointed out that this model fails to explain why some people who feel discontent, fail to take action and join social movements. "Some people are prone to conflict-avoidance"- is not a proper counter-argument. On the other hand, humanistic value restricts jealousy or envy to others, when this model indicates the inferences about that psychological state of participants without placing any direct evidence on the actual feelings of participants prior to protest participation.

## Resource Mobilisation Theory

Resource Mobilisation Theory (RM) was developed during 1960s in North America by John D. McCarthy and Mayer N. Zald (1977), with their other colleagues. Their approach drew particularly on Selznick's (1948, 1949) institutional approach to organisations as well as organisation theory more generally. The resource mobilisation theory takes as its starting point a critique of those theories that explain social movements are arising from conditions of social disorganisation and strain and are finding their recruits among the isolated and alienated portions of society.

By contrast, resource mobilisation theorists argue that the success of social movements rests mainly on the resources that are available to it; this means forming coalitions with already-existing organisations, securing financial support, and mounting effective and organised campaigns of political pressure. As a result of this emphasis, resource mobilisation theorists downplay the factor of ideology—and irrational factors generally—in the study of social movements. "Resource mobilisation theory, as originally conceived, self-consciously minimized the role of ideas and beliefs and their elaboration" (Mueller, 1992: 13). According to this theory, people, motivated to create a social movement, must have access to necessary resources to succeed (Jenkins, 1983).

This is an organisational-entrepreneurial model of social movements that McCarthy and Zald have formulated. In their (1977: 1217-1218) view, "a social movement is a set of opinions and beliefs in a population which represents preferences for changing some elements of the social structure and/or reward distribution of a society." This definition includes both organisational factors and the struggle for power. Mayer N. Zald and John D. McCarthy (1987), in crafting their *resource mobilisation* perspective, privileged the existence of organisational structures and processes to analyze SMs. Drawing on developments in organisational studies (OS), these theorists stressed that movements, if they are to be sustained for any length of time, require some form of organisation: leadership, administrative structure, incentives for participation, and a means for acquiring resources and support. Embracing an open systems perspective, the importance of the organisation's relations to its environments – social, economic, political – were underscored.

This theoretical perspective focuses on role of power and power struggles by assuming a liberal pluralistic political structure where there is continual political realignment, i.e. it assumes that there will always be grounds for protest in modern societies, and it de-emphasises the roles of mass discontent which is considered as a constant figure. This perception considers social situation as a condition where society now possesses the resources (money, political influence, access to media and workers) to mobilise variety of change efforts (Klandermans, 1984). In viewing participants as rational decision-makers, who have weighed costs and benefits of collective action and have decided that goals of protest are worth time and effort, this theory emphasises on the ongoing transformation in movement processes through interaction of competing SMOs and leadership in broader political environment.

Resource mobilisation theory is one that means sociologists use to explain the characters and outcomes of social movements. Here the mobilisation process: (1) creating a potential base of support in the population; (2) forming recruitment networks to tap potential members; (3) arousing motivation among targeted individuals through framing issues; (4) removing barriers to participation; (5) once activated, commitment is maintained by building a collective identity and continuing to nurture interpersonal relationships. Thus, the resource mobilisation perspective captures two essential elements of and theoretical approaches to social movements in (post) industrial societies. Firstly, it emphasises on the ways that social movements mobilise available economic, political and communications resources to address the issues; and secondly, the impacts are clearly identifiable in political issues.

This perspective differs sharply from previous ones by explicitly excluding actual conflict, mobilisation, and social change activities. This view explores the dynamics between various groups of society with their preference structures for changes. Any beneficial resource can be accepted; i.e., the support of powerful persons, aid from previously established social movement organisations, and assistance from important moral figures who can bestow legitimacy on the movement and its goals. For example, the civil rights movement was benefitted with the support of many African American churches (Morris, 1984) and their leaders, including Martin Luther King Jr.

This resource mobilisation tradition drew on organisational analysis to argue in part that social movement organisations, like many types of organisations, tend toward bureaucratisation, professionalisation, and conglomeration, and these organisations often adjust their goals in order to better fit their resource environments and survive (Kriesi, 1996). Other sociologists have proposed the resource mobilisation theory, arguing that social movements result from the availability of resources for mobilisation, but fail to explain how groups with limited resources can succeed in bringing social change.

According to this theory, what sparks a movement is not breakdown-frustration, but the availability of such mobilisation resources as strong organisation, effective leadership, money, and media access. But this theory has, in turn, been criticised for virtually ignoring the place of frustration in social movements (Mayer, 1995; Piven and Cloward, 1995; Oberschall, 1992). It also neglects some macro sociological issues, like identity, culture, etc. The critics also argue that it does not assign sufficient weight to grievances, and fails to explain the real existence of social movement communities, which are large networks of individuals and other groups surrounding social movement organisations and providing them with various services.

For all their disagreements, however, a particular image of organisation is shared by the feminist no-organisationists, the old institutionalists, and scholars in the resource mobilisation tradition.

In each case, the oppressiveness or the efficacy of formal organisation was attributed to traits such as centralisation and hierarchy. As Myra Marx Ferree and Carol Mueller (2004: 593) argued, resource mobilisation theory "guided social movement thinking in the United States toward theorising the hierarchical, centralised, formalised organisation as the normative 'SMO.'" Fed by diverse streams of work – feminism, the old institutionalism, among others – this growing attention to variation in organisational form represented a partial break from the core imagery of resource mobilisation theory.

Long the major point of conjuncture between organisational and social movement research, resource mobilisation theory built on assumptions that contrasted sharply with "no-organisationism" and the "iron rule of oligarchy." Like the case studies of the older institutionalist tradition just discussed, proponents of resource mobilisation theory (McCarthy and Zald, 1977) portrayed formal organisation as an asset that enhanced collective action and protected against the evanescent character of many protest efforts. In contrast there is another view, in which organisations master their members, and organisations are understood as resources to be deployed by activists.

## Political Process Theory

The political process theory is also known as political opportunities theory. This complementary *political process* perspective was pursued by Charles Tilly and his associates in the middle of 1970s. Though probably best known for its stress on shifting "political opportunities" (and constraints), this "external" focus on the political environment was always joined with an "internal" analysis of the "critical role of various grassroots settings – work and neighbourhood, in particular – in facilitating and structuring collective action" (McAdam, McCarthy and Zald, 1996: 4).

Like resource mobilisation theory (RM), the political process model is still useful tool for understanding the large social structures. In many situations, the seedbed of collective action is to be found in preexisting social arrangements that provide social capital critical to the success of early mobilising processes when warmed by the sunlight of environmental opportunities that allow members to exploit their capital (Tilly 1978; Tilly, Tilly and Tilly, 1975). Thus, concurs with resource mobilisation theory in emphasising existence of resources, political opportunities theory emphasises more on the existence of favourable structures of political opportunity. According to this model, the political context is the key in explaining social movements and their effects on society. It argues that success or failure of social movements is affected primarily by political opportunities. From 1970s onwards, *political process theorists* followed Tilly's lead in focusing on the political opportunities and constraints that structure contentious politics (Tarrow, 1994).

Political process theorists address the issue of timing of emergence and success of SM. It explains why SMs often are in waves or cycles, and why some SM are unsuccessful for long periods of time. And then suddenly appear to grow and succeed by developing political opportunity structures, which refers to the receptivity or vulnerability of the political system to organise protest by challenging groups (Amenta, 2006). When such structures expand, there is intense movement mobilisation that can take many forms, such as, growth of political pluralism or decline in effectiveness of repression.

Political scientists focused on interest groups as "normal" parts of the political process, while collective behaviour theorists saw movements as exceptions to normal political processes – virtually as part of abnormal psychology. In this point, Charles Tilly (1979: 12) defines social movement as "a sustained series of interactions between national power holders and persons successfully claiming to speak on behalf of a constituency lacking formal representation, in the course of which those persons make publicly-visible demands for changes in the distribution or exercise of power, and hack those demands with public demonstrations of support." For Tilly the focus is sustained interactions rather than the "social movement" as a phenomenon *sui generis*.

Tilly (1978: 49) breaks from previous definitions by refusing to treat the social movement as the unit of analysis, arguing instead that a movement is not a group that emerges and transforms over time. There are three vital components for movement formation: (1) *insurgent consciousness*: feelings of deprivation generate grievances directed at a system that people perceive as unjust; the development of collective sense of injustice motivates people to become movement members. (2) *organisational strength*: as a structural strength, the social movement must have strong and efficient leadership and sufficient resources. (3) *political opportunities*: the political context of society stresses the movement members to push through a social change. Indeed, the definitional points of political opportunity depict consistent, but not necessarily formal or permanent, dimensions of the political struggle that encourage people to engage in contentious politics.

From these three components, there emerges what proponent Doug McAdam (1982) terms "cognitive liberation," the ability of those active in political protest to recognise their collective strength and take advantage of political opportunities as they become available to them. As political opposition to the movement's demands weakens, members may feel a collective sense of symbolic efficacy, the capacity to enact significant change within the political arena. This opens up significant opportunities for movements to both recruit members and mobilise under a concentrated and effective cycle of demands. This theory argues that the actions of the activists are dependent on the existence or the lack of a specific political opportunity. The vulnerability can be the result of: (1) increasing political pluralism; (2) decline in repression; (3) power of political elite is undermined by internal fragmentation; (4) elite disunity translates into a net gain of political opportunity; (5) increased political enfranchisement; and (6) the fragmented disunity can lead to a crisis of legitimacy and thus, revolutionary movement can erupt.

The political opportunity theory has much in common with the related resource mobilisation theory, particularly when it is seen as focusing on mobilisation of resources external to the movement. This theory stresses on a process in which movement runs. It negates the conditions of alienation. Alienation, feelings of powerlessness, hopelessness, and estrangement from society may predispose an individual to participation. Some sociological scholars argue, however, that there are different kinds of alienation. One type leads merely to apathy and resignation. Political alienation, however, reflects a loss of faith in the political community and predisposes the individual to join a movement that challenges it.

Political process models are intended to analyze how actors respond to political environments in flux. Authors like Doug McAdam (1982) have demonstrated that it is often when environments shift by opening up new opportunities, movements emerge. But even models attentive to the dynamism of political opportunities often assume that the evolving environment continues to be predictable and transparent. In short, political opportunity structure models assume institutionalised environments. Both resource mobilisation and political process approaches in studying social movements and collective action have been criticised for their inattention in linking the ideational with the structural (Snow et al., 1986).

Studying field transformation and using theory from both institutional and social movements is consistent with the suggestion that social movement scholarship move away from narrow studies of the internal processes of movements (McAdam, Tarrow, and Tilly, 2001). A focus on processes also has methodological implications. New settlements generate through contentious social and political processes. The more the established arrangements are disrupted, the more contentious the process is likely to be.

This approach suggests the examination of questions such as: what the rules of the game were before the field was thrown into crisis, how the field became unsettled, who the various actors with stakes in new framings of the field were, how the interests and identities of these actors were reconstructed through the political process, how actors constructed events to be consequential, what the alternatives were that actors were promoting, how one solution or another succeeded at organising the field, and how the processes unfolded through time.

Political process theorists tended to narrow their attention to opportunities and forget about threats. This model is too narrow a focus on structural factors, and it ignores the role of culture and ideas in any political context. Critics contend that theorists place too great an emphasis on the role of social networks and often almost entirely ignore the cultural underpinnings that allow the networks to form and subsist. Another weak point suggests that political process theorists use overly-broad definitions as to what constitute political opportunities, and those definitions vary widely based on the historical context of the social movement itself.

### New Social Movement Theory

The idea of "new" in social movement studies had developed in Europe, and it was related to the emergence of environmentalism and the women's and peace movements of the 1970s. The term new social movements (NSMs) is a theory of social movements that attempts to explain the moral and quality-of-life issues and the establishment procedures of new collective identities. (Inglehart, 1990; Melucci, 1995). Loosely organised groups of people, who come together for a common local purpose in order to change some aspect of their life-situation, can be considered as new social movement. These NSMs are distinguished from interest groups, which represent a small group pursuing a narrow interest, and political movements, such as political parties which aim at social transformation through the political process. The NSMs are not bothered about changing the distribution of power in society, but they aspire about quality-of-life issues, such as having a clean environment. Examples of NSMs are ecological, feminist and racial justice movements.

The NSMs were developed in the late 1960s on issues such as environmental protection, racial identity, women's rights, gender relations, ethnicity and migration, peace and international solidarity – with a strong (new) middle-class basis and a clear differentiation from the models of working-class or nationalist collective action that had historically preceded them. In post-industrial society, this new theoretical dimension introduces the concept of anti-movement, which is illustrated with the contemporary cases of "global" anti-movements such as global terrorism or global anti-Semitism. (Bell, 1974; Wieviorka, 2005). While there are surely continuities between those movements and the current wave of global justice campaigns, there are also many suggestions that the overall patterns of collective action they display are significantly different from those we had grown accustomed to.

The new social movement theory is derived from an intellectual dissatisfaction with the predominantly Marxist view that treats social movements as reflecting a fundamental struggle among classes organised around economic production. That theory, it is argued, has become less relevant as these classes have been drawn into collective bargaining, the welfare system, and other social advancements within the state (Edwards, 2004). The NSMs that have arisen in their place are interpreted as struggles against the social inequalities, the dominance of the mass media, and other features of post-industrial capitalism and the welfare state. These include youth, feminist, peace, and ecological movements, as well as the rise of group conflicts based on ethnicity and race. The German sociologist Jürgen Habermas (1981, 1987) interpreted such movements as protests against the excessive size and rationality of the state and its bureaucracies and their intrusion into the private worlds of individuals.

NSMs are new because they contain new kind of conflicts, which arise in areas of cultural reproduction, social integration, and socialisation. Emphasis is given on the consciousness structure and cultural praxis with generalised beliefs, values. The new conflicts, thus, arise at the seam between system and life-world. The exchange between private and public sphere, on one hand, and economic and administrative system, on the other, takes place via media of money and power. This new reasonable content and its possibilities for the future differentiate and distance those spheres in which alone personal and collective identities could be formed as the *environment* of the system.

In this particular dynamic of the economic and political-administrative system of action, the new conflict is also directed against the process whereby services, relations and time become monetary values against the consumerist redefinition of private life spheres and personal life styles. The central conflicts of advanced capitalist societies have shifted away from the "capital-labour" struggles of the Labour Movement (now seen as "old" politics) towards grievances surrounding the "colonisation of the life-world" (Habermas, 1981: 35-37). In that over-complex everyday life, NSMs respond to questions about the legitimacy and accountability of governments, and in-turn, raise them. What is "new" about these movements, Habermas argues, is the conflict around which they organise. Doug McAdam (1982) explains that the Internet makes it easy for new social movements to disseminate their information broadly.

Alain Touraine, one of the French sociologists, recently studied social movements in depth, and suggests a theoretical model which is designed to analyze their action as well as their structure. Liberation movements, from peasant movements and popular revolutions to workers' strikes and the NSMs that already demanded cultural rights are not only undermined or abolished forms of social domination. The NSMs are certainly highly diverse, and all demands of recognition of new type of rights are cultural rights (Touraine, 2002). Alain Touraine (2007: 155) proposed that the "new social movements for their part do not have the transformation of economic situations and relations as their guiding principle; they defend the freedom and responsibility of each individual, alone or collectively, against the impersonal logic of profit and competition – and also against an established order that decides what is normal or abnormal, permitted or prohibited."

According to Touraine, there are three principles that must coexist in any social movement: (a) The principle of identity; (b) The principle of opposition; and (c) The principle of totality. The ideological contexts are different in NSMs. Here an ideology is shaped by values about self-actualisation, community and personal satisfaction. Identity is framed by concerns about individual and cultural rights, and articulating claims about fundamental economic justice or human or political rights. In NSMs, the principles of opposition are framed with internal diversity, distrustfulness of politics, favouring small scale and decentralised organisations, anti-hierarchical, advocating for direct democracy (Rudig, 1990). The NSMs must consider the revival of civil society as absolutely necessary to avoid a totalitarian world that explains the necessity to study the conditions of formation of new social movements.

The NSMs are associated not with grievances of lower status and economic groups but with rise of new upper-middle class of educated professionals (engineers, upper-middle functionaries, professionals), whose expertise is cultural or social rather than technocratic, thus have insight into threat posed by pursuit of non-material goals by material conditions of production and institutional framework of welfare state (Castells, 2010b). Having dreamed of a "new daily life" in the "exclusive" residential condominiums promised by the real-estate publicity, they are now discovering the mediocre quality of these places and the scarcity of facilities; the boredom of these depersonalised spaces and their social emptiness as well as the growing density of the neighbourhood with its repetitiously monotonous buildings. So the residential complexes have formed civic associations uniting the demands of the neighbours, proposals for neighbourhood social and cultural activities, and political information and discussion (Castells, 2010c). These social sectors form one of the most promising wings of the NSMs. The new social movements, in their diversity, react against globalisation, and against its political agents, and act upon the continuing process of informationalisation by changing the cultural codes at the root of new social institutions.

Castells locates the new social contradictions within the sphere of collective consumption (housing, education, health) and suggests that they are most clearly manifested at the urban level (Hannigan, 1985). Urban problems are, in his view, increasingly at the heart of political debate in industrial capitalist societies and this is because of the contradiction between the increasing socialisation of goods and the fact that they are managed in the interests of capital (Elliott, 1980:155). Similarly, Touraine (1981: 6-7) argues that "what is crucial is no longer the struggle between capital and labour in the factory but that between the different kinds of apparatus and uses"; in other words, between a highly centralised, technology-dominated state and a populace fighting to exercise a degree of self-management in the various spheres of the programmed society. As one reads Touraine and Castells, it becomes increasingly clear that beneath the language of neo-Marxist social theory, there are strong currents of the traditional mass society perspective.

New social movements have been identified in terms of four features, (1) *Aims:* these tend to be to do with the alteration of social and cultural values, especially those concerned with individual autonomy, rather than the transformation of social structures. (2) *Social base:* traditional political movements are based in social classes; NSMs are based in other groupings, women for example. (3) *Means of action:* NSMs do not use the traditional political means of influencing the state but rely on mass mobilisation to change values and attitudes, as in the deployment of Green social action. (4) *Organisation:* NSMs repudiate formal and bureaucratic modes of organisation, preferring loose, flexible modes that actively involve ordinary members, the grass roots.

The distinctiveness of NSMs may be exaggerated. They do use traditional political processes, they are often middle class and their mode of organisation is becoming more formal. A major criticism of new social movements (NSMs) theory is that it took certain traits as foundational characteristics of new social movements that were not necessarily new and far from generalisation – such as activists' middle class origins, or loose organisational forms (Calhoun, 1993; Kriesi et al., 1995).

NSMs have complex agendas that go beyond single issue limited by types of movements it tries to explain. In contemporary welfare states, such movements are more diverse than a theory purports. For example, many movements are for group rights or for basic human rights. Axel Honneth (1995) and many others deny the existence of new social movements (born after the 1960s). According to them, they are merely arbitrarily isolated elements in a complex of attitudes or demands mixing all kinds of objectives: economic, cultural, national, generational, sexual. From that position, the left-wing activities of NSMs have thrown considerable light upon the problematic relationship between the state and civil society. Their very emergence as a political force can be explained by a distrust of the ability of the state to govern civil society in ways which are democratic and inclusive.

## Concluding Remarks

The term social movement covers various forms of collective action aimed at social reorganisation. In general, it is not highly institutionalised, but arises from spontaneous social protest directed at specific or widespread grievances. As a collectivity, a social movement is characterised by an emergent social structure and a culture. The social structure is reflected in the relationship between leaders and followers, and in the culture between values and norms. Success is most apparent when a movement manages to acquire its power legitimised as authority. In other instances, the movement achieves power through secession (Tilly, 1963). In a successful revolution the social movement becomes the new source of authority and respectability, and opposition to those values, which are defined as counter-revolutionary.

Social movements may also be categorised on the basis of the general character of their strategy and tactics; for instance, whether they are legitimate or underground. The popular distinction between radical and moderate movements reflects this sort of categorisation. An obvious difference between types of movements depends upon their reliance on violent or non-violent tactics. But a non-violent movement may also be defined as revolutionary or radical because it accepts civil disobedience, rather than legal or parliamentary maneuver as a major feature of its strategy. It should be added that the distinction between violent and non-violent movements is a relative one because a movement may shift rapidly from one to the other as it develops.

A movement that appears to threaten the values of powerful and significant interest groups within the society is publicly defined as revolutionary and encounters violent suppression. As a result, it is denied access to legitimate means of promoting its programme. Another type of movement is defined as neither respectable nor dangerous but peculiar; this type, seen as odd but harmless, encounters ridicule and has limited access to legitimate means. A commonly used but highly subjective distinction is that between "reform" and "revolutionary" movements.

Such a distinction implies that a reform movement advocates a change that will preserve the existing values but will provide improved means of implementing them. The revolutionary movement, on the other hand, is regarded as advocating replacement of existing values. Several attempts to characterise movements involve the direction and the rate of change advocated. Adjectives such as radical, reactionary, moderate, liberal, and conservative are often used for such purposes. In this context the designations "revolutionary" and "reform" are often employed in a somewhat different sense than that described above, with the implication that a revolutionary movement advocates rapid, precipitous change while a reform movement works for slow, evolutionary change.

The culture of a movement encompasses norms and values. Norms are standardised expectations of behaviour developed by members. Values include the programme and the ideology. The programme is the scheme of change of the new social order that the movement proposes to bring about. The ideology is a body of ideas justifying the programme and the strategy of the movement. Propaganda is also important for maintaining morale and unity by encompassing action strategy. It usually includes a reinterpretation of history, a projection of the utopia that the success of the movement will introduce, a projection of the disastrous consequences of failure, and a reevaluation of the relationship between population segments and the movement.

The end products of social movements as collectivities attempting to change the social order cannot be analyzed simply in terms of success or failure. Failure may come as a result of ruthless suppression of the movement or through widespread apathy. A movement may wither away because too few take it seriously and it does not develop enough power to force its programme on society. Sometimes the remnants may linger for a long time as a cult, oriented inward toward the gratifications that the members obtain from participation but making no serious effort to change the social order.

Failure of a movement to gain a large number of converts, combined with indications that it has at its disposal effective means of coercion, leads to a shift to this type of strategy. Strategy and changes in strategy are strongly influenced by the relationship of the social movement to the larger society and to other social movements. The functional structure of society may lead to develop the feelings of deprivation and discontent, which are related to a desired point of reference. The social structure and the prevailing belief system may suggest either that change can be brought about by changing the hearts and minds of the individual members or that individuals have little effect on the social order. The idea of resource mobilisation shows us that the social movements arise from long-term changes in a group's organisation, available resources, and opportunities for group action. On the other way, the political processes have begun to look more closely at how, why and when stories are used and to what effect.

More general theories of the origin of social movements, such as those of Smelser, Turner and Killian, suggest that social change may result in strains or conflicts in one or more crucial aspects of the social order. Normative strain arises when changing conditions create a situation in which the established norms no longer lead to the attainment of important, accepted values. Strain in values arises when the values themselves seem to interfere with the satisfaction of important needs of a segment of the society. This sort of strain often arises when different groups, such as immigrants, minorities, or the younger generation, develop values that conflict with those of more established groups. Even with little change in norms and values, changes in social structure reflected in the failure of important functionaries to play their roles adequately may lead to discontent.

Role of ideology is important in old social movement. The ideology may lead a loyal member (the committed participant in a social movement) to view all governmental authorities as villains, while the ordinary citizen views them as legitimate leaders with some good and some bad qualities. The end product of this surrender of autonomy may be an altered world-view. Some things are taken for granted before becoming part of the movement will never seem the same again, even after leaving the discipline of the movement. New social movement breaks this commitment perspective and develops a socio-cultural space for social change.

In fact, Touraine's analysis of new social movements has still a more general goal. He proposes an analytical method of historical action, which he calls actionalist analysis. This aims to explain how values are created, the logic on which they are based, and by what means they appear, are expressed and provoke the action of collectivities. Touraine emphasises that he is not setting up his actionalism in opposition to functional and structural analysis; while these start with existing values, taking them as given, actionalism proposes going back to their origin and source.

In this actionalist analysis, Touraine gives social movements a privileged position. To him they appear to be the strategic place where new values are created and made explicit. Because of this, they become particularly central to the analysis of historical action and social change. It is mainly in and through social movements that innovating actors, as well as their opponents, organise their action and seek to influence the history of their society. New social movements are, thus, those in which political action is organised with respect to the recognition of the rights and differences of the segregated groups (for example "Black is beautiful"), with a corresponding decline in emphasis on universal principles of common humanity (for example, integration of the races). The social movements with a more fluid and transitory structure are also proposed as new for their self-actualisation goal.

Sociologists have also examined the ways that stigmatise identities and groups that are organised around them have become the source of political consciousness and attendant of social movement activity. For example, in the latter part of the twentieth century, those sustaining the gay and lesbian movement, the prostitutes' rights movement, the disabilities movement, the movement to advance fat acceptance, and the movement to normalise mental illness have sought to de-stigmatise the very attributes, identities, and behavioural actions that bind them together as a discernible socio-political group. By breaking with traditional social movements, they radically challenged perceived truths about how social movements operate. The sociology of education deals with a social movement by considering it as a process of mobilisation of large numbers of people to work together to deal with a social problem.

# Chapter - 7

# The Issues in the Sociology of Education

Issues in sociology of education are generally considered as public. The public issues lie beyond one's personal control and they are rooted in society instead of individual level. Most public issues are becoming a space of direct interest for sociological research. The sociologists, just as they draw their professional attention, public issues can prompt research interest in sociological thinking, what C. Wright Mills called a "sociological imagination"—that is, an ability to see private troubles as *public issues* and public issues as *private concerns*. By applying sociological analysis to familiar public issues, researcher shows others that a sociological imagination can be valuable, both personally and intellectually.

Public issues are ideal for teaching sociological principles, because they are both complex and intriguing. Our everyday life is often said to be the laboratory for sociology (Nock and Kingston, 1990). The activities, in the best possible ways, are performed by us in our daily life by acquiring new skills and knowledge from education. Education makes us dutiful and impacts directly on the development of leadership potentialities in our daily life. Albeit of this, one may be tempted to ask: do sociological perspectives really have any relevance to the study of education? What are the basic issues in sociology of education? Does a study of some public issues really have any impact on the "real world" of education – on classrooms, pupils, teachers and school organisation?

It is not difficult to reveal some evidences of such relevance and impact. Consider, for example, the controversy concerning gender inequality in education. Through a lens of sociology, we can best explain and react to the relative under representation of girls and young women at all levels of schooling in certain sections of a country. In a micro-level, patriarchy as a specific school culture may be examined through sociological perspectives. Indeed, discussion on public issues rarely proceeds without some reference to social science research. The researchers know that all educational issues are not public, as all public issues are not related to education. But, when we focus on knowledge, then all public issues are very much associated with the level of conscience and consciousness, i.e. education. Thus, a research itself has become an issue, especially when it attempts to quantify what goes on in social life.

The sociology of education attempts to interpret the issues in social life through three distinct levels of analysis. The first one is macro-sociological issue of education that deals with the explanatory accounts of whole societies, educational structures at large, and educational system. It is that of the "consensus" system or structural theorists represented by Emile Durkheim, Talcott Parson and Robert King Merton, who, as George Ritzer (1996) pointed out, focus on the invisible larger structures of society which they perceive as determinants of the actions of people and the society as a whole. Under this perspective, the shared norms and values are fundamental to study the whole educational system and to the maintenance of social order; social change occurs only in a slow and orderly manner.

The second extreme interprets society and social life in terms of purely human or social action. It is that level of analysis in which the focus is on face-to-face interactions in everyday life. This agency position considers the whole system as the product of the construction of meaning by its members. This micro-sociological issue is often concerned with understanding individual meanings and the actions or relationships through which a member attempts to impose that meaning on their historical situation (Dawe, 1970). Max Weber was the first sociologist to advocate such a social action approach. With such an interactionist view, the important issue is not so much the instance of an individual's compliance to large structures of society which act upon him, but his genuine creative ability to build such structures and ascribe meaning that are significant to them (Meighan and Siraj-Blatchford, 1986).

Within these two extremes, there is a middle path that represents a group of theorists such as Karl Marx, Georg Simmel, Ralf Dahrendorf, and so on, who although adopted a structural approach to the study of social life, nonetheless, rejected the methodological persuasions of the consensus theorists. They reject the notion of value consensus in society and stress the existence of fundamental differences of interest between social groups resulting in conflict being a common and persistent feature of society (Haralambos, Holborn and Heald, 2004). The issues in meso-level consider that the behaviour of agent is ultimately determined by the economic infrastructure.

Sometimes this level based division of perspectives does not maintain a strict differentiating line. Overlapping problems are there. For example, it can be seen that repetition, imitation, the application of rewards and punishments, and trial and error are the four main procedures through which learning operates. Whether in training children, in teaching, education or socialisation in general, the socialising agent and/or the person being socialised resorts constantly to one or another of these learning processes (Rocher, 1990[1968]).

Education and socialisation would consist above all in the learning of appropriate responses to situations, events and external objects which acted as stimuli; this learning would be carried out mainly by repetition and the interplay of sanctions. Behavioural perspective has often been criticized for the fact that its definition of human conduct and education is too molecular or atomized; it has also been accused of neglecting the goal that is pursued by the human subject in his behaviour and actions, and of tending to treat the human subject as an automaton or a machine. Human nature, therefore, is not completely fixed by human biology. It is shaped through learning and education hence must be regarded as both open and flexible (Scott, 2006). The motives that inform human actions are culturally formed and vary considerably through history and from one place to another.

Educational and teaching methods differ a great deal between rural and urban families. The education of children in the country is more uniform than is the case in the city. The education of the rural child is characterised by alternating freedom and constraints, depending on his age, and by the greater importance attached to duty. The city child succeeds in achieving his autonomy at an earlier stage and in a more complete way, but he is also subjected to a multiplicity of influences which are less homogeneous and less coherent than in the case of the country child. This micro-macro linkage through a meso-level of analysis also focuses on a fourth type, that is, a global level of analysis. Globalisation processes are examined here, where a migrant child of global metropolis may be focused to multiculturalism and global environment of technology based knowledge exchange with a racial segregation of social life.

Without specifying an issue on the locus of this micro-meso-macro model, present analysis incorporates twenty issues of the sociology of education. Here is a brief explanation of those issues, along with other co-related issues, in ten niches:

1. Education, Everyday Life and Leadership
2. Education, Schools and Teachers
3. Education, Inclusive Learning and Socialisation for Atypical Children
4. Education, Leisure and Community Development
5. Education, Class Identity and Inequality
6. Education, Stratification and Social Mobility
7. Education, Gender and Empowerment
8. Education, Culture and Multiculturalism
9. Education, Technology and Social Change
10. Education, Environment and Globalisation

## 1. Education, Everyday Life and Leadership

Everyday life is habitual daily life (Chattopadhyay, 2013). This routine life comprises the ways in which people typically think, feel and act on a daily basis. As a key concept in cultural studies, everyday life involves how people generate, establish, and interpret meaning. "The realm of everyday life simply *is* repetitive, being largely defined by monotony, routine, and habit" (Felski, 2000: 20). It is the realm of the eternal daily round, which may also be considered as an enigma with its stability.

Alfred Schutz (1971) defines everyday life by its "taken-for-grantedness." Not only Schutz, but also the philosophers and sociologists such as Lukács, Heidegger, Heller, Goffman, Habermas, Bech Jorgensen and others propose that everyday life is not simply interchangeable with the popular, and it is not the exclusive property of a particular social class or grouping. Sociologically it is that mundane space where the definition of self is constructed and the people conceptualise relationships to the world and others.

Thus, everyday life is created as doubleness. On one hand, it is of continuity, trust and certainty, which is made possible by the norms, rules and routines of everyday life, and on the other hand, change and a more or less frightening and joyful urge for autonomy. Change in everyday life may occur through the mediated tensions that arise from the conflicts of everyday life. For this reason, everyday life is the place of desire, and also the non-place [u-topia] of desire; it is the place where desire dies of satisfaction and reemerges from its ashes.

Henri Lefebvre (1984) argues that everyday life is a distinctively modern phenomenon that only emerged in the nineteenth century. It is true that everyday life became increasingly important in the nineteenth century as an object of critical reflection and representation in literature and art. The impact of capitalism and industrialisation on human existence and perception helps to develop a new awareness of the mundane that creates everyday life as a secular and democratic concept. Secular because it conveys the sense of a world leached of transcendence, and democratic, because it recognises the paramount shared reality of a mundane, material embeddedness in the world.

In the nineteenth century as a form of expert codified knowledge of everyday life, education became an elite issue with a procedural initiative whereby all forms of magical, mystical, traditional explanations are stripped from the world, open and amenable to the calculations of technical reason. The qualitative and theoretical orientations of the school develop the new habitual everyday practices and the constitution of images of the deviant cases as, in Garfinkel's terms, the "seen but-unnoticed background features" of everyday life.

Not only Harold Garfinkel, it were ethnomethodologists, who considered that everyone in society is essentially a sociologist in his or her everyday life, because we are constantly trying to understand and explain the social world that is going on around us. Contrasts with more encompassing institutional orders, like bureaucracy, markets, and states, the sociology of everyday life refers to the analysis of the interaction order or the forms of activity where participants are either co-present or in immediate communication with one another.

After WW-II, specifically in 1960s, the rigid disciplinary techniques of societalisation in school system has changed and the expansion of social security, rising wages, and the growth of the education system helped to develop free subjectivity. The mobilisation of this subjectivity intends to make a productive use of individual capacities for cooperation and communication. Everyday life sociologists move from studying interaction and communication in two directions. First, they move inward, to consciousness, deriving a model of the actor based on people's everyday life attitudes and behaviour. Second, they employ a view of social structure and social order that is derived from interaction and is also characterised by a reciprocal relation to it.

Pierre Bourdieu (1980) finds something that can unify above two directions by adjusting practices to structures and by explaining the gaps remaining between them. He locates it in a process which is his forte as a specialist in the sociology of education, the acquisition of knowledge; this is the sought-for mediation between the structures that organise it and the "dispositions" it produces. This "genesis" implies an interiorisation of structures (through learning) and an exteriorisation of achievements (what Bourdieu calls the habitus) in practices.

Thus, the production and acquisition of art become central in the sociology of education to study everyday life. The art is enlightened through reflection, but reflection is not its essential element, since art can exist without it. But there is no single art in which everything is reflective. The reflective art, within a time-space contextualisation, denotes the quality of leadership. Leadership in sociology of education is a culturally and contextually bounded educational process (Dimmock and Walker, 2005). It is subject to the cultural practices and values of the curriculum in which it is constructed.

In a common-sense approach, leadership refers to the ability of an individual or an organisation to guide individuals, teams, or organisations toward the fulfillment of goals and objectives. Education should train the educands in democratic leadership. The formal educational institution based leadership ensures an effective climate for learning. Thus, in everyday life discourse, the sociology of education views leadership not only from the perspective of technical skills of a learner, but it is also viewed more as a process of influencing relationships and modelling what are deemed to be "desirable" behaviours.

In 21$^{st}$ century, the nature of educational organisations and leadership is also under revision. The race, caste, class and gender based discourses of lifelong learning have encouraged seamlessness between educational sectors to facilitate smooth pathways for students. Educational organisations are part of a "constellation of sites, spaces and opportunities for learning" (Arnot, 2002: 258), with multiple configurations "locally" (multi-site campuses and community and industry partnerships) and "internationally" (offshore campuses) (Blackmore, 2010: 313). So, as education as a field is increasingly subject to markets and the economy, the profession is losing autonomy. Global relations have shifted the locus of power upwards and outwards from educational organisations owing to externally driven demands for accountability and market forces.

## 2. Education, Schools and Teachers

A school is an organised system of learning. In the second chapter of this book, we have already discussed about school as a special environment, or as an institution as well as an organisation of society. To avoid repetitive discussion, here we go through the issues of education in relation to schools and teachers.

Sources of children's education lie foremost in protecting children from possible harmful impact of natural and social environment. German pedagogue Friedrich Frebel, the founder of the original system of pre-school education, in his "kindergarten" (1840) planned to exemplify an enlightened educational institution for training of local children (Andriyivna, 2014). This educational institution, as a pre-school model had developed children's ability on the one hand, and a training for pre-school teachers to enhance practical knowledge, on other hand. These two ways attended to control school phobia and vulnerability in community life (Hamblin, 1974; Pritchard and Butler, 1978). In the case of the school phobic, social withdrawal and phobias are generally found in adulthood.

The elementary school experiences shape the kind of identity taken on by kids and by attaining to the eighth grade, these identities are usually firmly established. Dropout may change a kid's school identity to a street identity. Street kids' disconnection from school is marked by drastic changes in their behaviour that express their discontent with the student role. In *School Kids/Street Kids: Identity Development in Latino Students,* Nilda Flores-Gonza´lez (2002) proposes that the identity-threats, such as perceptions of unfairness of street culture, became an issue for the street kids and impacted their perceptions of school. Changes in education policy or through the motivational programmes organised by the teachers of a school can change the scenario of street identity among the drop-outs. It is also evident that some unprofessional teachers engaged in actions, emotionally hurt the leavers and returners. School climate has a direct impact on kids to select socially bestowed identity.

The quality of school climate emerges as an important variable to the quality of the teachers' identity. The school climate is remembered as very formal, austere and repressive. Relationships between educands and teachers are seen as inclusive with a distant and threatening relationship. But the relationships between peers are viewed as amusing and competitive. Peer grouping in school is an "informal group" that contains a place of self development in leisure times as well as a support group in preparing for examinations or in doing homework. It is related to children's academic lives at school. There are five types of peer statuses that most schools conform to: popular children, average children, neglected children, rejected children, and controversial children (Wentzel and Asher, 1995).

The teacher education is commonly known as teacher training that refers to the process by which a person attains education or training in an institution of learning in order to become a teacher. It also refers to the policies, procedures, and provision designed to equip (prospective) teachers with the knowledge, attitudes, behaviours, and skills they require to perform their tasks effectively in the classroom, school, university and wider community (Lopes and Pereira, 2012). There are two basic perspectives in this professional skills achievement process. Firstly, the formal curriculum, in which the teachers concentrate on the new teaching and learning perspectives of the school, and that have a great influence in their professional identity construction. Secondly, in regards to informal curriculum, they stress in teamwork and dynamics as the nuclear source of personal and professional growth.

The teachers are trained in such a manner that their work expectations are not different from the way things actually are at campus. They are not shocked by the reality of the situation. They can try to extent an applied knowledge system in education programme or to prove sprawling vocational education by job training in everything from mobile-repairing shop to fast food-restaurant worker. In praxis, they can objectively and scientifically compare their institution with others and may propose two versions of educational initiatives in particular: *reform* and *intervention* (Ebert and Culyer, 2011). A reform is a programme that seeks to replace some aspects of the current educational operation. It could be a matter of philosophy, administrative style, curriculum, instruction, or conceptualisation. On the other side, interventions typically are in response to some specific need, and though they can be a permanent change, they often do not have the intended longevity of a reform. The betterment programmes that pull specified children out for remedial reading instruction exemplify an intervention.

Presently the educational system is going to adopt an "open concept" approach of teaching, which is also run by an instructional method of learning in higher education and negates the issues like school refusal. Perhaps it is one of the most intriguing possibilities for the reconceptualisation of educational institution in the world of electronic technologies. Distance education, or the delivery of instructional programmes to educands in sites remote from the "school," originally began as correspondence courses by mail. Eventually, the advent of television and home videotape machines allowed distance education to become a multimedia—though still not "interactive"—experience. Global high speed internet access with smart phones explores a vast scope of participation in this type of courses of networked society. The potential power of electronic technology and its capacity for expanding education to a global enterprise may well influence that reconceptualisation of future schools and tomorrow's teachers.

## 3. Education, Inclusive Learning and Socialisation for Atypical Children

Socialisation is a lifelong process. It begins at the time of birth and ends with death. This process makes us conscious about society. We become a normative participant in social phenomenon and thus society runs. But for the atypical child, what would be the action frame of reference to continue this lifelong process? Is there any disruption to continue this process smoothly in a formal level? This analytical portion searches answers of such questions with others and go beyond the prescribed structure of inclusive schooling.

A key aspect of the term, "special educational need" is, of course, a "need" itself. To clarify the concept "need," one may begin with comparing and contrasting it with the notion of "want." In certain contexts, the terms "need" and "want" can be used almost interchangeably. The concept of "need" mostly conveys standing in want of something (Farrell, 2004: 14). But "need" is not "want." An uncontrolled social situation makes "need" more viable than "want." To "want" something implies a desire to have something, and it is generated by "id" or "ego." The expression of "need" can be justified by "super ego" and is used in a way that necessitates a particular goal. Thus, "need" exposes an inability and demands a support system which is run by others.

A child has special educational needs if he or she has a learning difficulty which calls for special service provision meant for him or her. A wide range of disabilities contribute to child's atypical condition. That condition may range from mild to severe, physical to mental, educational to social, or any combination of these conditions. Atypical child syndrome is a term borrowed from the medical profession and is no longer in common usage. The current term referring to this group is exceptional children. An exceptional child is one who deviates from the norm and can be categorised on the basis of a set of physical and/or behavioural characteristics (Chattopadhyay, 2014a). There are varieties of specific disorders in the area of special education that use the term syndrome as a part of the classification. Hunter syndrome, Down syndrome, Turner syndrome, Lesch-Neyhan syndrome, Cornelin deLange syndrome, Sturge-Weber syndrome, and Klinefelter's syndrome are but a few that are discussed in the special education literature.

It is difficult to fit an individual into a specific category, as each individual has a different combination and severity of disability. Disability classifications are set up according to the characteristics of the children who are different from the average or normal child and should be helped by educational programmes to meet the individual's needs. Samuel Kirk *et al* (2009: 6) describe six categories: (1) *intellectual differences,* including children who are intellectually superior (gifted) and children who are slow to learn (have intellectual and developmental disabilities); (2) *communication differences,* including children with learning disabilities, speech and language disabilities, or autism; (3) *sensory differences,* including children with auditory or visual impairments; (4) *behavioural differences,* including children who are emotionally disturbed or socially maladjusted; (5) *multiple and severe handicapping conditions,* including children with combinations of impairments (such as cerebral palsy and mental retardation, or deafness and blindness); and (6) *physical differences,* including children with nonsensory impairments that impede mobility and physical vitality. Although these categories have been used in psychology, sociology, physiology, and the medical profession, they would be briefly addressed from the educational standpoint also.

Atypical individuals tell us something important about human development. By studying and teaching children who are remarkably different from the normal, we learn about the many ways in which children develop and learn, and we inform ourselves more thoroughly about the developmental processes of all children; in this way, we tend to believe that his or her exceptional or atypical behaviour is the result of whatever disability the child possesses. However, such behaviours could well be the cumulative response of the child to the reactions of family, school, peers, and neighbourhood towards his or her disability.

When considering basic family responsibilities, it is important to realise the enormous diversities of families. There has been a substantial increase in the number of nuclear families, or working-parent families, single-parent families, poverty ridden families. Albeit of these situational adversities, family members, who react to a child with disabilities, have a natural tendency to respond in a nonproductive way to the overt behaviours shown by that child (Cox and Paley, 1997). Such coercive cycle tends to compound and extend the original problem, and this means that these families need to become aware of more productive responses to the original behaviour of the child. Increasingly, the approach that educators are taking to cope with the milder forms of exceptionality is to try to aid the child's adjustment by modifying the life circles around the child. Here professionals should attend to family priorities for goals and services, even when those priorities differ substantially from professional priorities. If we expect to be effective in special education, we need to work with all the members of the family in which the child lives, not just with the atypical child and the child's mother (Turnbull and Turnbull, 2004: 92). Involving and supporting families is likely to be a more powerful intervention than one that focuses exclusively on the child.

There is general agreement on the need to form partnerships with parents, but the real question is how that partnership is forged and how that changes the traditional professional-parent relationship (Roberts, Rule, and Innocenti, 1998). Teaching the professional to respect the family as an equal partner and helping parents carry out an action plan for their child requires a different kind of training than has been the style in education or special education. In this respect in recent years, we have become so accustomed in seeing the terms "inclusion," "inclusive education" and "inclusive schools" used interchangeably that it is tempting to see inclusion as being synonymous with the creation of inclusive schools (Barton and Corbett, 2002; Corbett, 2001). A child has a learning difficulty if he or she has a significantly greater difficulty in learning than the majority of children of the same age, or has a disability which prevents or hinders the child from making use of educational facilities of a kind generally provided for children of the same age in schools within the area of the local education authority. Children with disabilities and special needs also have the right to education just as normal children.

Inclusive education strives to address the learning needs of the special children, with a particular focus on those who are subject of being isolated and excluded. The philosophy behind inclusive education is to promote opportunities for all children to participate, learn and have equal treatment, irrespective of their mental or physical abilities. While the awareness on inclusive education in schools throughout the country is still at a stage of infancy, educational institutions are somewhat skeptical about having both normal and special children studying in the same classroom. And in circumstances, where a former excluded child is given admission into a mainstream classroom, the outcome of the action is questionable.

Underpinning inclusive education is the principle that each and every child, regardless of gender, ethnicity, social class, ability or disability, has the basic right to be educated in the regular classroom (Westwood, 2003: 2). This principle has been accepted in varying degrees in most of the developed countries and it has influenced educational policy-making in the developing countries. However, in many of these countries the implementation of inclusive classroom practice is still lagging well behind the stated policies—and often the rhetoric of "education for all" is far behind of the reality in schools (Kavale and Forness, 2000). Some countries are slow to promote integration and inclusion in part because many teachers and principals are not strongly in favour of teaching all children in the mainstream (Soodak and Podell, 1998). Sometimes there has been opposition from parents of both disabled and non-disabled children, as they think that classrooms, containing a very wide range of ability, may end up in failing to meet the needs of any of the children (Farrell, 2001). Other obstacles are lack of funds for providing an adequate system of support to integrate children and their teachers, and difficulties in providing sufficient additional training for teachers to enable them to teach students with special needs (Rose, 2001).

Interaction between the child and his or her surroundings begins at birth and continues and increases as time passes. In classroom or in play ground or in community life the environment is not the same for a child with disabilities as it is for the nondisabled peers. Here inclusion is primarily designed to promote social relationships between children with disabilities and without disabilities and to facilitate optimal access in learning opportunities. The use of blended practices that draw from general early childhood and early childhood special education allows the teacher in the inclusive classroom to meet the needs of all of his or her children (Grisham-Brown et al., 2005: 160). In this practice, assumptions often made about groups with a child with disability are that the nondisabled members are inevitably neglected because the instructors or elders must pay much attention to the child with disabilities and for this reason, the nondisabled members become resentful of the child with disabilities (Voeltz, 1980). Sometime the nondisabled members indulge the atypical one and try to exclude him or her from group activity.

To meet a socialisation goal of inclusion, instructors or educators endorse inclusion that has devised series of activities which enhance social contact and learning. In *peer-buddy systems,* a classmate may help another classmate with disabilities to negotiate the school day; *peer support networks* help students to become part of a caring community; and in *circles of friends,* an adult facilitator helps potential peer buddies sensitize peers to the friendship needs of students with disabilities (Kirk, 2009: 168; Villa and Thousand, 1995). This type of group instruction may actually be more advantageous than one-on-one instruction because of the economy of teacher effort, students learning as how to interact with peers, and students learning from peers. Small-group instruction is the mode for the regular classroom if the students with special needs are to be included (King-Sears and Carpenter, 2005).

Many atypical children not only engage in non-adaptive behaviours which cause them trouble with their peers and teachers but also lack positive social skills. Some students may have little opportunity in their neighbourhoods or in their families to see positive social skills in use. One specific goal of a special education programme, therefore, is to enhance the use and practice of socially acceptable behaviours for community development. The role of neighbourhood groups is very important not only for the nondisabled children, but for the atypical children also. Out of formal school activities neighbourhood community performs greater role to co-opt atypical children in normal course of social life (Shonkoff and Phillips, 2000). It includes a multicultural curriculum, informal literacy development, and supportive or affectionate creative thinking, as well as health and social services.

In many developing countries, for example, in India, and in many least developed countries of Sub-Saharan Africa, a majority of children with special needs do not receive any formal education, inspite of the practice of inclusive education in some schools. This is because children with disabilities and learning deficiencies are segregated from mainstream schools and other regular routines and social activities of typical children. It is quite evident in rural life than the urban areas. Other contributing factors to this situation are lack of affordability and awareness on the kind of educational choices available to children with special needs. However, if these children participate in this formal agency in their childhood and make them quite capable of socio-cultural settings, after completion of formal education they face another problem in greater community life where there are no such supportive teachers who can give them special professional support, except their family members. One way to think about this issue is to rethink of leisure education in community life.

## 4. Education, Leisure and Community Development

Leisure is being defined as time, free from paid work, and education is considered as enlightening experience. Sociologically, leisure refers to a specific area of human experience with its own benefits, including freedom of choice, creativity, satisfaction, enjoyment and greater amount of pleasure and happiness. It embraces comprehensive forms of expression or activity whose elements are often physical in nature as they are intellectual, social, artistic or spiritual. The sociology of leisure avoids important social aspects that influence leisure. Chris Rojek (1985) advocates that leisure research deals with forms of leisure and its characteristics, but not enough attention is paid to the field of social processes that affect leisure. He argues that the term "free time" does not have a meaning of its own, and that freedom should not be connected with leisure, for leisure is not free activity, but is heavily dependent on how systems of social legitimisation allow people to behave. His main example is the different ways of change in leisure time and leisure space, when gender is concerned.

Societies are complex and interrelated, and leisure cannot be separated from other life goals. To reach a state of physical, mental and social well-being, an individual or group must be able to identify and realise aspirations, satisfy needs and interact positively with the environment. It is important to explain at this point that power relations and manipulations are expressed through daily routine practices, with no awareness of the consequences of their outcomes. There is no central intention, no conspiracy, which regulates social processes. Actually the disciplinary society where we live, exercises discipline and ensures obedience by manipulating human bodies effectively through time and space.

Michel Foucault (1980) speaks about social exclusion as a general strategy, which is executed by several means. For example, by "enclosure", people are made to be relatively secluded from their environment and from each other. Hospitals and prisons are extreme examples, but other social institutions like schools, factories, offices and caravan sites act in similar ways. The practice is to enclose people in separate spaces in order to control and regulate their lives and behaviours more efficiently and more scientifically. Another example of spatial manipulation given by Foucault is "partitioning". Each individual is allocated in an individualised location that is his/hers for periods of the day, the year or for life. In this way an "analytical space" is created where people are viewed as they are placed in rows, lines or cells, with permanent spatial and temporal partitions between them.

These time–space partitions have two exclusionary outcomes: firstly, they help to avoid the creation of large groups that might be a source of the creation of independent will or opposition, e.g. they oppress collective efforts and voluntary organisation. And secondly, they enable direct manipulation of individual activities and avoid waste created by idle human encounters. They are productive and efficient in action.

Anthony Giddens (1984) noticed that Max Weber, as well as Foucault have dealt with the separation of units of space and time, and the control of these units. Weber stressed a phenomenon that is important for the discussion of leisure as no work – the importance of the complete separation between the locations of the workplace and the worker's home. In the same way Foucault's anti-psychological analysis interrogates the discourse of the human and the conditions of its emergence, arguing that people become individuals through discourses and institutions of culture. Thus, Foucault's problematisation of the psy-function helps us to bring into question the essentialism that underpins the doctrines of fundamental human needs which inform theories and policies of leisure. Actually Weber and Foucault have undergone a simultaneous internalisation and externalisation, individuation and collectivisation. Giddens adds that the journey to work (or to school) is another important mechanism of partition and control and is used to manipulate and control people in the disciplinary society (Meštroviæ, 1998).

Research indicates that the people, most likely to participate in leisure activities defined as "public activity," in voluntary organisations and in political activism, belong to the higher socioeconomic groups, in which self-fulfillment is developed during paid work as well (Sadan, 2000: 132). From this point of view leisure education should impart knowledge which is relevant to the leisure domains that pertains to the individual, to the individual's immediate environment, and to society at large. Here leisure education is an enabling process of society that employs the same differential mechanisms like all other social intervention systems, such as school education, training, employment and institutions (Parker, 1979). It deconstructs social structure with its power, authority and dominating roles and influences all aspects of human lives. This is why the splitting of life into work and leisure, does not always result in a quest for more leisure activities in order to compensate for frustrations generated during paid work.

The field of leisure education is a social function and as such it adheres to the same social rules and norms, and takes place in the same power arenas as all social relations. Leisure education does not have a different social role by merely claiming to have one. In fact, the early concept of community education was predominantly school based, but over the course of time, community education has become a system that provides for all the educational needs (including leisure education) of all its community members (including the members with special needs) by using the resources in them and helping people to gain power and control over their own lives.

Implementation of leisure education in the community involves the process of community development (Mundy, 1998). Sociologists argue that leisure education for community development should include concepts such as empowerment of individuals and groups to enhance the quality of life; accessibility, which is meant to minimize barriers and optimize access to leisure services; lifelong learning; social participation which creates opportunities to develop social networks needed in the community; diminishing constraints which prevent one from fulfilling personal, family and community needs; inclusivity – which means recognising the multicultural, socio-cultural (underprivileged), gender, age, ability and other constituent groups in society; civic and moral responsibility which develops a sense of community through responsible leisure behaviour; and preservation and conservation of natural resources which should be enhanced.

Leisure in the life of people has profoundly affected established institutions and one of the vitally affected has been the institution of public education. An important contribution that schools may offer to the common means of enjoyment is to provide leisure opportunities in an environment where people find it conducive for learning. Here leisure is a highly valued component of community development, and awareness about its advantages and benefits is essential. Leisure literacy should be considered as a societal goal, since community development depends, along with other things, on the personal development of its members.

The basic purpose of education is to develop people's values and attitudes and equip them with the knowledge and skills that will enable them to feel more secure and get more consensus and satisfaction from life. This implies that not only the education becomes relevant to work and economy, but it becomes equally important for the development and improvement of the quality of life. Thus, leisure education as a lifelong learning process incorporates the development of leisure attitudes, values, knowledge, skills and resources with an inclusive community vision.

Embodying a clear value of commitment to enhance access to leisure opportunities of individuals with special needs, this inclusive community vision should include all its individuals. Therefore, it should be recognised that leisure education programmes for people with special needs play important roles in improving the quality of community life (Sivan and Ruskin, 2000). Leisure is, therefore, seen as a resource for improving the quality of life, when increased dissatisfaction, stress, boredom, lack of physical activity, lack of creativity and alienation in people's day-to-day lives characterise many societies throughout the world. All these characteristics may be alleviated by leisure behaviour, and leisure behaviour may be moulded by leisure education.

Community is defined as a geographical location and an aggregate of interests which have an affinity with the interconnections between them. Community development refers to a process using formal, informal and non-formal education as well as leadership to enhance the quality of life of individuals (including the members with special needs) and groups living within the community. Indeed, communities encompass a variety of people, including people with special needs of all ages, such as those with developmental disabilities and impairment of adaptive behaviour at various levels, as well as physical, emotional and social disabilities. These people with special needs must have the legal, moral, ethical and economic public policy support to lead self-determined and authentic life plans within diverse cultural frameworks. Leisure education, for the most part, should centre on facilitating these life plans by the attainment of optimal and meaningful leisure experiences.

Therefore, all services, programmes and institutions, addressing the needs of people with special needs should be planned, implemented and evaluated in terms of specific belief systems. A fundamental belief supports the idea that all people, regardless of their condition in life or ethnic identities, should have the right to develop their human capacities to an optimal level. This deeply embedded concept is no less valid for persons with disabilities. This all inclusive process indicates that people with disabilities can benefit from participation in recreational activities during their leisure. The universality of need for leisure and its positive use demands such opportunities to be made available to all.

## 5. Education, Class Identity and Inequality

In our global village we live in uncertain social conditions except knowledge, which is only certain. Knowledge is found not only in demonstrations, but also in social lore, cultural creations, narrative accounts, institutional regulations and political decisions. Learning as a second job, gets preference in continuing the search of information, internalisation and shake-up knowledge in everyday social life. This refers to an identity of mature students, who generate economy by working in a full or part-time basis and study when they are free. Leisure as a concept now upholds the sense of a life of enjoyment, where entertainment makes a conscious space of praxis.

Identity is socially bestowed, or not – is the dominant question. The mechanism that causes individuals to be "constituted through social structures" is variously referred to as "socialisation", "internalisation" and "identification" (Widdicombe, 1998: 192). Traditionally identity is viewed as an individual's "ego" perception as reflected from his membership in social groups or categories. An individual's identity is assumed to be a combination of characteristics, roles, and beliefs culturally and commonly associated with the group he belongs to. The "content" of the individual's identity is more or less taken as stable and consequential to the individual's self conception and behaviour (Woodward, 2002). The earlier conceptions of identity as propounded by early psychoanalysts focused on identity as a sense of self - a big part of which is located deep in the subconscious mind of man.

It is noteworthy that identity is marked through symbols, involving an understanding of rational choice. In organisational research, identity is studied as a variable in the relationship between the organisational member and the organisation. Identity formation involves setting up boundaries which locate the parameters of difference and of symmetry. Those with whom we share an identity are marked out as the same, in contrast to those who are different (Chattopadhyay, 2014b). In this respect the study of schools as social organisations and bureaucracies is a well-established field in the sociology of education which provides the framework for studies of processes that occur within the school, such as the acquisition of attitudes, values, identity, achievement, discipline, and the like.

Anthony Giddens (1991) argues that self-identity is a distinctively modern project within which individuals can reflexively construct a personal narrative for themselves. If we discuss the relationship between emotion and identity, it may be seen that expressions of emotions are always in a contradictory flux and tend to disrupt identities (Craib, 1998). Identity travels, but it is about belonging. Identity crisis is relative and it includes both personal (i.e., individual/relational) and social (collective) levels, and both personal and social identities are shaped by social context. Difference and sameness involve the marking of boundaries and the identity story is characterised by the moments at which boundaries are constructed, deconstructed and transgressed. This is part of the dynamics of identity, as it is in class identity.

Race, caste, gender and class receive a good deal of attention in sociology, not only to study social strata and social inequality, but also for understanding the reproductive nature of social organisations. In sociology of education, race and ethnicity are important in so far as they provoke prejudice and discrimination in others, but they themselves do not constitute cultural formations that affect the ways in which their members operate in the world. But the class factors have primacy in determining people's life chances, which can be changed through acquiring effective knowledge by educative learning (Chattopadhyay, 2017a). The sense of class identity is shaped by the economic position of individual's life chances, which is objectively determined by the levels of social inequality. Indeed, as Pierre Bourdieu (1984[1979]) suggests, class is an identity term, which is organised primarily around an economic axis of social inequality.

The feminist perspectives of sociology of education examine an account of the gender-specific experience of class identity and expression of class culture, and assist in exploration of how gender meanings shape class formation. Kath Woodward (2000) proposes that the traditional views of identity, including the Marxist and Weberian approaches to class, have emphasized the role of social structures in shaping people's identities. More recent approaches have stressed the interaction between the social and the personal, such when individuals and groups negotiate their identities and represent themselves through patterns of consumption.

The sociology of education thus tries to understand the formation of subjective class identity among groups of educands. Here, the concept of class identity holds students' interests, tastes, attitudes, metaphors in language, and dispositions, which are linked to their socio-economic class position. From this perspective, the sociologists of education relate individuals' class positions with language patterns in school culture, where identity marks individual. Here, slang can be viewed as a marker of an individual's identity. For example, it may be perceived as a distinguishing mark, revealing private information about someone's age, gender, attitude, condition, education, special interest, etc. Schooling subdivides slang into two forms: one is specific and the other is general.

Basically, the general slang is language that speakers deliberately use to break with the standard language and to change the level of discourse in the direction of informality. Specific slang, on the other hand, is language that speakers use to show their belongingness to a group and establish solidarity or intimacy with the other group members. It is often used by speakers to create their own identity, including aspects like social status and geographical belonging, or even age, education, occupation, life style and special interests. It is largely used by people of similar age and experience to strengthen the bonds within their own peer group, keeping outsiders out. It is most common among the teenagers of college campus.

Inkeles and Smith (1974) found strong correlations between educational attainment and individual modernity in their study on adults of Argentina, Chile, East Pakistan (now Bangladesh), India, Israel and Nigeria. In their study, it is evident that the women, who are housewives and mothers of small children, are seen as having no prescribed work schedule, and consequently are assumed to be able to adjust their open and distance course studies quite easily into a daily routine of housework and childcare. Distance education, therefore, is often considered to be especially suited to mature women who want to pursue education while raising a family, or continuing to work in a lower level job, or both (Prummer, 2000). Women from higher middle class represents more in number than the lower class households.

However, such educational development can prove to be imbalanced with respect to the requirements of the productive system that gives rise to unsatisfied expectations and widespread frustrations among educated young people who are either unemployed or underemployed and who often become especially inclined to mass protest and political radicalism (Martinelli, 2005). These consequences restructure the class and status strata of society in a new form, which is very much related to the new pedagogical dimension of education. At the same time, subjective perception of risk is emphasised by the fading of beliefs in religion and magic, the rise in educational levels (which increase awareness of dangers to one's health and safety), and the recognition of the limits of scientific-technical capabilities and abstract systems.

A necessary component of the neoliberal mechanisms of globalisation, migration addresses the economic and labour needs of post-industrial countries while producing new modes of social fragmentation and inequality (Crompton, 2008). As migrant students insert themselves into segmented spaces, countries of origin are themselves implicated in a global class hierarchy, often positioning them in ways that refract this world economic order (Kelly, 2012). Operating in these transnational contexts, social class plays a significant role in determining life trajectories and the ways by which migrant students of diverse social classes exercise agency.

By affirming that migrant students come with valuable transnational informations and skills, teachers can help migrant students claim more-powerful identities from which to navigate investments in the language practices of their new classrooms and communities (Darvin and Norton, 2014). The analysis of the processes of identity formation, of the limits and possibilities of creating social change through educational reform and of the role of the state in regulating social categories and socio-economic relations are becoming central to the discipline of sociology of education in the present decade. Difference, therefore, emerges as central to inequality theories of education.

## 6. Education, Stratification and Social Mobility

Society, to maintain its homoeostasis equilibrium, arranges its elements into groups on different horizontal and vertical levels or strata. The internal inequalities among strata are maintained by social distances and systematic exclusions. Albeit of its internal antagonistic nature, through social differentiation and social stratification, society maintains its ordered life. This social differentiation is not social stratification. Because it involves the formation of horizontal social divisions, when social stratification involves vertical or hierarchical ranking of social strata. But social differences become social stratification when people are ranked hierarchically along some dimensions of inequalities on the basis of income, wealth, power, prestige, age, ethnicity, or some other characteristics.

Essentially, the topic of stratification concerns inequality (Kirby, 1999). Members of the various strata which constitute each level of the stratification hierarchy tend to have common life-chances and life-styles and may display an awareness of communal identity, and these characteristics further distinguish them from other strata. Sociologists normally identify four major types of stratification: slavery, estate, caste and class. There are basically two debates (Fuller and Hannum, 2004). The first one considers stratification as universal, and the second one considers the caste and class by unifocal lenses. For example, the French structuralist Louis Dumont (1970) wanted to uncover the underlying principle of Hindu caste, which he argued is hierarchical in nature, but this does not mean social stratification. Rather, caste hierarchy explains a relation of opposites that can nevertheless cohere within a cultural unity.

Some sociologists also contrast stratification, which implies gradation, with social class divisions, which are seen as polar and antagonistic. Stratification implies persistent gradation of social classes, occupational groups, and ethno-racial categories (Davis, 1949). Sociologists also distinguish closed stratification systems, such as the Hindu caste system, from open ones, such as modern occupational or class systems. In the former, social mobility (movement of an individual or a group from one stratum to another) is discouraged and restricted by traditional conventions. In the latter, mobility is typical, intense, and socially approved. In the functional theory of stratification, sociologists portray stratification as socially beneficial and consensual. Conflict theorists perceive stratification as contested and accompanied by domination (Collins, 1971; 1979).

What are the effects of education on social stratification and social mobility? Without asking this question, we can take a break and look at it little differently by asking: What are the effects of social stratification on education? This question focuses on some different outlooks. It also touches on some of the ways in which an individual of a social class affects the educational opportunities of her/his children. We have, for example, alluded to the fact that parents with low socio-economic status may be either unaware of the benefits which the parents of high status know by virtue of both their educational and occupational exposure, or unable to provide certain school like or school supportive activities for their children at home due to poverty.

Sociologists have agreed in this regard that parental support of education and the provision such as home tuition, access to home libraries, ability to learn the language of the school at home, an early start in education and access to most prestigious schools are not only crucial to children's success in school, but also responsible for the emergence of an obvious class division in children's education life chances. It is also evident from empirical studies in sociology of education that social stratification promotes obvious class division in educational life chances (Tumin, 1967). Children of the middle and upper class parents are better prepared for school education more adequately than children from the low social class structure.

However, children of middle and upper class parents and the elites are at an advantage over those from the poor or low socio-economic status parents as well as children of the uneducated or illiterates. A person who has attained higher level of education is likely to have higher chances of getting good jobs, which in return, determines an individual's social class and culture. This notion is based on Bourdieu's idea (Bourdieu and Passeron, 1977) that those with economic capital can purchase cultural capital: in simple terms, well-paid professional workers are in a position to secure a good education for their children.

Inequality shapes a person's life chances, and other socio-economic status variables that have traditionally been used to gauge the division in social well-being—quality of health and access to healthcare, homeownership and quality of housing, access to education and educational achievement, transportation, distribution of the tax burden, effectiveness of the social safety net, adequacy of retirement savings, the digital divide, and finally, income residential segregation and neighbourhood quality (Dasgupta, 2015). Education is thus a sound investment that is expected to enhance the economic growth of individuals. It is a known fact that education is a strong factor of social mobility (Tumin, 1953). This situation tends to create the socio-economic problems in the society, thereby, widening the gap between the rich, elites on one hand, and the poor, as well as the illiterates on the other.

Higher education is now becoming costlier day by day. The trend of privatisation will make it all the more costly each year in the coming decade. This will deprive many poor and lower middle class students to receive higher education in colleges of repute and universities. This will create class differences and spark off many agitations. Already many groups are clamouring for reservations and special privileges and rights. Banking loan facilities are creating a "new fearful middle class," who borrow money from bank for his/her kin's higher education. After completion of final grade, a jobless future may cause a downward social mobility for the whole family.

The rule of law changes the power balances in modern societies in favour of the lower strata by increasing their bargaining power and widening their access to welfare (Gupta, 1991). Therefore, social stratification in advanced societies is multidimensional and complex, and power hierarchies are open. For example, when a caste system is a form of social stratification in which castes are hierarchically organised and separated from each other by rules of ritual purity, then caste based reservation policy in India helps people of low caste ranks to get easy access in educational fields and also in job market.

Another example may be cited from American society, where the level of racial segregation is too high. Black live matter exposes the reality that lower-class nonwhite students showed better school achievement when they went to school with middle-class whites. Racial segregation, therefore, hindered the educational attainments of nonwhites. African American parents attributed the ineffective instruction at the schools attended by their children to one of two causes. If the schools were all-black, failure was attributed to the racially segregated character of those schools (Lareau, 2002). If whites were attending the schools, African American parents concluded, conditions would be better. This has been the dominant theme in American educational contexts.

In a stratified social setting, education helps people to occupy inconsistent statuses. For example, in multi-dimensional systems of stratification, individuals with a high level of educational attainment that provides a high social status along one stratification dimension, may be employed in occupations that are poorly paid and carry low prestige, indicating low status along other dimensions. Gerhard Lenski (1954) coined this term *status crystallisation,* which denotes consistency between an individual's various statuses. This status crystallisation identifies a qualitative difference in education with certain space specific social mobility. Thus, social stratification affects education in many ways, such as the promotion of obvious class division in educational life chances, qualitative differences in education, socioeconomic problem, over proliferation of class and private school rural-urban imbalance in education and gender bias in education. Rural girl children are more inclined to their household work and remain inattentive in school – a painful gender issue in Third World countries.

## 7. Education, Gender and Empowerment

The sociology of human action and organisation inhere many basic and complex theoretical issues, such as, the nature of social order and power, social equality and inequality, justice and the nature of man. These issues are strategic to sociology and also influence the postulates and presuppositions of other social sciences like history, economics, political science, anthropology, psychology and jurisprudence. In sociology, these issues are very much related to the concept construction and theory or model building, and also related to the analysis of conflict and consensus processes of social life.

Scientific ways of life, logical deduction and new innovative methods help man to moderate traditional orthodox techniques, but some traditional practices remain in modern social life across the globe. For example, "Halloween" customs and traditions, including its ancient Christian and Pagan roots act in the liturgical year in post-industrial and postmodern Western world. On the Eastern side, modern Indian "caste," as a cultural phenomenon, is merely a special form of the general system of status-based social hierarchy, which forms the basis for social ranking of persons and groups (Ghurye, 1961). Ranks are ordered on the basis of power position, where power *(Macht)* is the ability to fulfill one's will over others.

Power should be considered as a medium through which selections, made in one part of society could be transmitted to others, and thus could become analogous to resources. For this chance factor the question of powerlessness becomes relative. One, who is unable to mobilise economic resources and holds an identity as powerless, can be politically a powerful person. Political movement can alter the power hierarchy in social order. A unique aspect of subaltern movement of communities in the threshold of disempowerment into empowerment is that it inverts our presuppositions with regard to modern India (Wakankar, 2010). However, higher social status can also be a supplement of power. By acquiring knowledge, or by achieving economic or political resources, one can be accredited as powerful. For example, as a policy of poverty alleviation, microfinance can be a helpful measure. This economic measure partially helps to empower the poorest part of society (David, 2000; Horrell, Johnson and Mosley, 2008; Karmakar, 2008; Roy, 2010). But without education, innovation, and inclination to participation, the process will not take an organised form. The power in empowerment should not be derived from authority (legitimised power) but from brainpower.

Empowerment refers broadly to the expansion of freedom of choice and action to shape one's life. It implies control over resources and decisions. For poor people, that freedom is severely curtailed by their voicelessness and powerlessness in relation particularly to the state and markets. There are important gender inequalities manifested within the household. Powerlessness is also embedded in a culture of unequal institutional relations, when "*empowerment is the expansion of assets and capabilities of poor people to participate in, negotiate with, influence, control, and hold accountable institutions that affect their lives"* (Narayan, 2002: 14).

In the era of globalisation, empowering people of lower strata or poor men and women requires the removal of formal and informal institutional barriers that prevent them from taking action to improve their well-being—individually or collectively—and limit their choices (Elliott, 2008). The key formal institutions include the laws, rules, and regulations upheld by states, markets, civil society, and international agencies; informal institutions include norms of social solidarity, customary sharing, social exclusion, and corruption, among others. From these two institutional dimensions empowerment approaches focus on augmenting powerless people's freedom of choice and action. From formal institutional point of view, empowerment is not a stand-alone strategy, but a way of development, grounded in the conviction that marginality itself is the most invaluable partner in the task of deprivation and depression. Empowerment approaches, from informal institutional settings include behaviours, that construct people's self-confidence and their belief in themselves, and respect their dignity. Both perspectives view empowerment of powerless as an end in itself and also critical for development effectiveness.

The definition of empowerment as a means to achieve a democratic distribution of power and knowledge within society has many implications for gender. Gender is understood as a socio-cultural construct rather than a biological one where women and men are ascribed with specific social roles within society (Haider, 1996). Being dependent on culture, gender relations in society can be transformed and changed through the transmission of empowering values and education. Followed from this, the concept of empowerment as applied to gender implies a change toward a democratic distribution of power within society.

Empowerment also implies more participatory, bottom-up approaches to development objectives. Here empowerment is the act of completely taking control of one's life in all critical and vital areas of his/her existence. For example, when one is not the author of a digital work, sharing it with others is a step towards cultural empowerment. Here sharing is not the same thing as access, rather it is an act of making something available to others (Aigrain, 2012). However, empowerment in terms of citizen inclusion and participation at the local level can help to ensure that basic services can reach poor people, and can minimize operation and maintenance costs in comparison with centrally managed activities.

Gender discrimination, whether legal or customary, is a particularly important aspect of inequality (Agnaou, 2004; Rothchild, 2007). Empowerment involves women awareness of their conditions, their capability and belief that they can successfully act at personal and societal levels to improve their conditions, and finally their ability to analyze and criticize their environment in both social and political terms.

Empowerment must include cognitive, psychological, political and economic components (Stromquist, 1993). The cognitive component is related to address women's condition of subordination. The psychological component would involve the development of feelings so that women can act to improve their conditions. The political component encompasses the ability to organise and mobilise society for social changes. Finally, the economic component of empowerment embodies the aptitude to obtain some degree of financial autonomy. For the cognitive and psychological components the politics of inclusion makes the productive/innovative linkage of the politics of redistribution and the politics of recognition, which over a longer time span creates sustainable paths to democratic and social development by increasing the capacity to handle conflicts arising from economic resources and life-chances as well as conflicts about identities (Andersen and Siim, 2004). The politics of empowerment concerns the agency and mobilisation dimensions of social and political change.

A critical aspect of an empowering approach is to reduce inequality by broadening human capabilities (through, for example, universal basic education and healthcare, together with adequate arrangements for social protection) and improving the distribution of tangible assets (such as land or access to capital). Such an approach can maximize the poverty reducing impact of growth-inducing policies and investments by enabling poor people to participate in markets more effectively.

The converse is also probable. When inequality is high, poor people lack capabilities and assets (ranging from literacy to collateral for credit) and thus have difficulty in taking advantage of economic opportunity. This limits a society's potential for growth in general and pro-poor growth in particular, and consequently the effectiveness of development efforts. Microfinance projects, from an institutional venture, block the applicability of converse condition. Formal macro-enterprise like state intervention, collective organisation (trade unions and social movements) and wealth redistribution would eventually wither on the vine as alternatives. Through an informal microenterprise, and with the help of microfinance, the poor could be left to articulate individually their own exit from poverty (Robinson, 2001).

The converse becomes reality when microfinance appears as a "poverty trap" and an "anti-development policy" that ultimately destroys the potential for sustainable local economic and social development, and so also for sustainable poverty alleviation. "Put it very simply, within the context of expensive loans, rural producers are unable to produce their way out of poverty" (Bateman, 2010: 51). The rural poor are prone to be caught in a local 'poverty trap', vainly striving to produce and earn more in order to escape their expensive loans, but never quite getting there. When poor people associate only with each other in the neo-liberal empowerment process, they bring only their own meager resources to the table. Poor people understand these constraints and affirm that there is a limit on how much one hungry man can feed another.

Electronic media, like Internet empowers the disadvantaged by increasing their sense of community feeling. The members of this "imagined community" are obviously literate in global languages (Anderson, 1991). They may be crucial for co-ordination of widely dispersed nodes of political opposition, that is, by creating this sense of "we-feeling" among persons and groups (of women), who may otherwise feel relatively diffused and disempowered. Moreover, this imagined community is proven to be essential in facilitating their convergence at particular times and places for collective acts of resistance in globally networked society.

Education and development serve as key signifiers for women's dislocated subjectivity that open up space for discussion of some of the women's deepest gender-based desires and fears. The term "empowerment" as used in the 1990s, seems above all to be about being vocal, having a right to "voice" (Cheater, 1999:4). These voices maintain ethical and moral orders, which are always proven as networks of relationships with commodities. Commodity signifies material culture that involves taking on cultural practices in relation to material objects and defines the uses and values of those objects in everyday life.

In every corner of our globe, the ultimate objective of development is to empower people in general and women in specific. Historically, even when the forces of globalisation were not so strongly present worldwide, institutions remained the vital force for guiding development processes and empowering people grossly. But now globalisation has, in fact, been helping the underdeveloped societies and the territories to incorporate some changes in their social institutions to carry forward the agenda for development of women with renewed vigour. By this process it preserves and reinforces the global hegemony, with a policy framing tendency based on the blending of native social principles with material interests as focused by imperialist strategy.

Disempowerment and disentitlement have become "key features of globalisation" (Bleiker, 2005: 198). We hear of a neoliberal gendered-world order that is increasingly run by a few powerful multilateral institutions and multinational corporations–big, unaccountable structures, whose strategic leitmotifs and decision-making processes reflect the imperatives of short-term material objectives rather than principles such as protection of women and survival of an increasingly stretched global ecosystem.

Is empowerment somehow related to economic development, gender and environmentalism? If yes, then more complex paradigm can be constructed. Economy, society, politics, culture, environment are thus aspects, levels, elements, or "moments" of empowered or disempowered reality. This binary system of empowered and disempowered touches those who can relate with the complex structure of the above elements that cohere in terms of their inherent attributes (Shiva, 1988). A sense of inarticulacy and powerlessness represent this process of relation as everyday value dichotomy. Doing well for the children, or guarding the health of family life, or arranging cheap nutritious food for malnourished members indicate that more complex ethical concerns with the construction of social reality that can be disregarded with the consequence of a trivialised public discourse.

Interestingly, while in the mid-1990s empowerment was associated particularly with women, gender, health, education and development especially in Africa and also in Asia, the objective and subjective concepts of empowerment became more relevant in this decade and began to direct human activity from a multi-level process framework. This "Third Worldist" approach to power may be the most effective argument against Foucault's preference for 'a non-economic analysis' which sees power as "not build up out of 'wills' (individual or collective), nor…derivable from interests" (1980: 188), "neither given, nor exchanged, nor recovered, but rather exercised…in action" (1980: 89) in a curiously agentless way within "an unequal and relatively stable relation of forces" (1980: 200).

At least in its zero-sum conception, power clearly implies control of resources rather than—or in addition to—"voice." To those using the zero-sum conception of a fixed quantum of power, a Foucauldian approach is not only unattractive, but it is also dangerously mystificatory, as Cynthia Cockburn (1994:111) has noted—it is totally insensitive to the ways in which power is gendered, racialised, and classified. More generally, the very discourse of empowerment itself, particularly but not only in the global context of Third World inequality and development, may obscure the "real" or hegemonic relations of power linking states, developers and empowerers to poor people lacking resources and thereby render the already vulnerable even less capable of defending their self-identified interests.

From this point of view, domestic labour that moves to trivialise child bearing, home making, and performing roles as wives and mothers, is used to discriminate women from the world of employment. This explanation is veiled in arguments about how women's traditional roles impede them from their engagement in activities that would lead them to access power, without pointing out the dearth of acknowledgement to women on their own rights and thus denies women power. Another explanation for lack of power among women draws on research on race, gender, ethnicity, and disability, and has consistently argued that women's social and cultural positions have disempowered them because they often find themselves inferior to men and capitalist ideology where men and a larger patriarchal society have access to and benefit from women's labour, both in the processes of reproduction and production (Gordon, 1996).

In their review of empowerment frameworks, Charles Browne and Charles Mills (2001:24) identify four central concepts that are inherent in all empowerment theories in 21st century. These are: (1) Development of [clients'] attitudes, values, and beliefs around self-efficacy that extend from feelings of individual competency to the betterment of the community; (2) validation of people's stories and the collective experience; (3) knowledge and skills for critical thinking, access to information, and action based on critical analyses of structural forces that affect life and opportunity; and (4) individual-focused and social-justice-oriented strategies of intervention and action that as praxis in the empowerment tradition can help clients and client communities to recognize their strengths and use these strengths to engage in advocacy.

This advocacy of new century begins with a sense of faith in one's own strength, advances to activity in inter-personal domains, and continues from there to activity for social change. These meta-narratives contend that women have power and agency, and these are seen in their everyday lives and activities, but are not acknowledged or supported by others. To empower women and to restore their power and agency, society needs to acknowledge women's activities and knowledge and look for ways through which these can be applied in action and policies.

Violence, domination, coercion, inferiority etc. are sensitising and opening up fresh grounds to understand the cultural-historical development of women's disempowerment in the Third World countries. Beyond all of these, however, is the finding that takes into account the issues of Westernised powerful women and confirms the importance of acknowledging women's traditional knowledge systems in order to avoid evisceration of their power and agency. To empower is to understand and to be able to question the rules and laws of society that are oppressive.

Women's participation in development projects planned by the government within the context of empowerment is, in fact, a way to disempower women. The colonial project was predicated on gaining profit by all possible means, including fabricating lies to exploit the labour of native women. Socialising women into domestic roles and dependency was a sure way of acculturating women in Asia and Africa into European lifestyle and was the part of the large scheme of disempowering and dislocating colonised women.

The missionary and colonial schools played the same role of pacifying women. Those who did not comply with the objectives of colonial education were demonised as ignorant and illiterate. Educated women are more empowered than uneducated ones. Colonisers were aware that women's traditional knowledge in birth control and production was contrary to the colonial project of exploitation of women and their labour.

Women's knowledge systems in colonised societies have been marginalised and sidelined, and by doing this, the binary opposition between women's empowerment and disempowerment moves on. To go beyond the division of literacy and illiteracy, empowerment and disempowerment, the question of how knowledge brings empowerment is considered primal. Considering larger social, economic, cultural and political processes and practices, when the debate centers around "women and power," the discussion takes into account the operation of power in marginalising women's traditional knowledge systems, which is not discussed adequately. Without understanding the coded messages in the women's stories, social workers cannot understand their plight and forms of disempowerment that they experience.

These aspects in the debate on women's empowerment argue that the discourse of literacy, empowerment, and socialisation processes create a form of subjecting women into powerless position, and they are constantly in need of knowledge for empowerment. On the other side women's sense of disempowerment is far from simply being a result of lack of contemporary world-view, but is part of ongoing social and cultural insistence of the late modern era without acknowledging or appreciating women's traditional knowledge systems.

Postmodern fluidity of 'self' does not result in a loss or weakening of the "self," rather has a liberating effect on the individual (Bennett, 2005:40). The central feature of postmodernity is its "empowering of the individual subject" (MacCannell and MacCannell, 1993:126). This kind of empowerment allows individual to construct identities which are free from the confines and restraints of class and tradition. Does this rootless empowerment depict the shadow of disempowerment? The question remains.

## 8. Education, Culture and Multiculturalism

Following the Industrial Revolution, the concept of culture went from meaning the growth of something, like horti*culture* or agri*culture*, to signifying the creative aspirations of the human mind. These early notions of culture, as a series of increasingly superior manifestations of human creativity and intellect were closely tied to other prevalent modes of thought at the time—Eurocentrism and evolutionism in particular. Consequently, the idea of culture with a superior-inferior sense was associated with late-19th- and early-20th-century ideas about the progression of evolutionary stages that ranked racial groups in terms of levels of intelligence or development (Convertino, Levinson, and González, 2013: 27).

In response to the racism embedded in this concept of culture, using a historical comparative method, the German-born American anthropologist Franz Boas replaced the "theory of progress" with a theory of "cultural relativism" by demonstrating that cultures are neither superior nor inferior; they are just different from one another (Visweswaran, 2010: 77). This ethnographic tradition based description of culture has changed in 21st century by proposing that culture refers to the symbolic meanings by which the members of a society communicate with and understand themselves, each other, and the world around them and the human beings are, above all, great symbol makers and manipulators.

For 21st century educators, education is the process by which culture is constantly transmitted and produced. One cannot conceive of education in the absence of culture. Thus, the meaning of culture is deeply implicated in education. The educational process, which is much broader than *schooling*, fundamentally oscillates between an emphasis on continuity and an emphasis on change. In the broadest sense, then, education underwrites every human group's ability to adapt to its environment and thereby reproduce the conditions of its existence (Chattopadhyay, 2018). In historical sense, informal teaching was conducted through simple mechanisms of imitation or rote memorisation. Anthropologists have also emphasised the educative role of ritual for binding members of a society to a common cultural vision. The sociology of education considers that the cultural beliefs and values shape what occurs within the institutional structure of formal education systems. From this cultural point of view, education can just as likely serve as the mechanism for domination of one group over another in the pursuit of its own interests.

In present context of a rapidly changing world, *adaptive knowledge*—"the development of flexible knowledge and dispositions that facilitate effective navigation across varied settings and tasks" (Nasir et al., 2006: 490)—is increasingly important and necessary for both educators and students. Learning is now inscribed in shifting and multiple practices situated within dynamic and changing contexts and it is mediated through and with cultural practices and processes that are themselves diverse, partial, and fluid. This diversified fluid nature of society cannot rely on the one-dimensional views of teaching and learning; rather, it must cultivate the capacity to view the students and the ways of learning and teaching as multidimensional.

In the context of 21st century global world, which is characterised by an expanding multiculturalism through the constant circulation of ideas and people, the social relations that mediate learning and the production of knowledge cannot be reduced to a singular or normative reference (e.g., an individual, a nation-state, or a bounded cultural group). Now the individuals are considered as a part of collectivities that provide meaning to their lives. School practices and policies are now increasingly interested in addressing some categories of difference, i.e., different categories of identity such as race, caste, class and gendered minority sexuality

(Chattopadhyay, 2015). LGBTQ, queer, and gender-identity issues are not always considered part of multicultural education, as because schools have long seen sexuality as controversial or because "there is still acceptance of homophobia in schools and communities" (Mayo, 2013: 161). In multicultural education, the educational policies are framed to endorse cultural diversity.

In multicultural education, the dynamic and complex processes of cultural construction create an educational reform movement, and a process whose major goal is to change the structure of educational institutions so that male and female students, exceptional students, and students from varied racial, ethnic, language, and cultural groups will have an equal chance for academic achievement in school (Homans, 2020). It is necessary to conceptualise the school as a social system in order to implement multicultural education successfully. It involves changes in the total school or educational environment which is not limited to curricular changes. Thus, it phenomenalises multiculturalism, which refers to the co-existence of diverse religious, ethnic or cultural groups in a society without any domination-subjugation relations.

In a multicultural classroom, "history stands sentinel. It watches us, it covers us, it has the power to taunt and divide us. Only with effort can we make history work in our own interest, make it allow us to build to some degree, a history of our own" (Dilg, 2003: 38). Understanding these ways in which culture and power support or impinge upon teaching and learning can help teachers engage in a more thoughtful approach to curriculum and pedagogy. This becomes inevitable in diaspora culture. The asylum-seekers, refugees, exiles, forced migrants, immigrants, expatriates, guest workers, trading communities, and ethnic communities of various kinds, have come to be described as in diaspora or as tokens of a single diaspora. In the predominantly "white" societies of the European diaspora in the USA, Canada, Australia and New Zealand, that have both practised colonialism and have been shaped by it, populations are inevitably characterised by immense cultural diversity (Anne, 2003). They consist of indigenous people and of the descendants of the Europeans who displaced and dispossessed indigenous people in the colonial adventure. They also consist of waves of migrants from all over the globe, who augmented this population of the European invaders and settlers.

James A. Banks (1992: 35) proposes that multicultural education is necessary to help all the future citizens of a nation to acquire knowledge, attitudes, and skills, which are needed to survive in the 21st century.

Nothing less than the nation's survival is at stake. The rapid change in the national composition of population by the people of colour or caste, the escalating importance of nonwhite nations such as China and Japan, and the widening gap between the rich and the poor make it essential for our future global citizens to have multicultural literacy and cross-cultural skills. In the 21st century, a nation, whose citizens cannot negotiate with the world's multicultural global stage, will be tremendously disadvantaged, and its very survival will be imperiled.

India is a unique land in the whole world for this reason. It is the only land where religion of humanity or *Manab Dharma* has not only been shaped but perfected and practiced before any civilisation came into existence. Apart from it, the religious faiths which came to India from outside though at times tried to accommodate Indian religious faiths yet failed and had to co-exist with indigenous faiths and knowledge and became a part of enlightened Indian culture and civilisation (Sharma, 2002; Chauhan, 2004). Contemporary theories of multicultural society and education offer a poor start for understanding the dynamic flow and complex experience of cultural sustainability as it is actually lived. If we are to succeed in the study of cultural education and sustainability, we must change the academic starting point—to move beyond the particular/universal distinction to an expanded vision that incorporates the complexity of everyday life experience.

Members of minority, ethnic, and indigenous groups continually engage multiple others and in doing so they construct personal narratives that weave elements of their narrower and broader cultural identities in an ongoing process, whether it is formal or informal (Rao et al., 2013). The result is often confident and accepting those individuals, who are agents of cultural groups seeking survival, but at the same time, embody the negation of the idea that culture and identity are fixed and primordial. This process constellates a school, in India, by the dominant form of interactions between teachers and students. Thus, a challenge that multicultural education faces is how to help students from diverse groups mediate between their home and community cultures and the school culture. Students should acquire the knowledge, attitudes, and skills needed to function effectively in each cultural setting. They should also be competent to function within and across other micro-cultures in their society, within the national macro-culture, and within the world community.

The tension between the processes of cultural autonomy and cultural homogenisation is a central dilemma in the information age when anyone concerned with cultural education–educational sustainability must be tackled. The analysis presented here does not refer to the continuing presence of education as a basic feature of societies around the world in the twenty-first century, but to its decisive role in nurturing the construction of resistance identities against the "dominance of market values and the so-called Western culture in the process of globalisation" (Castells, 2010b: xxi). On the contrary educational perspective of imperialist culture may ask: what is the extent of the obligations that the state should impose on "faith-based schools" in order to ensure the sustainability of common public norms that bind all citizens to a common public sphere?

The concept of "communities of practice" enables us to see that individuals do not fashion identity in a vacuum, but within a trajectory as they move within and between communities. School subcultures constitute and are constituted within the web of multiple-communal memberships. The result is a sophisticated understanding of the interaction of the state, national origins of immigrant groups, and the place of educational institutions within minority communal life, all of which enable an understanding of the role schools play in reproduction of educational and social inequalities and their capacity to help or hinder social and political integration.

## 9. Education, Technology and Social Change

Social change, a collective phenomenon, is seldom an orderly procedure. It is a common fact of human life and many people embrace it, equal numbers fear it. As common as social change may be, rebelling against it is also common. The relationship between education and social change can be analyzed from two points of view. Firstly, the position of education and technology as active agents of social change and secondly, its dealing of changes that occur in educational institutions due to the installation of new technology and searches the effects of those accepted changes on other social institutions.

In the nineteenth century, the key argument was made in favour of education that stressed on its civilising impact. The potential power of education was assured to create committed and compliant citizens. Specialised skills were sometimes encouraged and considered as the "end of education" that developed all the "perfection" of which individual is capable of. Then educational institutions and teachers were engaged in transmitting a way of life to the new generation. During those days, education was more a means of social control than an instrument of social change. Following Emile Durkheim (1956: 71-72), education consists of a methodological socialisation of the young generation. It creates in man a new being. For education "individual being" connects with "social being," which denotes the totality of religious beliefs, moral values and practices, national or professional traditions, collective opinions of every kind.

This creative quality is considered as a special prerogative of human education. This social character of education, in promoting skill and efficiency, has often been invoked during the twentieth century. In the context of rising youth unemployment, successive governments have proclaimed the necessity to make education a retainer of the economy. This venture makes educational system to be more scientific. When this scientific knowledge is applied to the problems of life, it becomes technology. It is a product of civilisation.

Albeit different innovations through educational cultivation, technology appears as a foreign invention to deliver changes in society by restructuring environments to which man in turn adapt. "In such an atmosphere technology appears as a strange intrusion" (Ogburn, 1949: 16). Thus, technology makes possible certain human achievement, and anyone can also admit that without those material aids these achievements would not be possible. Here technology, as a form of systematic knowledge, is put into practice and helps to serve human purposes. Education, at the present time, aims at imparting empirical knowledge and has been chiefly instrumental in preparing the way for the development of science and technology.

The term "technology" should be understood in sociology in a much wider sense than the meaning usually attributed to it. Conceptually it does not simply mean machines, tools and scientific instruments; it also implies an appropriate attitude, habits, thoughts and actions. Similar to education, as a complex process, technology brings about changes in the behaviour of social animals. Lewis Mumford (1934: 109-110), in his *Technics and Civilisation,* has used the state of technology as a criterion for the construction of a classification of historical societies. Each of these phases represent "a period of human history" and characterised significantly by the fact what he designates as "a technological complex." It is the nature of real civilisation that denotes the history of technology. "Each phase has its origin in certain definite regions and tends to employ certain special resource and raw materials. Each phase has its specific means of utilising and generating energy."

The technology and education cannot be divorced from their larger social pattern; for it is this pattern that gives them meaning and purpose. Every period of civilisation carries a specific type of education that refuses the insignificant past and cultivates new ones (Chattopadhyay, 2016a). In today's society a highly educated man has become the centre of any resource. Education has brought about phenomenal changes in every aspect of human life. Peter Drucker, (2010: 35) intends that "if an educated man of those days of the first technological revolution—an educated Sumerian, perhaps, or an educated ancient Chinese—looked at us today, he would certainly be totally stumped by our technology. But he would, I am sure, find our existing social and political institutions reasonably familiar. They are, after all, by and large not fundamentally different from the institutions he and his contemporaries first fashioned."

Futurist scholars have provided insight into this process. For example, Daniel Bell (1974) wrote about a new "postindustrial" society, characterised by increased affluence, automation, and too much leisure. Alvin Toffler (1970) wrote about the modern society being in a permanent state of "future shock," that means technological and social change can take place faster than people's ability to adjust to it. William Ophuls (1992) described a "scarcity society," in which depletion of resources leads to a lower standard of living and a strong, authoritarian state that regulates conflicts between groups struggling to share the scarce resources. Although these writers focused on American and European societies, the predictions apply elsewhere. In the end of last century, Asian and African societies and social institutions, including school, have changed greatly by interacting with the outside world through space research, international trade, political associations, terrorist or military activity, cyber communication and education exchanges.

In his *Cities in Evolution,* Patrick Geddes (1915: 60-83) suggests the industrial age as twofold: "Paleotechnic" and "Neotechnic." The paleotechnic era was that of the coal and iron revolution of the eighteenth century and the neotechnic phase was that of electricity at the end of the nineteenth century. The neotechnic era had two strengths. Firstly, it reflected the fundamental trend of a system – endless expansion, continuous adaptation of form but permanent reproduction of substance, along with the prospect of universal participation in the good society, however, unequal it still was. Secondly, based on ideology, it permitted the long-term reinforcement of the state structures, the strategic underpinning of a functioning capitalist world-economy. In geotechnic era "the acolytes of culture assert the intrusion of human agency, as intrinsic possibility, or as source of collective hope" (Wallerstein, 1991: 12).

Accepting Geddes idea and terminology, Mumford added a third phase, preceding and preparatory to these two phases, which he called "eotechnic phase" (Mumford, 1934: 107-150). This phase is characterised by eotechnic economy that had started in the sixteenth century and continued until the end of the eighteenth century. Replacing slavery, eotechnic era used water and wind power to run mills and transportation. The invention of printing press and the clock, destined to exert a great influence on social life. Adopting Mumford's analysis, Guy Rocher (1990[1968]: 162-163) offers the study of Henri Janne, who added two more preceding phases to these three stages: the lithotechnic phase and the anthropotechnic phase. In the lithotechnic era the archaic tools were made out of elementary materials – wood, bone, skin and flint. This phase is characterised by local barter economy with low rate of production and limited exchange. The anthropotechnic era is characterised by slavery based agrarian economy on a vast scale. Business and commerce were initiated and city-states were ruled by the rational urban milieu. Espousing this typology, we can append another one stage that goes after neotechnic phase and characterises by the challenge to the geopolitics and geoculture of the capitalist world-economy and it may be considered as "geotechnic era."

In the neotechnic age, the sources of energy had appeared as a form of fossil fuel, electricity, petroleum, gas and atomic energy. All these sources create waste that affects environment in a harmful manner. In the geotechnic era, the sources of energy are renewable, solar and bio-power. Climate change and global warming are the burning issues of the geotechnic era. Education with technological innovation includes, in this phase, those procedures which are applied to prevent or to mitigate the damage caused by natural calamities, such as avalanches, mud flows, volcanic eruptions, etc. It embraces educational research on the field of soil chemistry, rock mechanics, geophysics and other pure and social sciences.

In geotechnic era, education is used as the deliberate instrument of technological and social change. Here the involvement of education in public life is more obvious than any time before. The geotechnic era is that of the technological revolution, communicating the information/ knowledge with one part of the globe to other. It is that phase to which we have entered from the beginning of the twenty-first century. It is an era that is commonly known as geotechnic, which replaces the Fordist organisation of industrialism and applies the scientific methods, technology and engineering principles to design the problem solving works.

In the geotechnic era, knowledge creating processes are necessarily context-specific, in terms of who participate and how they participate in the process. The context here does not mean "a fixed set of surrounding conditions but a wider dynamical process of which the cognition of an individual is only a part" (Hutchins, 1995: xiii). The context is not a physical setting, nor created in combinations of personnel; rather, it is the people who interacted and created the environment for them. Thus, team work is given priority in the geotechnic era.

The geotechnic era is characterised by work teams, increased effectiveness and efficiency levels of the actors, time for reflection and learning incorporated into work tasks, longer time cycles or work units, and in decentralises the team works on decision-making processes in relation to product quality, production planning, process improvements, and general self-management (Linger and Burstein, 1997). A description of the changing nature of work practices address a fluidity of dynamic environment and its internal needs to adapt to the changing environment. The geotechnic work practices involve workers taking responsibility for analyzing, reflecting, and innovatively changing their work tasks. Trade unions are merely becoming a peripheral voice of geopolitics and geoculture.

In the geotechnic era, the sociology of education as an important scientific discipline, maintains the task that educational institutions perform to create new knowledge and apply that knowledge to all areas of social, cultural and economic life. In this new age a technological paradigm organises a series of technological discoveries around a nucleus and a system of relationships that enhance the performance of each specific technology (Chattopadhyay, 2017b). This paradigm is a conceptual pattern that sets the standards for performance. It integrates innovations into a coherent system of relationships characterised by its synergy; that is, by the added value of the system vis-à-vis its individual components. Thus, this era is characterised by increasingly interconnected processes of auto-centred production within an increasingly clearly defined matrix of reproduction in which the basic economic characters make an inevitable context, where the rich becomes richer and the poor becomes poorer.

The geotechnic era is characterised by social innovations that hold the promise of offering solutions to a range of today's social problems. "Social innovations such as microfinance, fair trade, and emission trading have proven to be impactful instruments for social change" (Choi and Majumdar, 2015: 7). Inducing social change has become the forte of social enterprises and social entrepreneurs. Social entrepreneurs play the role of change agents, and pursue social innovations with the aim of developing and implementing new ideas (products, services and models) to meet social needs using innovation at different stages of the process. In this era, social entrepreneurship is not simply about creating an enterprise; it is about finding novel solutions to social problems (Bornstein, 2004). Here social entrepreneurship pursues opportunities for transformative social change and the acts are characterised by innovation (Roberts and Woods, 2005).

The creation of some new methods and models, for providing products and services to cater to the unsatisfied basic human needs, is the primary goal of this geotechnic era. By being proactive and innovative, it creates better social value, where technology alone does not create the desired social change (Mort et al., 2003). Even technology alone cannot remove poverty, redress injustices, provide a panacea and solve advancement problems. Technology needs to be adapted or made appropriate for the local ecosystem to create the desired social change (Damani and Sardeshpande, 2015: 128). Technology is only a sub-system of society, and the development of society hinges, not only on technology, but also on the other crucial social subsystems like education. Thus, the geotechnic knowledge helps to transform the geopolitics and the shaky world-economy, and expose a lifestyle which is characterised by hypersociability with fear.

Thus, the more important issue in geotechnic age is the possibility that the increased visibility and reach of informal learning practices threatens to deepen the divisions between the informal learning cultures of different groups of young people outside school. "*The challenges educators will face, then, are not those of responding to a single overwhelming flood of new generational practice, but of deciding how to respond to very visible different experiences of learning outside the school setting. This is a very old problem in a new form*" (italics in original, Facer, 2011: 20).

In this geotechnic era the decisions go global in a big way, while being facilitated by government policies of deregulation, risk management and privatisation of service in international scenario would not have been possible without computer networking, telecommunications, and information technology-based transportation systems. The network enterprise became the most productive and efficient form of doing contemporary transactions. While it is true that the internal decentralisation of multinational corporations and networks of firms began in neotechnic era, based on the fax, telephone, and electronic exchange systems, the full networking of segments, the digitalisation of manufacturing, the networked computerisation of services and office work, turned on full-fledgedly from the 1980s onwards on the basis of the new Information and Communication Technology (ICT).

ICT is an umbrella term that includes any communication device or application, encompassing radio, television, cellular phones, computer and network hardware and software, satellite systems and so on, as well as the various services and applications associated with them, such as videoconferencing and distance learning (de Sousa and Monteiro, 2011: 8). The network society of the geotechnic era is "characterised by a pattern of networking, flexibility, the recombination of codes, and ephemeral symbolic communication" (Castells, 2004: 29). Indeed, the "Internet" is itself an important piece of technology. The emergence of this internet as a new resource and communication medium has significantly changed many aspects of society, and, expectedly, it is having a similar impact on education in the geotechnic era.

The internet has become such an integrated part of students' lives that it is as ordinary to them as the television and the telephone were in neotechnic age. The geotechnic era feels quite comfortable with internet usage through mobile handsets. Transactions in every possible form of contexts are made possible between the participants, who are driven by "collective intelligence." It has led to a blurring of national knowledge boundaries leading to a take-off stage of "globalisation of education," with many educational institutions searching for new markets that were previously unobtainable. The geotechnic era is being realised by information technology, and characterised by user participation, openness, and network effects.

The exploitation of contemporary Information and Communication Technologies (ICTs) in the design process of advanced e-learning methods and systems is only one indispensable factor that needs to be addressed, considering that the principle need of students nowadays is the easy and straightforward access to educational material. In addition, the rapid technological revolution and the unceasing invasion of new technologies as a manipulator for the power of penetration render older technologies obsolete after only a short lifetime. Taking this into account, it becomes apparent in the geotechnic age that the cognitive material is affected in numerous ways and that the need to dynamically upgrade it is absolutely necessary in order to be constantly updated and to follow closely the technological innovations.

The emergence of the "Internet" as a new resource and communication medium has significantly changed many aspects of social life, and, expectedly, it is having a similar impact on education. The advancements of this Internet and ICTs affect everyday life in the geotechnic era to a great extent, and, expectedly, education is no exception. The use of educational technology at university and college campuses, or in nursery and primary level has grown and changed substantially in the last decades. The province of computer and other forms of technology are now being used for multiple functions in diverse educational settings. In many universities, the educators use the software available to organise lecture notes and e-mail and electronic forums to communicate students. Inside the classroom, computer projection systems are replacing traditional overhead transparencies and thus making it possible to harness the interactive and visual capabilities of the computer for lecture and group activities.

Web learning (or e-learning) is the result of the advancement of the Internet and the ICTs. It has completely changed education, the delivery of knowledge as well as the role of school of neotechnic era. Web-learning provides the opportunity to the user for distant learning through the Internet with multimedia means such as text, images, audio and video. This advance, combined with the popularity of the Internet among users has led to the exploitation of ICTs by network engineers towards the integration of ICTs and the Internet with traditional teaching-learning methods. This integration has led to what is commonly known as e-learning or web learning. Here the learners can access easily the resources and study wherever they are and at whenever they wish to engage in their studies. Prompt and reliable delivery has guaranteed by "virtual office support," which is also needed to ensure that students' queries and concerns are met as promptly and fully as possible. Students can submit further articles, information and links to the office. Students develop their skills and understandings in uses of ICT.

This usage of new way of life with new method of knowledge culture identifies social change, which refers to the alteration in patterns of social structure, social institutions, social processes, and human behaviour and interaction over time. Social change makes factual the journey of human creations from the lithotechnic era to the anthropotechnic era and then to the eotechnic era, and again to the paleotechnic era, and then to the neotechnic era. This is obviously a journey from archaic tools to electronic tools. Sometimes the stages of this linear social change are overlapping and interwoven to each other. Indeed, the beginning of twenty-first century makes it confirm the existence of new era as geotechnic, where the human is seen as an element directed with stronger forces outside their own power.

## 10. Education, Environment and Globalisation

Globalisation is a process always in a flux. Through this process a cosmopolitan human being is interconnected with his regional counterpart. A bridge between world knowledge and local knowledge was built up from the very beginning of human diaspora. In this journey, man has gradually casted off his integument of tradition and has been flowed in the tide of modernity to post-modernity of cultural settings. The neo-liberal globalisation introduced in the last decade of the 20$^{th}$ century has explored new dimensions in the field of economics. Privatised knowledge as the medium of exchange has strengthened the economic factors. Such an event has never taken place earlier in human history.

It is not surprising that the globalisation of the market and consumer economy, as well as the globalising effect of the Internet and other media, lead to a revival of the idea of a certain kind of cosmopolitanism — namely we are no longer only the citizens of a nation state, but the citizens of the world. A global citizen is a person who can live anywhere, but a signifier of global knowledge (Chattopadhyay, 2012). Here lies the question, why sustainability problems call for an educational response?

Sociological expeditions regarding environmental knowledge, international cultural homogenisation and the global population pressures that outstrip any foreseeable growth in basic commodities or public services are conspiring with other aspects of globalisation to transfer the focus of political philosophy to a world stage on which the fate of individual countries, let alone national minorities, is not in their own hands—a global stage on which a commitment to establish fair terms of cooperation in the survival of diverse ethnic groups may matter to the survival of a civilised way of life in general (Curren, 2010). Educational philosophy must follow, ensemble, and adopt a perspective that is both global and comprehensive in its understanding of the prospects for human well-being.

It has become commonplace to point the globalisation process in the explanation of the changes that reshape our societies on the economic, social, political and cultural dimensions. Large corporations increasingly think of their future in global terms, and governments now meet regularly. In an effort to coordinate a broad agenda of topics of mutual interest, the Public-Private-Partnership model is going to conquest the space of knowledge where the universities are among the engines of globalisation (Chattopadhyay, 2016b). For example, extraordinary proliferation of Canadian support for information technology projects suggests that knowledge or sharing of knowledge is becoming effectively border free (Baggaley, 1999). Returning students are extremely potent force for the internationalisation of campuses in Canada. Having spent time in another culture, they recognize differences that are salient to the education of other Canadian students who chose not to travel yet need to increase their intercultural knowledge.

In contemporary globalised world, education is one of the most crucial and critical resources for acquiring skills and capabilities needed to function in competitive capitalist job markets. Global capitalism and its disequalising dynamics reflect major structural imbalances in the distribution of global resources. 1990s saw the development of a culture of adult education in form of "lifelong education" as a key objective of governments concerned with balancing issues of economic development and competition in global markets. Moreover, in the developed countries this objective accelerates the method of "re-skilling." In the Southern countries the professionals and skilled individuals are seeking skills and educational credentials through adult education and communication technologies to enhance their employability in developed or high-income countries, thus causing brain drain and underdevelopment in their home countries (Shizha and Abdi, 2009).

In recent years they have moved toward a consensus that takes nature seriously. As opposed to prior weakness to part off the natural world from the recognised separate social world, analysts are struggling to create more useful ontologies and epistemologies for analyzing what has differently been termed "nature-culture," "hybrid objects," "quasi-objects", "cyborgs", or, most usefully, "socionature" (Latour, 1993). All of these theoretical interventions are attempts to close the "great divide" between society and nature that two decades ago William Catton and Riley Dunlap (1978) dubbed as "human exemptionalism paradigm."

According to Durkheimian tradition, *nature* is a social and cultural construction, and natural objects are made to embody social subjects. Australian Aborigines adopted almost any animal, plant or thing, but there was certain logic in their choice of an element of their material and biotic environment. The relationship with the natural world represented by totemism was nothing other than a projection and representation of the clan itself. Durkheim's (1976) analyses of totemic practices exemplify this approach. In totemic societies, social identity is concentrated in clans, typically individuals related to each other by sharing a common ancestor through male or female lineages. Typically, each clan claims a separate species of animal or plant or more rarely rocks, stars, planets and so as the ancestor from whom the clan descends (Franklin, 2002: 25). The social logic of kinship was drawn on to establish links between the key subjects, clans and species. Just as clan members are bound to support and protect one another so such a relationship was incurred between human clans and natural species.

Clan education, as basic forms of language, knowledge and culture thus undoubtedly emerged as distinctive adaptive traits of early human social cooperation (Chattopadhyay, 2014c). With the advent of industrial capitalism, certain kinds of formal and institutional educational processes, such as the teaching of an ethic of competitive individualism, may be adaptive in relation to the economic foundations of a capitalist nation, but not in relation to a self-sufficient community or, ultimately, in relation to the well-being of the Earth's biosphere. To establish environmental justice, the educators, activists, scholars, and independent researchers have strongly criticised the racial discrimination in environmental policy-making and enforcement of regulations for the destruction of environment in the name of development and empowerment. To wipe off environmental racism, higher education's initial focus is on the training in environmental protection (Sharpe, 1995). Increasing numbers of Environmental Information Systems (EIS) are being assembled worldwide for the purpose of monitoring and managing watersheds, bioregions, and other ecosystems.

As the second decade of the 21st century unfolds, the major issues in higher education, though perennial to some extent, now possess a radically different dimension due to the new context of global pandemic. This necessitates genuinely innovative approaches both to reflect and co-operate modalities by policy-makers, by the academic community and by society at large. The advent of the "Knowledge Society in a Virtual Level" has affected the development agenda of every nation in multiple ways. Consequently, there is serious pressure on each country to ensure the state's responsibility to support higher education institutions so that they may effectively respond to the escalating pace of social change. In a world where education has become borderless, countries must learn to operate in dual mode because national issues assume global ramifications.

Higher education develops and nurtures values. With the demise of value-oriented programmes such as the National Social Service, National Cadet Corps, and other extension activities universities are no longer concerned with social issues. It is important that special efforts are made to preserve and promote values such as thirst for knowledge, critical thinking, search for truth, and more importantly to inculcate universal human values such as peace, tolerance, nonviolence, love, patriotism, and social welfare through education. These values may, in the final analysis, reflect the true quality of our higher education. The inculcation of these values is perhaps more important in the era of globalisation, when national and traditional values are being rapidly replaced by global, and most prominently Western and market-oriented values (Sidhu, 2006). These are the educational and human values that are marked by the culture of universities. Here a university stands for humanism, for tolerance, for reason, for the adventure of ideas and for the search of truth. It stands for the onward march of the human race towards even higher objectives.

Globalisation is itself a complex force that affects all aspects of our global and national education systems. On one hand is the pull towards cooperation, social cohesion, social harmony, transparency, equity and encouragement to greater numbers to participate in higher education. On the other hand are the financial issues, the neo-liberal agenda, which call for competition, free trade, the dominance of the market. The flows of change move first in one direction, then in another: equity, inequality; convergence, divergence; change, non-change; inclusion, exclusion; the global, the local (Chaput, 2008). The recognition that higher education reforms are necessarily intertwined with the effects of globalisation may enable us to understand more clearly the knowledge education systems and their relationship to society as a whole. Without that the humanitarian global value of development becomes a rhetorical discourse. De-humanisation and exploitation befall a harsh reality, where man cannot turn into the starter and end product of development.

# References


Abbott, P., Wallace, C. and Tyler, M. (2005). *An Introduction to Sociology: Feminist Perspectives.* New York: Routledge.

Abdi, A. A., and Cleghorn, A. (2005). "Sociology of Education: Theoretical and Conceptual Perspectives," in Ali A. Abdi and Ailie Cleghorn (eds.), *Issues in African Education: Sociological Perspectives.* New York: Palgrave Macmillan Ltd. Pp. 3-23.

Abes, E. S., and Kasch, D. (2007). "Using queer theory to explore lesbian college students' multiple dimensions of identity," in *Journal of College Student Development*, 48(6): 619–636.

Adorno, T. W. (2000). *Introduction to Sociology.* Stanford: Stanford University Press.

Adorno, T. W., Frenkel-Brunswik, E., Levinson, Daniel J., and Sanford, R. N. (1950). *The Authoritarian Personality.* New York: Harper and Brothers.

Agger, B. (1979). *Western Marxism: An Introduction.* Santa Monica, Calif: Goodyear Pub. Co.

Agnaou, F. (2004). *Gender, Literacy, and Empowerment in Morocco.* New York: Routledge.

Aigrain, P. (2012). *Sharing: Culture and the Economy in the Internet Age.* Amsterdam: Amsterdam University Press.

Alexander, J. C. (1990). "Analytic Debates: Understanding the Relative Autonomy of Culture," in Jeffrey C. Alexander and Steven Seidman (eds.), *Culture and Society.* Cambridge: Cambridge University Press.

Alexander, R. (2008). *Education for All: The Quality Imperative and the Problem of Pedagogy*. London: CREATE.

Alon, S. (2009). "The Evolution of Class Inequality in Higher Education: Competition, Exclusion, and Adaptation," in *American Sociological Review,* 74 (5): 731–755.

Althusser, L. (2006). *Philosophy of the Encounter: Later Writings, 1978-87*. London: Verso.

Amenta, E. (2006). *When Movements Matter: The Townsend Plan and the Rise of Social Security*. Princeton, NJ: Princeton University Press.

Andersen, J., and Siim, B. (2004). "Introduction," in John Andersen and Birte Siim (eds.), *The Politics of Inclusion and Empowerment: Gender, Class and Citizenship.* New York: Palgrave Macmillan Ltd.

Anderson, B. (1991). *Imagined Communities.* London: Verso.

Andriyivna, K. I. (2014). "Role of Frebel course in formation of professional training for pre-school teachers in western Ukraine (last third of the XIX early XX centuries)," in *European Science Review,* 11(12): 42-44.

Angell, R. C. (1928). *The Campus: A Study of Contemporary Undergraduate Life in the American University.* New York: D. Appleton and Company.

Anne, H. H. (2003). "Multicultural Education and the Postcolonial Turn," in *Policy Futures in Education,* 1(2): 381-401.

Anyon, J. (2011). *Marx and Education.* New York: Routledge.

Apple, M. W. (1980). "Curricular form and the Logic of Technical Control," in Len Barton, Roland Meighan and Stephan Walker (eds.), *Schooling, Ideology and the Curriculum*. Lewes: The Falmer Press. Pp. 11-27.

———. (1982). *Education and Power*. London: Routledge.

———. (1996). "Power, Meaning and Identity: Critical Sociology of Education in the United States," in *British Journal of Sociology of Education,* 17(2): 125–44.

———. (2006). *Educating the 'Right' Way: Markets, Standards, God, and Inequality.* New York: Routledge.

Arce-Trigatti, P., Chukhray, I., and López-Turley, R. N. (2018). "Research–Practice Partnerships in Education," in Barbara Schneider (ed.), *Handbook of the Sociology of Education in the 21st Century.* New York: Springer International Publishing. Pp. 561–580.

Archer, M. S. (1995). *Realist Social Theory: The Morphogenetic Approach.* Cambridge: Cambridge University Press.

Arnold, M., et al. (1994). *Culture and Anarchy.* New Haven: Yale University Press.

Arnot, M. (2006). "Retrieving the Ideological Past: Critical Sociology, Gender Theory, and the School Curriculum," in Lois Weis, et al. (eds.), *Ideology, Curriculum, and the New Sociology of Education: Revisiting the Work of Michael Apple.* New York: Routledge. Pp. 17-36.

Aronowitz, S., and DiFazio, W. (1994). *The Jobless Future.* London: University of Minnesota Press.

Arum, R. (2003). *Judging School Discipline: The Crisis of Moral Authority.* Cambridge: Harvard University Press.

Arum, R., et al. (2015). "Introduction," in Richard Arum, Irenee R. Beattie, Karly S. Ford, (eds.), (2015). *The Structure of Schooling: Readings in the Sociology of Education.* New Delhi: Sage Publications India Pvt. Ltd. Pp. xi–xx.

Aslan, C. (2020). "An Analysis on the Development of Sociology of Education in USA and England," in *African Educational Research Journal,* 8(2): S186–S195.

Assie-Lumumba, N'dri T. (2011). *Cyberspace, Distance Learning, and Higher Education in Developing Countries: Old and Emergent Issues of Access, Pedagogy, and Knowledge Production*. Boston: Brill.

Atkinson, P. (1985). *Language, Structure and Reproduction: An Introduction to the Sociology of Basil Bernstein.* London: Methuen & Co. Ltd.

Baggaley, J. (1999). "The Impact of Information Technology on National and Transnational Education," in Sheryl Bond and Jean-Pierre Lemasson (eds.), *A New World of Knowledge: Canadian Universities and Globalisation.* Ottawa, Canada: International Development Research Centre. Pp. 183-200.

Ball, S. J. (1981). "The Sociology of Education in Developing Countries," in *British Journal of Sociology of Education,* 2(3): 301–313.

Ball, S. J. (2004a). "The Sociology of Education: A Disputational Account," in Stephen Ball (ed.), *The RoutledgeFalmer Reader in Sociology of Education.* London: RoutledgeFalmer. Pp. 1-12.

———. (2004b). "Performativities and Fabrications in the Education Economy: Towards the Performative Society," in Stephen J. Ball (ed.), *The RoutledgeFalmer Reader in Sociology of Education.* NewYork: RoudedgeFalmer. Pp. 143–55.

Ballantine, J. H. (2001). *The Sociology of Education: A Systematic Analysis.* Englewood Cliffs, NJ: Prentice-Hall, Inc.

Ballantine, J. H., and Spade, J. Z. (2012). "Introduction," in Jeanne H. Ballantine and Joan Z. Spade (eds.), *Schools and Society: A Sociological Approach to Education.* Thousand Oaks, California : Pine Forge Press. Pp. 1-7.

Banks, J. A. (1972). *The Sociology of Social Movements.* London: The Macmillian Company Ltd.

———. (1992). "Multicultural Education: Nature, Challenges, and Opportunities," in Carlos Diaz, (ed.), *Multicultural Education for the 21st Century.* Washington, DC: NEA Professional Library. Pp. 23-37.

Banks, O. (1971). *The Sociology of Education.* London: B.T. Batsford Ltd.

Barcan, A. (1993). *Sociological Theory and Educational Reality: Education and Society in Australia since 1949.* Kensington: University of New South Wales.

Barker, C. (2013). "Class Struggle and Social Movements," in Colin Barker, Laurence Cox, John Krinsky, and Alf Gunvald Nilsen (eds), *Marxism and Social Movements.* Boston: Brill. Pp. 41–62.

Barrett, B. D. (2012). "Knowledge, Pedagogy and Society: International Perspectives on Basil Bernstein's Sociology of Education," in *International Studies in Sociology of Education,* 22(1): 73–80.

Barton, L., and Corbett, J. (2002). *Inclusive Education: Difficulties and Possibilities,* London: University of London.

Bateman, M. (2010). *Why Doesn't Microfinance Work: The Destructive Rise of Local Neoliberalism.* London: Zed Books.

Bates, R. (1980). "New Developments in the New Sociology of Education," in *British Journal of Sociology of Education,* 1(1): 67-79.

Bautier, E. (2011). "The Analysis of Pedagogic Discourse as a Means of Understanding Social Inequalities in Schools," in Daniel Frandji and Philippe Vitale, (eds.), *Knowledge, Pedagogy and Society: International Perspectives on Basil Bernstein's Sociology of Education*. New York: Routledge. Pp. 108-125.

Beasley, C. (2005). *Gender & Sexuality: Critical Theories, Critical Thinkers*. London: Sage Publications.

Becker, H. S. (1973). *Outsiders: Studies in the Sociology of Deviance.* New Glencoe, Illinois: The Free Press.

Beckett, A. E., Bagguley, P., and Campbell, T. (2016). "Foucault, Social Movements and Heterotopic Horizons: Rupturing the Order of Things," in *Social Movement Studies*, 16(2): 169–181.

Bell, D. (1974). *The Coming of Post-Industrial Society*. London: Harper Colophon Books.

Belsey, C. (1980). *Critical Practice.* New York: Methuen.

Bendix, R., and Roth, G. (1971). *Scholarship and Partnership: Essays on Max Weber.* Berkeley, CA: University of California Press.

Bennett, A. (2005). *Culture and Everyday Life.* New Delhi: Sage Publications India Pvt. Ltd.

Bergquist, W. (1995). *Quality Through Access/Access with Quality.* San Francisco: Jossey-Bass.

Berkowitz, W. (1988). *Social Structures: A Network Approach.* London: Jai Press Inc.

Bernstein, B. (1961). "Social Class and Linguistic Development: A Theory of Social Learning," in A. H. Halsey, Jean Esther Floud and C Arnold Anderson, (eds.), *Education, Economy, and Society: A Reader in the Sociology of Education.* New York: The Free Press. Pp. 288–314.

———. (1971). "On the Classification and Framing of Educational Knowledge," in M. Young (ed.), *Knowledge and Control.* London: Collier-Macmillan. Pp. 47-69.

———. (1973). *Class, Codes and Control. Vol. II, Applied Studies Towards a Sociology of Language.* London: Routledge and Kegan Paul.

———. (1990). *Class, Codes and Control, Volume- IV: The Structuring of Pedagogic Discourse*. London: Routledge.

———. (1996). *Pedagogy, Symbolic Control and Identity: Theory, Research, Critique.* London: Taylor & Francis.

Bernstein, R. J. (1971). *Praxis and Action: Contemporary Philosophies of Human Activity*. Philadelphia: University of Pennsylvania Press.

Bhushan, V., and Sachdeva, D. R. (2012). *Fundamentals of Sociology.* Delhi: Pearson Education.

Bidwell, C. E. (1979). "The Sociology of the School and Classroom," paper presented at *American Sociological Association* meetings, Boston, August.

Bilton, T., Bonnett, K. et al. (1996). *Introductory Sociology.* London-Macmillan Press Ltd.

Birden, S. (2003). "Critical and Postmodern Challenges for Education," in Lisa M. Baumgartner, et al. (eds.), *Adult Learning Theory: A Primer.* Columbus: Center on Education and Training for Employment, The Ohio State University. Pp. 29-33.

Blackedge, D., and Hunt, B. (1985). *Sociological Interpretations of Education.* London, New Hampshire: Croom Helm.

Blackmore, J. (2010). "Educational Organisations and Gender in Times of Uncertainty," in Michael W. Apple, Stephen J. Ball and Luis Armando Gandin, (eds.), *The Routledge International Handbook of the Sociology of Education.* New York: Routledge. Pp. 306-317.

Bleiker, R. (2005). "Seattle and the Struggle for a Global Democratic Ethos," in Catherine Eschle and Bice Maiguashca (eds.), *Critical Theories, International Relations and 'the Anti-Globalisation Movement': The Politics of Global Resistance.* London: Routledge. Pp. 195-211.

Bloland, H. (1995). "Postmodernism and Higher Education," in *The Journal of Higher Education*, 66(5): 521-559.

Blumer, H. (1951). "Collective behavior," in Alfred McClung Lee (ed.), *Principles of Sociology*. New York: Barnes & Noble. Pp. 199–212.

———. (1969). "Social Movements," in Barry McLaughlin (ed.), *Studies in Social Movements: A Social Psychological Perspective*. New York: The Free Press. Pp. 8–29.

Boocock, S. S. (1973). "The School as a Social Environment for Learning: Social Organisation and Micro-Social Process in Education," in *Sociology of Education*, 46(1): 15–50.

Bornstein, D. (2004). *How to Change the World: Social Entrepreneurs and the Power of New Ideas*. Oxford: Oxford University Press.

Bourdieu, P. (1967). "Systems of Education and Systems of Thought," in *International Social Science Journal*, 19(3): 338-358.

———. (1973). "Cultural Reproduction and Social Reproduction," in Richard Brown (ed.), *Knowledge, Education, and Cultural Change*. London: Tavistock Publications. Pp. 71-84.

———. (1974). "The School as a Conservative Force: Scholastic and Cultural Inequalities," in John Eggleston (ed.), *Contemporary Research in the Sociology of Education*, London: Methuen. Pp. 32-46.

———. (1977). *Outline of a Theory of Practice*. Cambridge and New York: Cambridge University Press.

———. (1980). *The Logic of Practice*, (Translated by Richard Nice). Stanford, Calif.: Stanford University Press.

———. (1984[1979]). *Distinction: A Social Critique of the Judgment of Taste* (trans. by R. Nice). Cambridge, Mass.: Harvard University Press.

———. (2004). "The Forms of Capital," in S. J. Ball (ed.), *The RoutledgeFalmer Reader in Sociology of Education*. London, UK: RoutledgeFalmer. Pp. 15–29.

Bourdieu, P., and Passeron, J. C. (1979). *The Inheritors: French Students and Their Relation to Culture*. Chicago: University of Chicago Press.

———. (1990[1977]). *Reproduction in Education, Society and Culture*. London: Sage Publications Ltd.

Bowles, S., and Gintis, H. (1976). *Schooling in Capitalist America: Educational Reform and the Contradictions of Economic Life*. New York: Basic Books.

Bredo, E., and Feinberg, W. (1982). "Introduction: Competing Modes of Social and Educational Research," in Eric Bredo and Walter Feinberg (eds.), *Knowledge and Values in Social and Educational Research*. Philadelphia: Temple University Press. Pp. 3-11.

Breuing, M. (2011). "Problematizing Critical Pedagogy," in *International Journal of Critical Pedagogy*, Vol. 3 (3). Pp. 2-23.

Britzman, D. (1995). "Is There a Queer Pedagogy? Or, Stop Reading Straight," in *Educational Theory*, 45(2): 151-165.

Brom, L., and Selznick, P. (1963). *Sociology*. New York: Harper & Row Publishers.

Brookover, W. B., and Erickson, E. L. (1975). *Sociology of Education.* Homewood, Ill: Dorsey Press.

Broom, M., and Klein, D. (1999). *Power: The Infinite Game.* Monterey, California: Sea Otter Press.

Brown, F. J. (1954). *Educational Sociology.* New York: Prentice-Hall, Inc.

Brown, H. C. (1893). *Froebel and Education by Self-Activity.* New York: Charles Scribner's Sons.

Browne, C., and Mills, C. (2001). "Theoretical Frameworks: Ecological Model, Strengths Perspective, and Empowerment Theory," in R. Fong & S. B. C. L. Furuto (eds.), *Culturally Competent Practice: Skills, Interventions, and Evaluations.* Needham Heights, MA: Allyn and Bacon. Pp. 10–32.

Burgess, R. G. (1985). *Education, Schools and Schooling.* London: Macmillan Education.

Burkhead, J. (1967). *Input and Output in Large-city High Schools.* Syracuse, N.Y.: Syracuse University Press.

Butler, J. (1990). *Gender Trouble: Feminism and the Subversion of Identity.* London: Routledge.

Calhoun, C. (1993). "New Social Movements of the Early 19th Century," in *Social Science Journal,* 17(3): 385–427.

Cameron, W. B. (1966). *Modern Social Movements: A Sociological Outline.* New York: Random House.

Card, B. Y. (1976). "A State of Sociology of Education in Canada: A Further Look," in *Canadian Journal of Education,* 1(4): 3–32.

Castells, M. (2004). *The Network Society: A Cross Cultural Perspective.* Massachusetts: Edward Elgar Publishing, Inc.

———. (2010a). *The Information Age: Economy Society and Culture, Volume I: The Rise of the Network Society.* Oxford: Blackwell Publishing Ltd.

———. (2010b). *The Information Age: Economy Society and Culture, Volume II: The Power of Identity.* Oxford: Blackwell Publishing Ltd.

———. (2010c). *The Information Age: Economy Society and Culture, Volume III: End of Millennium.* Oxford: Blackwell Publishing Ltd.

Catton, W. R., Jr., and Dunlap, R. E. (1978). "Environmental Sociology: A New Paradigm," in *The American Sociologist,* 13(1): 41–49.

Chaput, C. (2008). *Inside the Teaching Machine: Rhetoric and the Globalisation of the U.S. Public Research University Rhetoric Culture and Social Critique.* Tuscaloosa: The University of Alabama Press.

Chattopadhyay, K. (2012). "Environment and Sociology: A Conceptual Framework," in *Edulight,* 1(2): 115-122.

———. (2013). "Understanding Everyday Life: A Sociological Construct," in *Edulight,* 2(3): 209-223.

———. (2014a). "Inclusive Schooling and Children with Special Needs: The Sociology of Leisure Education," in *Journal of Educational Thoughts,* 1(1): 257-264.

———. (2014b). *The Sociology of Family Life.* Kolkata: Books Way.

Chattopadhyay, K. (2014c). "Tribal Life in the Era of Globalisation: A Socio-Educational Outlook," in *Journal of Knowledge,* 2(5): 175-188.

———. (2015). "Queer Theory, Higher Education and Social Change: A Sociological Interpretation," in Ajit Mondal and Jayanta Mete (eds.), *Higher Education: Emerging Issues and Concerns.* New Delhi: APH. Publishing Corporations. Pp. 221-239.

———. (2016a). "Globalizing Perspective of Tribal Life: A Sociological Understanding," in V. P. Sharma, P. K. Bhowmick, and P. C. Coomar (eds.), *Globalisation: The Missing Roads of Tribals.* Delhi: Kalpaz Publications. Pp. 43-48.

———. (2016b). "Cultural Globalisation in Twenty-First Century: A Marxist Interpretation," in *Shinjan,* 2(3): 19-36.

———. (2017a). "New Class Relations in Education: Sociology of Pedagogy Today," in *Journal for Educational Reserch Perspective*, Special issue, pp. 97-106.

———. (2017b). "Education, Technology and Social Change," in Rajib Saha and Jayanta Mete (eds.), *ICT in Education: A 21st Century Phenomenon.* New Delhi: APH Publishing Corporation. Pp. 1-11.

———. (2018). "Culture and Education," in Ajit Mondal and M. Narula, (eds.), *Education in Emerging India.* New Delhi: Atlantic Publishers. Pp. 306-397.

Chauhan, C. P. S. (2004). *Modern Indian Education: Policies, Progress and Problems.* New Delhi: Kanishka Publishers, Distributors.

Choi, N. and Majumdar, S. (2015). "Social Innovation: Towards a Conceptualisation," in Satyajit Majumdar, Samapti Guha, Nadiya Marakkath, (eds.), *Technology and Innovation for Social Change*. New Delhi: Springer. Pp. 7-34.

Cheater, A. (1999). *The Anthropology of Power: Empowerment and Disempowerment in Changing Structure.* London: Routledge.

Clark, B. R. (1964). "Sociology of Education," in Robert E. L. Faris (ed.), *Handbook of Modern Sociology.* Chicago: Rand-McNally. Pp. 734-769.

Cockburn, C. (1991). *In the Way of Women: Men's Resistance to Sex Equality in Organisations.* London: Macmillan.

Coleman, J. (1968). "The Concept of Equality of Educational Opportunity," in *Harvard Educational Review,* 38(1): 7-22.

Coleman, J., and Hoffer, T. (1987). *Public and Private High Schools: The Impact of Communities.* New York: Basic Books.

Collins, R. (1971). "Functional and Conflict Theories of Educational Stratification," in *American Sociological Review,* 36(6): 1002-1019.

———. (1979). *The Credential Society: An Historical Sociology of Education and Stratification.* New York: Academic Press.

Conant, J. B. (1963). *The Education of American Teachers.* New York: McGraw-Hill.

Connell, R. W., Ashenden, D.; Kessler, S. and Dowsett, G. (1982). *Making the Difference: Schools, Families and Social Division*. Sydney: Allen & Unwin.

Connerton, P. (1980). *The Tragedy of Enlightenment: An Essay on the Frankfurt School.* Cambridge: Cambridge University Press.

Convertino, C., Levinson, B. A. and González, N. (2013). "Culture, Teaching and Learning," in James A. Banks, Cherry A. McGee Banks, (eds.), *Multicultural Education: Issues and Perspectives*. NY: John Wiley & Sons, Inc. Pp. 25-41.

Corbett, J. (2001). *Supporting Inclusive Education: A Connective Pedagogy*. London: Routledge Falmer.

Corwin, R. G. (1965). *A Sociology of Education*. New York: Appleton-Century-Crofts.

———. (1977). *Perspectives on Organisations: The School as a Social Organisation*. Washington: American Association of Colleges for Teacher Education.

———. (1987). *The Organisation-Society Nexus: A Critical Review of Models and Metaphors*. New York: Greenwood Press.

Cox, M., and Paley, B. (1997). "Families as Systems," in *Annual Review of Psychology*, 48(1): 243–267.

Craib, I. (1998). *Experiencing Identity*. New Delhi: Sage Publications India Pvt. Ltd.

Crompton, R. (2008). *Class and Stratification*. Cambridge, United Kingdom: Polity.

Crossley, N. (2002). *Making Sense of Social Movements*. Buckingham: Open University Press.

Crowder, J., and Shaw, M. (1997). "Social Movements and the Education of Desire," in *Community Development Journal*, 32(3): 266-279.

Curren, R. (2010). "Education for Global Citizenship and Survival," in Yvonne Raley and Gerhard Preyer (eds.), *Philosophy of Education in the Era of Globalisation*. London: Routledge. Pp. 67-87.

Dahrendorf, R. (1958). "Out of Utopia: Toward a Reorientation of Sociology Analysis," in *American Journal of Sociology*, 64(2):115-127.

———. (1959). *Class and Class Conflict in Industrial Society*. Stanford, Calif: Standford University Press.

Damani, B., and Sardeshpande, V. (2015). "Social Change Using Innovation and Technology," in Satyajit Majumdar, Samapti Guha, Nadiya Marakkath, (eds.), *Technology and Innovation for Social Change*. New Delhi: Springer. Pp. 125-142.

Dasgupta, K. (2015). *Introducing Social Stratification: The Causes and Consequences of Inequality*. Boulder, CO: Lynne Rienner Publishers.

Dasgupta, R. K. (2011). "Queer Sexuality: A Cultural Narrative of India's Historical Archive," in *Rupkatha Journal on Interdisciplinary Studies in Humanities*, 3(4): 651-670.

Darvin, R., and Norton, B. (2014). "Social Class, Identity, and Migrant Students," in *Journal of Language, Identity & Education*, 13(2): 111-117.

David, H. (2000). *Microfinance: A Reader*. London: Routledge.

Davis, J. A. (1966). "The Campus as a Frog Pond: An Application of the Theory of Relative Deprivation to Career Decisions of College Men," in *American Journal of Sociology*, 72(1): 17-31.

Davis, K. (1949). *Human Society*. New York: The Macmillan Company.

Davis, K., and Moore, W. E. (1945). "Some Principles of Stratification," in *American Sociological Review*, 10 (April): 242–249.

Dawe, A. (1970). "The Two Sociologies," in *The British Journal of Sociology,* 21(2): 207-218.

de Sousa, F. C., and Monteiro, I. P. (2011). "A Benchmarking Study on Organisational Creativity Practices in High Technology Industries," in Anabela Mesquita (ed.), *Technology for Creativity and Innovation: Tools, Techniques and Applications.* New York: Information Science Reference. Pp. 1-25.

Delaura, D. J. (1973). *Matthew Arnold: A Collection of Critical Essays.* Englewood Cliffs, N.J.: Prentice-Hall, Inc.

della Porta, D., and Diani, M. (2006). *Social Movements: An Introduction* (2nd Ed). Malden, MA: Blackwell Publishing.

Dewey, J. (1959). *Dewey on Education: Selections,* (With an introduction and notes by Martin S. Dworkin). New York: Teachers College Press.

———. (1997[1938]). *Experience and Education.* New York: Simon & Schuster.

———. (2004[1915]). *Democracy and Education: An Introduction to the Philosophy of Education.* New Delhi: Aakar Publication.

Dilg, M. (2003). *Thriving in the Multicultural Classroom: Principles and Practices for Effective Teaching.* New York: Teachers College.

DiMaggio, P. J., and Powell, W. W. (1991). *The New Institutionalism in Organisational Analysis.* Chicago: University of Chicago Press.

Dimmock, C., and Walker, A. (2005). *Educational Leadership: Culture and Diversity.* New Delhi: Sage Publications India Pvt. Ltd.

DiPaola, M., and Hoy, W. (2008). *Principals Improving Instruction: Supervision, Evaluation, and Professional Development.* Boston, MA: Pearson.

Dore, R. J. (1976). *The Diploma Disease: Education, Qualifications and Development.* London: Allen and Unwin.

Douglas, J. D. (1970). "Understanding Everyday Life," in Jack D. Douglas (ed.), (1970). *Understanding Everyday Life: Toward the Reconstruction of Sociological Knowledge.* Chicago: Aldine Publishing Company. Pp. 3-44.

Douglas, J. W. B. (1967). *The Home and the School.* London: Panther.

Drucker, P. (2010). *The Drucker Lectures: Essential Lessons on Management, Society and Economy.* New York: McGraw-Hill.

Dumont, L. (1970). *Homo Hierarchicus: The Caste System and its Implications.* New Delhi: Oxford University Press, Inc.

Durkheim, É. (1956[1922]). *Education and Sociology,* (Translated by S. D. Fox). Chicago: The Free Press.

———. (1961[1925]). *Moral Education: A Study in the Theory and Application of the Sociology of Education*, (Translated by E. K. Wilson and H. Schurer). New York: The Free Press.

———. (1974 [1914]). "The dualism of human nature and its social conditions," in R. N. Bellah (ed.), *Emile Durkheim on Morality and Society*. Chicago: University of Chicago Press.

———. (1976). *The Elementary Structures of the Religious Life*. London: George Allen & Unwin.

Durkheim, É. (1977[1938]). *The Evolution of Educational Thought: Lectures on the Formation and Development of Secondary Education in France*. London: Routledge.

Ebert, E. S., and Culyer, R. C. (2011). *School: An Introduction.* Belmont, CA: Wadsworth, Cengage Learning.

Edwards, G. (2004). "Habermas and Social Movements: What's 'New'?" in *The Sociological Review,* 52(s1): 113–130.

Elliott, B. (1980). "Manuel Castells and the New Urban Sociology," in *British Journal of Sociology,* 31(1): 151–158.

Elliott, C. (2008). *Global Empowerment of Women Responses to Globalisation and Politicized Religions Routledge Research in Gender and Society.* New York: Routledge.

Ellwood, C. A. (1911). "The Sociological Basis of the Science of Education," in *Education,* 32(3): 133-140.

———. (1914). *Sociology in Its Psychological Aspects.* New York: D. Appleton and Company.

———. (1927). "What is Educational Sociology?" in *Journal of Educational Sociology,* 1(1): 25-30.

Engels, F. (1970[1884]). *The Origins of the Family, Private Property and the State.* New York: Int. Publishers.

———. (1958 [1845]). *The Condition of Working Class in England.* Stanford: Stanford University Press.

———. (1925[1847]). *Principles of Communism.* Chicago: The Daily Worker Publishing Co.

Etzioni, A. (1995). *Modern Organisations.* New Delhi: Prentice-Hall of India Pvt. Ltd.

Facer, K. (2011). *Learning Futures Education, Technology and Social Change.* New York: Routledge.

Farrell, M. (2004). *Inclusion at the Crossroads: Special Education - Concepts and Values.* London: David Fulton Publishers Ltd.

Farrell, P. (2001). "Special Education in the Last Twenty Years: Have Things Really Got Better?" in *British Journal of Special Education,* 28(1): 3–9.

Felski, R. (2000). *Doing Time: Feminist Theory and Postmodern Culture.* New York: New York University Press.

Ferguson, I., and Smith, L. (2012). "Education for Change: Student Placements in Campaigning Organisations and Social Movements in South Africa," in *The British Journal of Social Work*, 42(5): 974–994.

Ferree, M. M., and Mueller, C. (2004). "Feminism and the Women's Movement: A Global Perspective," in David A. Snow, Sarah A. Soule, and Hanspeter Kriesi (eds.), *The Blackwell Companion to Social Movements*. New York: Blackwell. Pp. 576–607.

Flores-Gonza´lez, N. (2002). *School Kids/Street Kids: Identity Development in Latino Students.* New York: Teachers College Press.

Foucault, M. (1974a). "Human nature: Justice versus power," in A. J. Ayer and Fons Elders (eds.), *Reflexive Water: The Basic Concerns of Mankind*. London: Souvenir Press. Pp. 133-197.

———. (1974b). *The Archaeology of Knowledge.* London: Tavistock Publications.

———. (1980). *Power/Knowledge: Selected Interviews and Other Writings 1972–1977* (Edited by Colin Gordon; Translated by Colin Gordon, Leo Marshall, John Mepham, Kate Soper). New York: Pantheon Books.

———. (1981[1976]). *The History of Sexuality: An Introduction.* New York: Pantheon Books.

———. (1984). *The History of Sexuality: An Introduction.* Harmondsworth: Penguin.

———. (1986[1975]). *Discipline and Punish: The Birth of the Prison.* New York: Vintage Books.

———. (1986[1984]). *The Care of Self.* New York: Pantheon Books.

———. (1990[1984]). *The Use of Pleasure.* New York: Vintage Books.

Fowler, H. W. (1965). *A Dictionary of Modern English Usage,* 2nd ed., revised by Sir Ernest Gower. Oxford: Clarendon Press.

Franklin, A. (2002). *Nature and Social Theory.* New Delhi: Sage Publications India Pvt. Ltd.

Freire, P. (1985). *The Politics of Education: Culture, Power, and Liberation.* Connecticut: Bergin & Garvey.

———. (2005[1970]). *Pedagogy of the Oppressed.* New York: The Continuum International Publishing Group Inc.

Fuller, B., and Hannum, E. (2004). "Introduction: Inequality Across Societies," in David Baker, Bruce Fuller, Emily Hannum, Regina Werum (eds.), *Inequality Across Societies: Famllies, Schools, and Persisting Stratification.* Oxford: Elsevier Ltd. Pp. 1-6.

Garfinkel, H. (1967). *Studies in Ethnomethodology.* Englewood Cliffs, NJ: The Prentice-Hall, Inc.

Geddes, P. (1915). *Cities in Evolution: An Introduction to the Town Planning Movement and to the Study of Civics.* London: Williams and Norgate.

Gerth, H., and Mills, C. (1948). *From Max Weber.* London: Kegan Paul.

Ghurye, G. S. (1961). *Caste, Class and Occupation.* Bombay: Popular Book Depot.

Giddens, A. (1984). *The Constitution of Society: Outline of the Theory of Structuration.* Cambridge: Polity Press.

———. (1990). *The Consequences of Modernity.* Cambridge: Polity Press.

———. (1991). *Modernity and Self-Identity: Self and Society in the Late Modern Age.* Stanford, CA: Stanford University Press.

———. (2009). *Sociology,* 6th ed. Cambridge: Polity Press.

Gill, J., and DeFronzo, J. (2009). "A Comparative Framework for the Analysis of International Student Movements," in *Social Movement Studies,* 8(3): 203–224.

Gintis, H., and Bowles, S. (1980). "Contradiction and Reproduction in Educational Theory," in Ten Barton, Roland Meighan, and Stephen Walker (eds.), *Schooling, Ideology and the Curriculum.* Barcombe, Lewes: Palmer. Pp. 51–65.

Giroux, H. A. (1981). *Ideology, Culture, and the Process of Schooling*, Philadelphia, PA:Temple University Press.

———. (1983). "Theories of Reproduction and Resistance in the New Sociology of Education," in *Harvard Educational Review,* 53(3): 257-293.

———. (1988). *Schooling and the Struggle for Public Life: Critical Pedagogy in the Modern Age.* Minneapolis: University of Minnesota Press.

———. (2005[1992]). *Border Crossings: Cultural Workers and the Politics of Education.* New York: Routledge.

Gitlin, T. (1995). *The Twilight of Common Dreams*. New York: Henry Holt.

Goodman, J. (1992). "Theoretical and practical considerations for school-based research in a post-positivist era," in *International Journal of Qualitative Studies in Education,* 5 (2): 117–33.

Goffman, E. (1982). "The Interaction Order," in *The American Sociological Review,* 48(1): 1-17.

Gorbutt, D. (1972). "The New Sociology of Education," in *Education for Teaching,* 89(1): 3-11.

Gordon, A. (1996). *Transforming Capitalism and Patriarchy: Gender and Development in Africa*. London: Lynne Rienner.

Gore, J. M. (1993). *The Struggle for Pedagogies: Critical and Feminist Discourses as Regimes of Truth.* New York: Routledge.

Gramsci, A. (1977[1917]). "The Revolution against 'Capital'," in Q. Hoare (ed.), *Antonio Gramsci: Selections from Political Writings (1910-1920).* New York: Int Publishers. Pp. 34-37.

Green, A. W. (1960). *Sociology: An Analysis of Life in Modern Society.* New York: McGraw-Hill Book Company, Inc.

Grisham–Brown, J., Hemmeter, M. L., and Pretti-Frontczak, K. (2005). *Blended Practices for Teaching Young Children in Inclusive Settings*. Baltimore: Brookes.

Gross, N. (1959). "The Sociology of Education," in Robert K. Merton, L. Broom, and L. S. Cottrell, Jr. (eds.), *Sociology Today: Problems and Prospects,* Volume-I. New York: Basic Books Inc. Pp. 128–152.

Gupta, D. (1991). "Hierarchy and Difference: An Introduction," in Dipankar Gupta (ed.), *Social Stratification.* New Delhi: Oxford University Press. Pp. 1-21.

Gurr, T. R. (1970). *Why Men Rebel.* Princeton, NJ: Princeton University Press.

Habermas, J. (1975). *Legitimating Crisis.* Boston: Beacon Press.

———. (1981). "New Social Movements," in *Telos*, 1981(49): 33–37.

———. (1987). *The Theory of Communicative Action Volume II: System and Lifeworld.* Cambridge: Polity.

Haidar, R. (1996). *Gender and Development*. Cairo: The American University Press.

Hamblin, D. (1974). *The Teacher and Counselling*. Oxford: Basil Blackwell & Mott Limited.

Hammersley, M., and Woods, P. (1976). "Introduction," in Martyn Hammersley and Peter Woods (eds.), *The Process of Schooling: A Sociological Reader.* London: Routledge & Kegan Paul.

Hannigan, J. A. (1985). "Alain Touraine, Manuel Castells and Social Movement Theory a Critical Appraisal," in *The Sociological Quarterly,* 26(4): 435–454.

Hansen D. A. (1967). "The uncomfortable relation of sociology and education," in D. A. Hansen and J. E. Gerstle (eds.), *On Education: Sociological Perspectives.* New York: John Wiley & Sons.

Haralambos, M., Holborn, M., and Heald, R. (2004). *Sociology: Themes and Perspectives.* London: HarperCollins Publishers Limited.

Harris, W. T. (1893). *Educational Review*, Vol. VI, June-December. New York: Henry Holt and Company.

Heberle, R. (1951). *Social Movements: An Introduction to Political Sociology.* New York: Appleton-Century-Crofts, Inc.

Hegel, G. W. F. (1967[1807]). *The Phenomenology of the Mind,* New York: Harper Colophon.

Hekman, S. J. (1983). *Weber, the Ideal Type, and Contemporary Social Theory*. Notre Dame: University of Notre Dame Press.

Henry, M. (1988). *Understanding Schooling: An Introductory Sociology of Australian Education.* London: Routledge.

Hoadley U., and Muller, J. (2010). "Codes, Pedagogy and Knowledge: Advances in Bernsteinian Sociology of Education," in Michael W. Apple, et al. (eds.), *The Routledge International Handbook of the Sociology of Education.* New York: Routledge.

Hobbes, T. (1951). *Leviathan.* London: Dent.

Hoffer, E. (1966). *The True Believer: Thoughts on the Nature of Mass Movements.* New York: Harper & Row.

Homans, M. (2020). "Reunions with Siblings in Search Memoirs across Cultures," in Jenny Heijun Wills, et al. (eds.), *Adoption and Multiculturalism: Europe, the Americas, and the Pacifc.* Michigan: University of Michigan Press. Pp. 69-96.

Honneth, A. (1995). *The Struggle for Recognition: The Moral Grammar of Social Conflicts,* translated by Joel Anderson. Cambridge: Polity Press.

Horkheimer, M. (1987 [1947]). *The Eclipse of Reason*. Athens: Kritiki.

Horrell, S.; Johnson, H. and Mosley, P. (2008). *Work, Female Empowerment and Economic Development.* New York: Routledge.

Howard, S. (1986). *Doing Things Together: Selected Papers.* Evanston, IL: Northwestern University Press.

Hoyle, E. (1969). *The Role of the Teacher.* London : Routledge and Kegan Paul.

Huffer, L. (2009). *Mad for Foucault: Rethinking the Foundation of Queer Theory.* New York: Columbia University Press.

Hunt, E. F. (1972). *Social Science*. New York: The Macmillan Company.

Hutchins, E. (1995). *Cognition in the Wild.* Cambridge, MA: MIT Press.

Inglehart, R. (1990). "Values, Ideology, and Cognitive Mobilisation in New Social Movements," in R. J. Dalton and M. Keuchler (eds.), *Challenging the Political Order: New Social and Political Movements in Western Democracies.* New York: Oxford University Press. Pp. 43–66.

Inkeles, A. (1964). *What is Sociology?* New Delhi: Prentice-Hall of India Ltd.

Inkeles, A. and Smith, D. H. (1974). *Becoming Modern.* London: Heinemann Education Books.

Ivinson, G. and Duveen, G. (2005). "Classroom structuration and the development of social representations of the curriculum," in *British Journal of Sociology of Education.* 26(5): 627–642.

Jackson, K. (1995). "Popular Education and the Sate: A New Look at the Community Debate," in Marjorie Mayo and Jane Thompson (eds.), *Adult Learning, Critical Intelligence and Social Change.* Wales: NIACE. Pp. 182-203.

Jackson, P. (1968). *Life in Classrooms*. New York: Holt, Rinehardt & Winston.

Jacoby, R. (1994). *Dogmatic Wisdom: How the Culture Wars Divert Education and Distract America*. New York: Doubleday.

Jagose, A. (1996). *Queer Theory: An Introduction.* New York: New York University Press.

Jameson, F. (1991). *Postmodernism or the Cultural Logic of Late Capitalism.* London: Verso.

Jasper, J. M. (2014). *Protest: A Cultural Introduction to Social Movements.* Cambridge: Polity Press.

Jenkins, J. C. (1981). "Sociopolitical Movements," in Samuel L. Long (ed.), *Handbook of Political Behavior,* Volume, IV. New York: Plenam Press. Pp. 81–153.

———. (1983). "Resource Mobilisation Theory and the Study of Social Movements," in *Annual Review of Sociology*, 9(1): 527–553.

Johnston, H. and Klandermans, B. (1995). "The Cultural Analysis of Social Movements," in Hank Johnston, Bert Klandermans (eds.), *Social Movements and Culture.* Minneapolis: University of Minnesota Press. Pp. 3–24.

Jones, S. M., and Dindia, K. (2004). "A meta-analystic perspective on sex equity in the classroom," in *Review of Educational Research, 74(4):* 443–471.

Judge, P. S. (2012). *Foundations of Classical Sociological Theory: Functionalism, Conflict and Action.* Delhi: Pearson Education India Ltd.

Karabel, J., and Halsey, A. H. (1977). "Educational Research: A Review and an Interpretation," in Jerome Karabel and A. H. Halsey (eds.), *Power and Ideology in Education*. New York: Oxford University Press. Pp. 1-85.

Karmakar, K. G. (2008). *Microfinance in India.* New Delhi: Sage Publications India Pvt Ltd.

Kavale, K. A., and Forness, S. R. (2000). "History, Rhetoric and Reality: Analysis of the Inclusion Debate," in *Remedial and Special Education,* 21(5): 279–96.

Kelly, F. J. (1914). *Teachers' Marks; Their Variability and Standardisation.* New York: Teachers College, Columbia University.

Kelly, P. (2012). "Migration, Transnationalism, and the Spaces of Class Identity," in *Philippine Studies: Historical and Ethnographic Viewpoints*, 60(2): 153–186.

Kerbo, H. R. (1982). "Movements of 'crisis' and movements of 'affluence': A critique of deprivation and resource mobilisation theories," in *Journal of Conflict Resolution*, 26(4): 645–663.

Killian, L. (1964). "Social Movements," in R. E. L. Faris (ed.), *Handbook of Modern Sociology.* Chicago: Rand McNally. Pp. 426–55.

Kincheloe, J. L. (2000). "Foreword," in Peter McLaren, (author), *Che Guevara, Paulo Freire, and the Pedagogy of Revolution*. New York: Rowman & Littlefield Publishers, Inc. Pp. ix-xii.

———. (2008). *Knowledge and Critical Pedagogy: An Introduction*. New York: Springer Science + Business Media B.V.

King, C. W. (1956). *Social Movements in the United States*. New York: Random House.

King, R. (1983). *The Sociology of School Organisation*. London and New York: The Chaucer Press.

King-Sears, M. E. and Carpenter, S. L. (2005). "Teaching Self-Management to Elementary Students with Developmental Disabilities," in Michael L. Wehmeyer and Martin Agran (eds.), *Mental Retardation and Intellectual Disabilities: Teaching Students Using Innovative and Research-Based Strategies*. Boston: Merrill/Prentice Hall. Pp. 235-253.

Kirby, M. (1999). *Stratification and Differentiation*. London: Macmillan Press Ltd.

Kirk, S. A. et al. (2009). *Educating Exceptional Children*. Boston: Houghton Mifflin.

Kirsch, M. H. (2000). *Queer Theory and Social Change*. London: Routledge.

Klandermans, B. (1984). "Mobilisation and Participation: Social-psychological Expansions of Resource Mobilisation Theory," in *American Sociological Review*, 49(5): 583–600.

Kohl, H. R. (1967). *36 Children*. New York: Signet Books.

Kokkinos, C. (2007). "Critical Theory and Education: Addressing the Educational Process in the Era of New Technology," in *The International Journal of Technology, Knowledge and Society*, 3(1): 79-82.

Krahn, H. and Harrison, T. (1992). "'Self-referenced' Relative Deprivation and Economic Beliefs: The Effects of the Recession in Alberta," in *Canadian Review of Sociology*, 29(2): 191–209.

Kriesi, H. (1996). "The Organisational Structure of New Social Movements in a Political Context," in Doug McAdam, John D. McCarthy, and Mayer N. Zald (eds.), *Comparative Perspectives on Social Movements*. New York: Cambridge University Press. Pp.152–184.

Kriesi, H., Koopmans, R., Duyvendak, J. W. and Giugni, M. (1995). *New Social Movements in Western Europe*. London: University of Minnesota Press.

Kugle, S. (2002). "Sultan Mahmud's Makeover: Colonial Homophobia and the Persian-Urdu Literary Tradition," in Ruth Vanita (ed.), *Queering India: Same Sex Love and Eroticism in Indian Culture and Society*. London: Routledge. Pp. 30-46.

Kumar, K. (1989). *Social Character of Learning*. New Delhi: Sage Publications India Pvt. Ltd.

Lachman, L. M. (1971). *The Legacy of Max Weber*. Berkeley: The Glendessary Press.

Lareau, A. (2002). *Unequal Childhoods: Class, Race, and Family Life*. Berkeley: University of California Press.

Latour, B. (1993). *We Have Never Been Modern*. Cambridge: Harvard University Press.

Latour, B. (2005). *Reassembling the Social: An Introduction to Actor-Network Theory.* Oxford: Oxford University Press.

Lauder, H., Brown, P. and Halsey, A.H. (2009). "Sociology of Education: A Critical History and Prospects for the Future," in *Oxford Review of Education*, 35(5): 569-585.

Lauer, R. H. (1972). "Social Movements: An Interactionist Analysis," in *The Sociological Quarterly,* 13 (3): 315–328.

Le Bon, G. (1896). *The Crowd: A Study of the Popular Mind.* New York: Macmillan & Co.

Lefebvre, H. (1984). *Everyday Life in the Modern World.* New Brunswick, N.J.: Transaction Books.

Lehrer, J. (2009). *How We Decide.* Boston: Houghton Mifflin Harcourt.

Lenski, G. E. (1954). "Status Crystallisation: A Non-Vertical Dimension of Social Status," in *American Sociological Review,* 19(4): 405-413.

Levy, M. J. (1952). The Structure of Society. Princeton, N.J.: Princeton University Press.

Linger, H., and Burstein, F. (1997). "Intelligent decision support in the context of the modern organisation," in *Proceedings of the 5th ISDSS International Conference,* Laussane.

Lofland, J. (1995). "Charting Degrees of Movement Culture: Tasks of the Cultural Cartographer," in Hank Johnston and Bert Klandermans, (eds.), *Social Movements and Culture*. Minneapolis: University of Minnesota Press. Pp. 188-216.

Lopes, A. and Pereira, F. (2012). "Everyday Life and Everyday Learning: The Ways in which Pre-service Teacher Education Curriculum can Encourage Personal Dimensions of Teacher Identity," in *European Journal of Teacher Education,* 35(1): 17-38.

Luhmann, S. (1998). "Queering/Querying Pedagogy? Or, Pedagogy Is a Pretty Queer Thing," in William F. Pinar, (ed.), *Queer Theory in Education.* London: Lawrence Erlbaum Associates, Inc. Pp. 120-132.

Lukacs, G. (1968[1922]). *History and Class Consciousness.* Cambridge, Mass: M.I.T. Press.

———. (1991[1918]). "Georg Simmel," in *Theory, Culture and Society,* 8(3):145-150.

Lukes, S. (1973). *Emile Durkheim. His Life and Work: A Historical and Critical Study.* London: Routledge.

Lynch, K. (2006). "Research and Theory on Equality and Education," in Maureen T. Hallinan (ed.), *Handbook of the Sociology of Education*. New York: Springer. Pp. 85-106.

Lyotard, J.-F. (1992). *The Postmodern Explained.* Sydney, Australia: Power Publications.

Mac an Ghaill, M. (1994). *The Making of Men: Masculinist Sexualities and Schooling.* Buckingham: Open University Press.

MacCannell, D. and MacCannell, J. F. (1993). "Social Class in Postmodernity: *Simulacrum* or Return of the Real?" in Chris Rojek and Bryan S. Turner (eds.) *Forget Baudrillard?* London: Routledge. Pp. 124-145.

Macionis, J. J., and Plummer, K. (2008). *Sociology: A Global Introduction.* New Delhi: Pearson Education Limited.

Madan, A., Sastry, R., and Ramdas, B. (2019). "Social Movements and Educational Change: A Case Study of the Adivasi Munnetra Sangam," in *Economic and Political Weekly,* 54(5): 45-52.

Majoribank, K. (1985). "Sociology of Education," in T. H. T. M. Postleithwaits (ed.), *The International Encyclopedia of Education, Research and Studies.* Oxford: Pergamon. Pp. 4680-4700.

Malinowitz, H. (1993). "Queer Theory: Whose Theory?" in *Frontiers,* 13(2): 168-84.

Malinowski, B. K. (1931). "Culture," in *Encyclopedia of the Social Sciences,* Vol. 4, pp. 621-645.

Mannheim, K. (1940). *Man and Society in an Age of Reconstruction.* London: Routledge & Kegan Paul.

———. (1943). *Diagnosis of Our Time: Wartime Essays of a Sociologist.* London: Routledge & Kegan Paul.

———. (1952). *Essays on the Sociology of Knowledge.* London: Routledge & Kegan Paul.

———. (1956). *Essays on the Sociology of Culture.* London: Routledge & Kegan Paul.

Mannheim, K., and Stewart, W. A. C. (1962). *An Introduction to the Sociology of Education.* London: Routledge & Kegan Paul.

Manton, K., and Moore, R. (2010). "Introduction: Coalitions of the Mind," in Karl Maton and Rob Moore, (eds.), *Social Realism, Knowledge and the Sociology of Education: Coalitions of the Mind.* London: Continuum International Publishing Group. Pp. 1-13.

Marcuse, H. (1958). *Soviet Marxism: A Critical Analysis.* New York: Columbia University Press.

Mare, R. D. (1991). "Five Decades of Educational Assortative Mating," in *American Sociological Review,* 56 (February issue) :15–32.

Marotta, T. (1981). *The Politics of Homosexuality.* Boston: Houghton Mifflin.

Marshall, H., Robinson, P., Germov, J., and Clark, E. (2009). *Teaching Sociology in Australia.* A Report to the Australian Learning and Teaching Council.

Martinelli, A. (2005). *Global Modernisation: Rethinking the Project of Modernity.* New Delhi: Sage Publications India Pvt. Ltd.

Marx, K. (1842/1977). "Communism and the Augsburger Allegemeine Zeitung," in D. McLellan (ed), *Karl Marx: Selected Writings.* New York: Oxford University Press.

———. (1847/1963). *The Poverty of Philosophy.* New York: Int. Publishers.

———. (1857/1974). *The Grundrisse: Foundations of the Critique of Political Economy.* New York: Random House.

Marx, K. (1867/1967). *Capital: A Critique of Political Economy*, Vol.1 New York: Int. Publishers.

Marx, K., and Engels, F. (1948[1848]). *The Communist Manifesto.* New York: International Publishers Co., Inc.

———. (1969). *Selected Works,* Vol. II. Moscow: Progress Publishers.

Matthews, M. R. (1980). *The Marxist Theory of Schooling: A Study of Epistemology and Education.* Sussex: Harvester Press.

Mauer, M. (1990). *Young Black Men in the Criminal Justice System.* Washington, D.C.: The Sentencing Project.

Mayer, M. (1995). "Social Movement Research in the United States: A European Perspective," in Stanford M. Lyman (ed.), *Social Movements: Critiques, Concepts, Case-Studies.* London: Macmillan Press Ltd. Pp. 168–195.

Mayo, C. (2013). "Queer Lessons: Sexual and Gender Minorities in Multicultural Education," in James A. Banks, Cherry A. McGee Banks, (eds.), *Multicultural Education: Issues and Perspectives.* NY: John Wiley & Sons, Inc. Pp. 161–175.

Mazzeno, L. W. (1999). *Matthew Arnold: The Critical Legacy.* Rochester, NY: Camden House.

McAdam, D. (1982). *Political Process and the Development of Black Insurgency, 1930–1970.* Chicago: University of Chicago Press.

McAdam, D., McCarthy, J. D., and Zald, M. N. (1988). "Social Movements," in Neil J. Smelser (ed.), *Handbook of Sociology*. Newbury Park, CA: Sage Publications. Pp. 695–737.

———. (1996). "Introduction: Opportunities, Mobilizing Structures, and Framing Processes – Toward a Synthetic, Comparative Perspective on Social Movements," in Doug McAdam, John D. McCarthy, and Mayer N. Zald (eds.), *Comparative Perspectives on Social Movements.* New York: Cambridge University Press. Pp. 1–20.

McAdam, J. D., Tarrow, S., and Tilly, C. (2001). *Dynamics of Contention*. New York: Cambridge University Press.

McCarthy, J. D. and Zald, M. N. (1977). "Resource Mobilisation and Social Movements: A Partial Theory," in *American Journal of Sociology,* 82(6): 1212–1241.

McFarland, D. A., et al. (2011). "Methodological Transactionalism and the Sociology of Education," in Maureen T. Hallinan, (ed.), *Frontiers in Sociology of Education*. New York: Springer. Pp. 87-110.

McLaren, P. (2000). *Che Guevara, Paulo Freire, and the Pedagogy of Revolution*. New York: Rowman & Littlefield Publishers, Inc.

Mead, G. H. (1962[1934]). *Mind, Self, and Society: From the Standpoint of a Social Behaviorist.* Chicago: The Chicago University Press.

Meighan, R., and Siraj-Blatchford, I. (1986). *A Sociology of Educating.* London: Cassell Educational.

Melucci, A. (1980). "The New Social Movements: A Theoretical Approach," in *Social Science Information,* 19 (2): 199–226.

Melucci, A. (1995). "The Process of Collective Identity," in H. Johnston and B. Klandermans (eds.), *Social Movements and Culture.* Minneapolis, Minnesota: University of Minnesota Press. Pp. 41–63.

Merton, R. K. (1968[1957]). *Social Theory and Social Structure.* New York: The Free Press.

Meštroviæ, S. G. (1998). *Anthony Giddens: The Last Modernist.* London: Routledge.

Milan, S. (2013). *Social Movements and Their Technologies: Wiring Social Change.* New York: Palgrave Macmillan.

Mintz, B., and Rothblum, E. (eds.), (1997). *Lesbians in Academia: Degrees of Freedom.* New York: Routledge.

Moir, A., and Moir, B. (1999). *Why Men Don't Learn.* London: Harper Collins.

Moore, R. (2013). *Basil Bernstein: The thinker and the field.* New York: Routledge.

Morris, A. D. (1984). *Origins of the Civil Rights Movement.* New York: Free Press.

Morrow, R. A., and Torres, C. A. (1995). *Social Theory and Education: A Critique of Theories of Social and Cultural Reproduction.* New York: State University of New York Press.

Mort, S. G., Weerawardena J., and Carnegie K. (2003). "Social entrepreneurship: toward conceptualisation," in the *Journal of Nonprofit Volunt Sect Mark,* 8(1): 76–88.

Mueller, C. M. (1992). "Building Social Movement Theory," in Aldon D. Mueller and Carol McClurg Mueller (eds.), *Frontiers in Social Movement Theory.* London: Yale University Press. Pp. 3–25.

Mumford, L. (1934). *Technics and Civilisation.* London: Routledge and Kegan Paul.

Mundy, J. (1998). *L'eisure Education: Theory and Practice.* Urbana, Illinois: Sagamore Publishing LLC.

Murdock, G. P. (1949). *Social Structure.* New York: Macmillan.

Musgrave, P. W. (1965). *The Sociology of Education.* London: Methuen.

Nambissan, G. B., and Rao, S. S. (2012). "Introduction: Sociology of Education in India—Trajectory, Location, and Concerns," in Geetha B. Nambissan and S. Srinivasa Rao (eds.), *Sociology of Education in India: Changing Contours and Emerging Concerns.* New Delhi: Oxford University Press. Pp. 1-21.

Narayan, D. (2002). *Empowerment and Poverty Reduction: A Sourcebook.* Washington, DC: The World Bank.

Nasir, S. N., Rosebery, A. S., Warren, B., and Lee, C. D. (2006). "Learning as a Cultural Process: Achieving Equity through Diversity," in Robert Keith Sawyer (ed.), *The Cambridge Handbook of the Learning Sciences.* Cambridge, UK: Cambridge University Press. Pp. 489–504.

Nock, S. L., and Kingston, P. W. (1990). *The Sociology of Public Issues.* Belmont, California: Wadsworth Publishing Company.

Oakley, A. (1972). *Sex, Gender and Society.* London: Temple Smith.

Oberschall, A. (1973). *Social Conflict and Social Movements.* Englewood Cliffs, NJ: Prentice-Hall, Inc.

———. (1992). *Social Movements: Ideologies, Interests, and Identities.* New Brunswick, N.J.: Transaction.

Offe, C. (1985). "New Social Movements: Challenging the Boundaries of Institutional Politics," in *Social Research,* 52(4): 817–868.

O'Gorman, P. (1993). "Codependency Explored: A Social Movement in Search of Definition and Treatment," in *Psychiatric Quarterly,* 64(2): 199-212.

Ogburn, W. F. (1949). "The Process of Adjustment to New Inventions," in William Fielding Ogburn, (ed.), *Technology and International Relations*. Chicago, Illinois: The University of Chicago Press. Pp. 16-27.

Ophuls, W. (1992). *Ecology and the Politics of Scarcity Revisited.* New York: W.H. Freeman.

Ottaway, A. K. C. (1955). "The Educational Sociology of Emile Durkheim," in *The British Journal of Sociology,* 6(3): 213–227.

———. (1960). "The Aims and Scope of Educational Sociology," in *Educational Review,* 12(3): 190-199.

———. (1962). *Education and Society: An Introduction to the Sociology of Education.* London: Routledge & Kegan Paul.

Parker, S. (1979). *The Sociology of Leisure*. London: George Allen and Unwin.

Parsons, T. (1942). "Some Sociological Aspects of Fascist Movements," in *Social Forces*, 21(2): 138–147.

———. (1951). *The Social System.* New York: The Free Press.

———. (1955). "The American Family: Its Relations to Personality and Social Structure," in Talcott Parsons and Robert F. Bales (eds.), *Family, Socialisation and Interaction Process.* New York: Free Press.

———. (1961). "Suggestions for a Sociological Approach to the Theory of Organisations," in Amitai Etzioni (ed.), *Complex Organisations.* New York: Holt, Rinehart and Winston. Pp. 32–47.

Pathania, G. J. (2013). "Sociology of Education," in *Economic & Political Weekly,* xlviii (50): 29-31.

Payne, E. G. (1928). *Principles of Educational Sociology: An Outline.* New York New: York University Press.

Pickering, M. (2009). *Auguste Comte: An Intellectual Biography,* Volume-3. Cambridge: Cambridge University Press.

Pickering, W. S. F. (1979). *Durkheim: Essays on Morals and Education*. London: Penguin.

Piven, F. F., and Cloward, R. A. (1995). "Collective Protest: A Critique of Resource-Mobilisation Theory," in Stanford M. Lyman (ed.), *Social Movements: Critiques, Concepts, Case-Studies.* London: Macmillan Press Ltd. Pp. 137–167.

Popkewitz, T. S. (1991). *A Political Sociology of Educational Reform: Power, Knowledge in Teaching, Teacher Education, and Research.* New York: Teachers College Press.

———. (1998). "The Sociology of Knowledge and the Sociology of Education: Michel Foucault and Critical Traditions", in Carlos Alberto Torres and Theodore R. Mitchell (eds.), *Sociology of Education: Emerging Perspectives.* New York: State University of New York. Pp. 47-90.

Pritchard, C., and Butler, A. J. (1978). "Teachers' perceptions of school phobic and truant behaviour and the influence of the youth tutor," in *Journal of Adolescence,* 1(3): 273-282.

Prummer, C. V. (2000). *Women and Distance Education: Challenges and Opportunities.* London: Routledge.

Pugh, T. (2008). *Sexuality and Its Queer Discontents in Middle English Literature.* New York: Palgrave Macmillan.

Queiroz, Jean-Manuel D. (2011). "The message and the voice," in Daniel Frandji and Philippe Vitale (eds.), (2011). *Knowledge, Pedagogy and Society: International perspectives on Basil Bernstein's sociology of education.* New York: Routledge. Pp. 49-61.

Rao, P., Patil, Y., and Gupte, R. (2013). "Education for Sustainable Development: Trends in Indian Business Schools and Universities in a Post Liberalisation Era," in Sandra Caeiro et al. (eds.), *Sustainability Assessment Tools in Higher Education Institutions*. New York: Springer, pp. 417-432.

Rao, S. S., and Singh, S. (2018). "Max Weber's Contribution to the Sociology of Education: A Critical Appreciation", in *Contemporary Education Dialogue*, 15(1): 73–92.

Renn, K. A. (2010). "LGBT and Queer Research in Higher Education: The State and Status of the Field," in *Educational Researcher,* 39(2): 132–141.

Ritzer, G. (1996). *Modern Sociological Theory.* New York: McGraw Hill Company, Inc.

Roberts, D., and Woods, C. (2005). "Changing the world on a shoe-string: the concept of social entrepreneurship," in *University of Auckland Business Review*, 7(1): 45–51.

Roberts, R., Rule, S., and Innocenti, M. (1998). *Strengthening the Family Professional Partnership in Services for Young Children*. Baltimore: Brookes.

Robinson, M. (2001). *The Microfinance Revolution: Sustainable Finance for the Poor.* Washington, DC: The World Bank.

Rocher, G. (1990[1968]). *A General Introduction to Sociology: A Theoretical Perspective,* translated from the French by Peta Sheriff. Kolkata: Academic Publishers.

Rojek, C. (1985). *Capitalism and Leisure Theory.* New York: Tavistock.

Rose, R. (2001). "Primary School Teacher Perceptions of the Conditions Required for Including Pupils with Special Educational Needs," in *Educational Review,* 53(2): 147–56.

Rothchild, J. (2007). *Gender Trouble Makers Education and Empowerment in Nepal.* New York: Routledge.

Roucek, J. S. (1956). "The Roots of American Educational Sociology," in *The American Catholic Sociological Review,* 17(3): 195–205.

———. (1958). "Changing Concepts and Recent Trends in American Educational Sociology," in *International Review of Education,* 4(2): 240–244.

Rowbotham, S. (1973). *Women's Consciousness, Man's World.* Middlesex, Eng.: Pelican.

Rowbotham, S. (1989). *Hidden from History: 300 Years of Women's Oppression and the Fight against it.* Winchester, Mass: Unwin Hyman.

Roy, A. (2010). *Poverty Capital: Microfinance and the Making of Development.* London: Routledge.

Rudig, W. (1990). *Anti Nuclear Movements*. London: Longman.

Runciman, W. G. (1966). *Relative Deprivation and Social Justice.* London: Routledge & Kegan Paul.

———. (1972). *A Critique of Max Weber's Philosophy of Social Science.* London: Cambridge University Press.

Ryan, B. (1992). *Feminism and the Women's Movement: Dynamics of Change in Social Movement Ideology.* New York: Routledge.

Sadan, E. (2000). "Community Empowerment, Poverty and Leisure Education," in A. Sivan and H. Ruskin (eds.), *Leisure Education, Community Development and Populations with Special Needs.* New York: CABI Publishing. Pp. 131-142.

Sadker, M., and Sadker, D. (1994). *Failing at Fairness.* New York: Touchstone.

Saha, L. J. (2008). *Sociology of Education, 21st Century Education: A Reference Handbook.* New York: Sage Publications.

———. (2015). *Educational Sociology. International Encyclopedia of the Social & Behavioral Sciences,* 2nd edition (Ed. James D. Wright). Elsevier: Oxford.

Schaefer, R. T. (2013). *Sociology: A Brief Introduction.* New York: McGraw-Hill Publications.

Schneider, B. (2005). "The Social Organisation of Schools," in Larry V. Hedges and Barbara Schneider (eds.), *The Social Organisation of Schooling*. New York: Russell Sage Publication. Pp. 1-12.

Schutz, A. (1971). "On Multiple Realities," in Alfred Schutz (auth.), *Collected Papers I: The Problems of Social Reality,* (edited by Maurice Natanson). The Hague: Martinus Nijhoff. Pp. 207-259.

Scott, J. (2006). *Social Theory: Central Issues in Sociology.* New Delhi: Sage Publication Pvt. Ltd.

Seidman, S. (1995). "Deconstructing Queer Theory or the Under-Theorisation of the Social and the Ethical," in L. Nicholson and S. Seidman (eds.), *Social Postmodernism: Beyond Identity Politics.* Cambridge: Cambridge University Press. Pp. 116-141.

Selakovich, D. (1984). *Schooling in America.* New York: Longman.

Selznick, P. (1948). "Foundations of the Theory of Organisation," in *American Sociological Review,* 13(1): 25–35.

———. (1949). *TVA and the Grass Roots*. Berkeley: University of California Press.

Shah, G. ([1990] 2004). *Social Movements in India.* New Delhi: Sage Publications India Pvt. Ltd.

Sharpe, B. (1995). "Environmental education and environmental information systems: A project on the Grand River Basin, Ontario," in *International Research in Geographical and Environmental Education,* 4(1): 101-106.

Sharma, Y. K. (2002). *The Doctrines of the Great Indian Educators*. New Delhi: Kanishka Publishers, Distributors.

Shimbori, M. (1972). "Educational Sociology or Sociology of Education?" in *International Review of Education,* 18(1): 3–12.

Shiva, V. (1988). *Staying Alive: Women, Ecology, and Survival in India.* New Delhi: Kali for Women.

Shizha, E., and Abdi, A. A. (2009). "Globalisation and Adult Education in the South", in Ali A. Abdi and Dip Kapoor (eds.), *Global Perspectives on Adult Education.* New York: Palgrave Macmillan. Pp. 17- 34.

Shonkoff, J., and Phillips, D. (eds.), (2000). *From Neurons to Neighborhoods: The Science of Early Childhood Development*. Washington, DC: National Academy Press.

Sidhu, R. K. (2006). *Universities and Globalisation: To Market, To Market.* London: Lawrence Erlbaum Associates, Inc.

Sieber, S. D., and Wilder, D. E. (1973). "Introduction: Classical Perspectives," in Sam D. Sieber and David E. Wilder (eds.), *The School in Society: Studies in the Sociology of Education.* New York: The Free Press.

Sinclair, M. E., and Lillis, K. (1980). *School and Community in the Third World.* London: Croom Helm.

Singer, M. S. (1992). "The Application of Relative Deprivation Theory to Justice Perception of Preferential Selection," in *Current Psychology,* 11(2): 128–144.

Singh, R. (2001). *Social Movements, Old and New: A Post-modernist Critique.* New Delhi: Sage Publications India Pvt. Ltd.

Sivan, A., and Ruskin, H. (2000). "Introduction," in A. Sivan, H. Ruskin, (eds.), *Leisure Education, Community Development and Populations with Special Needs.* New York: CABI Publishing. Pp. 1-12.

Skeggs, B. (1995). "Introduction," in Beverley Skeggs (ed.), *Feminist Cultural Theory: Process and Production.* Manchester: Manchester University Press. Pp.1-30.

Small, A. W. (1897). "The Meaning of the Social Movement", in *American Journal of Sociology*, 3(3): 340-354.

Smelser, N. J. (1962). *Theory of Collective Behavior*. New York: The Free Press.

Smith, W. R. (1917a). *An Introduction to Educational Sociology.* Boston: Hougton Mifflin Company.

———. (1917b). "The Foundations of Educational Sociology," in *American Journal of Sociology,* 22(6): 761-778.

Snedden, D. (1922). *Educational Sociology*. New York: The Century Company.

Snow, David A., Rochfold, E. B. Jr., Worder, Steven K., and Benford, Robert D. (1986). "Frame Alignment Processes, Micromobilisation, and Movement Participation," in *American Sociological Review,* 51(4): 464–81.

Sombart, W. (1909[1896]). *Socialism and the Social Movement.* London: J. M. Dent & Co.

Soodak, L. C., and Podell, D. M. (1998). "Teacher Efficacy and the Vulnerability of the Difficult-to-Teach Student," in Jere E. Brophy (ed.), *Advances in Research on Teaching*, Vol. 7. Greenwich, CT: JAI Press. Pp. 75-109.

Spargo, T. (1999). *Foucault and Queer Theory*. New York: Totem Books.

Sriprakash, A. (2012). *Pedagogies for Development: The Politics and Practice of Child-Centred Education in India*. London: Springer.

Stanley, W. R. (1983-1984). "The rights of gay student organisations," in *Journal of College and University Law*, 10(3): 397-418.

Stouffer, S. A., et al. (1949). *The American Soldier*, volume- I. Princeton: Princeton University Press.

Stromquist, N. P. (1990). "Women and Illiteracy: the Interplay of Gendered Subordination and Poverty," in *Comparative Education Review* 34(1): 95–111.

Sumner, W. G. (1906). *Folkways: A Study of the Sociological Importance of Usages, Manners, Customs, Mores, and Morals*. Boston: Ginn and Company.

Suzzallo, H. (1908). "Education as a Social Study," in *The School Review*, 16(5): 330-340.

Swidler, A. (1986). "Culture in Action: Symbols and Strategies," in *American Sociological Review*, 51(2): 273-286.

Swift, D. F. (1966). "Social Class and Achievement Motivation," in *Educational Research*, 8(2): 83-95.

———. (1969). *The Sociology of Education: Introductory Analytical Perspectives*. London: Routledge & Kegan Paul.

Szymanski, A. T., and Goertzel, T.G. (1979). *Sociology: Class, Consciousness, and Contradictions*. New York: Van Nostrand-Reinhold.

Tarrow, S. (2011[1994]). *Power in Movement: Social Movements and Contentious Politics*. Cambridge : Cambridge University Press.

Tawney, R. H. (1926). "Adult Education in the history of the nation," paper read at the Fifth Annual Conference of the British Institute of Adult Education.

Taxel, J. (1980). *The Depiction of the American Revolution in children's Fiction: A study in the Sociology of School Knowledge*. Doctoral dissertation, University of Wisconsin–Madison.

Taylor, M., and Coia, L. (2014). "Addressing Gender, Feminism, and Queer Theory Through Self-Study of Teacher Education Practices: A Literature Review," in M. Taylor and L. Coia (eds.), *Gender, Feminism, and Queer Theory in the Self-Study of Teacher Education Practices*. Rotterdam: Sense Publishers. Pp. 11-30.

Taylor, W. (1967). "The Sociology of Education," in J. W. Tibble (ed.), *The Study of Education*. London: Routledge & Kegan Paul.

Thornburg, H. D. (1984). *Introduction to Educational Psychology*. Eagan, Minnesota: West Publishing Company.

Tierney, W. G. (1994). "Self and identity in a post-modern world: A life story," in D. McLaughlin & W. G. Tierney (eds.), *Naming Silenced Lives: Personal Narratives and the Process of Educational Change*. New York: Routledge. Pp. 119–134.

Tierney, W. G., and Dilley, P. (1998). "Constructing Knowledge: Educational Research and Gay and Lesbian Studies," in William F. Pinar, (ed.), *Queer Theory in Education*. London-Lawrence Erlbaum Associates, Inc. Pp. 40-60.

Tilly, C. (1963). "The Analysis of a Counter-Revolution," in *History and Theory*, 3(1): 30–58.

———. (1978). *From Mobilisation to Revolution*. Reading, MA: Addison-Wesley.

———. (1979). "Social Movements and National Politics," in *CRSO Working Paper No. 197*. Ann Arhor, Michigan.

Tilly, C., Tilly, L., and Tilly, R. (1975). *The Rebellious Century, 1830–1930*. Cambridge: Harvard University Press.

Tilly, C., and Wood, L. J. (2009). *Social Movements, 1768–2008*. London: Paradigm Publishers.

Tobin, J. J., Wu, D. Y. H., and Davidson, D. H. (1989). *Preschool in Three Cultures: Japan, China and the United States*. London: Yale University Press.

Toch, H. (1965). *The Social Psychology of Social Movements*. Indianapolis: Bobbs-Merrill.

Toffler, A. (1970). *Future Shock*. New York: Random House.

Torres, C. A., and Mitchell, T. R. (1998). "Introduction", in Carlos Alberto Torres and Theodore R. Mitchell (eds.), *Sociology of Education: Emerging Perspectives*. New York: State University of New York. Pp. 1-18.

Touraine, A. (1981). *The Voice and the Eye: An Analysis of Social Movements*. New York: Cambridge University Press.

———. (1988). *The Return of the Actor*. Minneapolis: University of Minnesota Press.

———. (2002). "The Importance of Social Movements," in *Social Movement Studies*, 1(1): 89–95.

———. (2007). *A New Paradigm for Understanding Today's World*. New York: Polity Press.

Tumin, M. M. (1953). "Some Principles of Stratification: A Critical Analysis," in *American Sociological Review*, 18(4): 387-394.

———. (1967). *Social Stratification: The Forms and Functions of Inequality*. Englewood Cliffs, NJ: Prentice-Hall, Inc.

Turnbull, A. P., and Turnbull, H. R. (2004). *Individuals with Disabilities Education Act: Resources for Educators*. Paper presented at the Conference on Equity, Community, and Social Justice for Urban Students. New York.

Turner, R. and Killian, L. M. (1957). *Collective Behavior*. Englewood Cliffs, N.J.: Prentice-Hall.

Vanita, R. (2005). *Love's Rite: Same-Sex Marriage in India*. New York: Palgrave Macmillan.

Villa, R., and Thousand, J. (1995). *Creating an Inclusive School*. Alexandra, VA: Association for Society for Curriculum Development.

Vincent, G. E. (1897). *The Social Mind and Education*. Chicago: The University of Chicago Press.

Visweswaran, K. (2010). *Un/common Cultures: Racism and the Rearticulation of Cultural Difference*. Durham, NC: Duke University Press.

Voeltz, L. M. (1980). "Children's Attitudes toward Handicapped Peers," in *American Journal of Mental Deficiency,* 84(5): 455–464.

Wafer, J. (1997). "Muhammad and Male Homosexuality," in Stephen O. Murray and Will Roscoe (eds.), *Islamic Homosexualities*. New York: New York University Press.

Wakankar, M. (2010). *Subalternity and Religion: The Prehistory of Dalit Empowerment in South Asia.* New York: Routledge.

Walford, G., and Pickering, W. S. F. (1998). *Durkheim and Modern Education*. London: Routledge.

Waller, W. (1932). *The Sociology of Teaching.* New York: Wiley.

Wallerstein, I. (1991). *Geopolitics and Geoculture: Essays on the Changing World-System.* New York: Cambridge University Press.

Ward, L. F. (1883). *Dynamic Sociology.* New York: D. Appleton and Company.

Warner, M. (1993). "Introduction," in Michael Warner (ed.), *Fear of a Queer Planet: Queer Politics and Social Theory.* Minneapolis: University of Minnesota Press. Pp. vii-xxxi.

Wax, M. (1967). "On Misunderstanding Verstehen: A Reply to Abel," in *Sociology and Social Research,* 51 (3): 323-333.

Weber, M. (1978[1968]). *Economy and Society: An Outline of Interpretive Sociology. Vols. I and II*, (eds. Guenther Roth and Claus Wittich). Berkeley: University of California Press.

———. (1991[1904–1905]). *The Protestant Ethic and the Spirit of Capitalism.* London: Harper Collins.

Weiler, K. (1988). *Women Teaching for Change: Gender, Class and Power.* New York: Bergin and Garvey.

Wentzel, K. R., and Asher, S. R. (1995). "The academic lives of neglected, rejected, popular, and controversial children," in *Child Development,* 66(3): 754–763.

Westwood, P. (2003). *Commonsense Methods for Children with Special Educational Needs: Strategies for the Regular Classroom.* London: Routledge.

Wexler, P. (1982). "Structure, Text, and Subject: A Critical Sociology of School Knowledge," in Michael W. Apple (ed.), *Cultural and Economic Reproduction in Education Essays on Class, Ideology and the State.* New York: Routledge & Kegan Paul Ltd. Pp. 275-303.

———. (1987). *Social Analysis of Education: After the New Sociology.* London: Routledge & Kegan Paul.

———. (1992). *Becoming Somebody: Toward a Social Psychology of School*, London: Routledge.

———. (2009). *Social Theory in Education: Primer.* New York: Peter Lang Publishing, Inc.

Whitty, G. (1985). *Sociology and School Knowledge: Curriculum Theory, Research and Politics.* London: Methuen.

Widdicombe, S. (1998). "Identity as an Analysts' and a Participants' Resource," in Charles Antaki and Sue Widdicombe (eds.), *Identities in Talk.* London: Sage Publications Ltd. Pp. 191–206.

Wieviorka, M. (2005). "After New Social Movements," in *Social Movement Studies,* 4(1): 1–19.

Wilkinson, P. (1971). *Social Movement.* London: The Macmillan Press Ltd.

Willis, P. E. (1977). *Learning to Labor: How Working Class Kids Get Working Class Jobs*. New York: Columbia University Press.

Willmott, R. (1999). "School Effectiveness Research: An Ideological Commitment?" in *Journal of Philosophy of Education,* 33(2): 253–68.

Willower, D. J., and Carr, C. F. (1965). "The School as a Social Organisation," in *Educational Leadership,* 22(4): 251–255.

Windmeyer, S. L., and Freeman, P. W. (2001). "Uppercase Greek Alphabet," in S. L. Windmeyer and P. W. Freeman (eds.), *Secret Sisters: Stories of Being Lesbian and Bisexual in a College Sorority*. New York: Alyson Books.

Wink, J. (2005). *Critical Pedagogy: Notes from the Real World.* Boston: Pearson Education, Inc.

Woodward, K. (2000). "Afterword," in Kath Woodward (ed.), *Questioning Identity: Gender, Class, Nation.* New York: Routledge. Pp. 155-158.

———. (2002). *Understanding Identity.* London: Arnold Publication.

Woolgar, S., Coopmans, C., and Neylund, D. (2009). "Does STS mean business?" in *Organisation,* 16(1): 5-30.

Wright, R. (2014). "The Fourth Sociology and Music Education: Towards a Sociology of Integration," in *Action, Criticism & Theory for Music Education,* 13(1): 12-39.

Yixian, L. (1987). "A Probe into the Nature of Sociology of Education as a Discipline and Its Subject of Study," in *Chinese Education & Society,* 20(2): 10–23.

Youdell, D. (2010). "Recognizing the Subjects of Education: Engagements with Judith Butler," in Michael W. Apple, Stephen J. Ball, and Luis Armando Gandin (eds.), *The Routledge International Handbook of the Sociology of Education.* Abingdon, UK: Routledge. Pp. 132–142.

Young, K. (1934). *An Introductory Sociology.* New York: American Book Company.

Young, M. F. D. (1971). "An Approach to the Study of Curricula as Socially Organised Knowledge," in Michael F. D. Young (ed.), *Knowledge and Control: New Directions in the Sociology of Education.* London: Collier-Macmillan Publishers. Pp. 19-46.

———. (1998). *Curriculum of the Future: From the New Sociology of Education to a Critical Theory of Learning*. New York: Falmer Press.

Zald, M. N., and McCarthy, J. D. (1987). "Social Movement Industries: Competition and Conflict among SMOs," in Mayer N. Zald and John D. McCarthy (eds.), *Social Movements in an Organisational Society: Collected Essays*. New Brunswick, NJ: Transaction Books. Pp. 161–180.

# Index

## C

I



J

## O



## P

## Q



## R